MW00759782

Objects of Vision

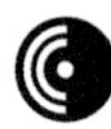

Perspectives on Sensory History

Books in the Perspectives on Sensory History series maintain a historical basis for work on the senses, examining how the experiences of seeing, hearing, smelling, tasting, and touching have shaped the ways in which people have understood their worlds.

Objects of Vision

Making Sense of What We See

A. Joan Saab

The Pennsylvania State University Press
University Park, Pennsylvania

Library of Congress Cataloging-in-Publication Data

Names: Saab, A. Joan, author.
Title: Objects of vision : making sense of what we see / A. Joan Saab.
Other titles: Perspectives on sensory history.
Description: University Park, Pennsylvania : The Pennsylvania State University Press, [2020] | Series: Perspectives on sensory history | Includes bibliographical references and index.
Summary: "Examines a series of linked case studies that not only highlight moments of seeming disconnect between seeing and believing, including hoaxes, miracles, spirit paintings, manipulated photographs, and holograms, but also offer a sensory history of ways of seeing"—Provided by publisher.
Identifiers: LCCN 2020035744 | ISBN 9780271088105 (hardback)
Subjects: LCSH: Visual perception. | Art—Psychological aspects.
Classification: LCC N7430.5 .S235 2020 | DDC 152.14—dc23
LC record available at https://lccn.loc.gov/2020035744

Printed in the United States of America
Published by The Pennsylvania State University Press, University Park, PA 16802–1003

The Pennsylvania State University Press is a member of the Association of University Presses.

It is the policy of The Pennsylvania State University Press to use acid-free paper. Publications on uncoated stock satisfy the minimum requirements of American National Standard for Information Sciences—Permanence of Paper for Printed Library Material, ANSI Z39.48–1992.

FOR STEVE, FINN, AND WILSON

Contents

Illustrations

Acknowledgments

My son jokingly suggested that I make sure to thank all the saints and spirits whose shrines and sites I visited while researching this project: the Virgins of Guadalupe, Fatima, Montserrat, and Lourdes in the Bronx, Saint Anne de Beaupré, Kateri Tekakwitha, Saint Jude, the Fox sisters, the mediums of Lily Dale, the witches of Enchantments magic candle store in the East Village, Stevie Nicks . . . the list goes on and on. It was my interlocutors here on earth, however, who enabled me to successfully write this book and that list is longer still.

My colleagues at the University of Rochester supported me in ways that are hard to fully capture. Nora Rubel, a kindred spirit, read the entire manuscript (some parts more than once) and pushed me to actually finish the thing. She, along with Rachel Haidu, constituted my perfect scholarly coven. John Michael, Janet Berlo, and Christopher Heuer read drafts of the introduction and helped me clarify my disparate thoughts to frame my argument. Joel Burges listened to me go on and on about the materiality of visions. Tanya Bakhmetyeva shared valuable material on Conan Doyle. Rio Hartwell assured me that the work made sense and, in some cases, showed me how it did so and Laura Smoller pointed me towards sources of wonder. I'd like to thank Joanie Rubin in the Humanities Center and Gloria Culver, Dean of Arts and Sciences, for suggesting me for the inaugural Nazarian lecture where I first presented some of this material (and to Ani and Mark Gabrellian for funding the series). Marty Collier, Lorna Maier, and Tricia DiQuattro provided invaluable administrative support (and blocked my calendar when I most needed it).

I had the very good fortune to work with some outstanding students in the Graduate Program in Visual and Cultural Studies. In particular I'd like to thank Ouma Amadou and Victoria Taormina who worked magic to locate images and permissions. I am also grateful for the students in my seminar on Digital Culture in the Material Age, who patiently let me test out some of my examples in class. They may not believe that precipitated paintings really appear out of thin air, but they were playful and very sharp discussants. Almudena Escobar Lopez and Mimi Chen were also a great help. Two former VCS students and now my co-editors, Aubrey Anable and Cat Zuromskis, were incredibly patient with me when I missed deadlines or privileged this project over our shared volume. For their understanding and tolerance, I am most grateful.

Andrea Reithmayr in the Rare Books Collection in the University of Rochester Library was an invaluable resource. Not only did she share my interest in nineteenth-century Spiritualism, she seemed able to conjure sources whenever I needed them. Shannon Taggart told me where to find an early spirit trumpet and

Brandon Hodge of the Mysterious Planchette confirmed my skepticism about the Fox sisters' table and pointed me toward other examples of séance tables in early Spiritualist literature.

I want to thank Mark Smith for having faith in me to write this volume, and Martin Berger for recommending me to Mark—as well as for reading drafts of grant applications along with Tom DiPiero. At Penn State University Press I want to thank Kendra Boileau and her super assistant Alex Vose for identifying two fantastic outside readers, one of whom was Lisa Cartwright, who has been an inspiration and a mentor to me since my first day on the job at the University of Rochester. Lisa's comments helped me to crystalize the project around the idea of objects of vision, and the work is much, much stronger for her care and attention. I would also like the production team at PSU, in particular Nicholas Taylor for his extraordinary copyediting skills.

Finally, I want to thank my family. As always, my parents Maureen and Richard Saab have been my biggest cheerleaders and still don't seem to think it weird when I go off in search of the seemingly bizarre. And to Steve, Finn, and Wilson Brauer, who joined me on my search. To Finn, who gamely came with me on an eight-hour pilgrimage to Canajoharie, New York, to see where Kateri was born. For Wilson, who didn't seem to mind when we left the Baseball Hall of Fame to see the Cardiff Giant. And to Steve, who visited more shrines, tracked down more spiritualist ephemera, and accompanied me to countless makeshift museums and random archives. For the three of you, in the words of Fox Mulder, "I want to believe."

Prologue
In Memory of . . .

On the evening of March 3, 1991, the Los Angeles Police Department pulled over an African American construction worker named Rodney King following a protracted high-speed chase. After King attempted to flee the scene, four white officers—Laurence Powell, Timothy Wind, Theodore Briseno, and Stacey Koon—retained King and repeatedly kicked him, Tasered him, and hit him with their metal batons. The incident was caught on videotape by George Holliday, a resident of a nearby apartment building. Holliday sent a copy of his tape to the LAPD. After receiving no response, he shared it with the Los Angeles television station KTLA, which edited the tape and broadcast it on the evening news. CNN picked up the clip the next day and soon the footage was everywhere. Indeed, as CNN Vice President Ed Turner asserted, "Television used the tape like wallpaper."[1] Following public outcry, the four officers were arrested for excessive use of force. Despite Holliday's video, which seemed to show in detail the officers' beating of King, the jury concluded that there was insufficient evidence to convict any of them.

Ironically, the video was key to the officers' acquittal. At the trial, which was moved from Los Angeles to the conservative suburb of Simi Valley, the defense attorneys for the police officers presented the short clip frame by frame to a predominantly white jury. By showing the beating in slow motion, they treated each of the fifty-six blows separately. According to one of the jurors, "A lot of those blows, when you watched them in slow motion, were not connecting. . . . Those batons are heavy, but when you looked at King's body three days after the incident, not that much damage was done."[2] The trial was broadcast on the newly launched Court TV. In addition to a "live, gavel-to-gavel, ringside seat" of the proceedings, what millions of viewers watched unfold in real time was a larger debate over the nature of evidence: in particular, how to see and interpret what was visible and hence seemingly legible in Holliday's pixilated video.[3] Terry White, a deputy district attorney and lead attorney for the prosecution, for example, approached the tape on its own terms, maintaining, "What more could you ask for? You have the videotape that shows objectively, without bias, impartially, what happened that night. The videotape shows conclusively what happened that night. It can't be rebutted." White ended his closing arguments with one more showing of the tape, followed by a question to the jurors: "Now who do you believe, the defendants or your own eyes?"[4]

The attorneys for the accused, however, deployed the videotape as part of a larger story about the dangerous nature of police work in an attempt to justify the actions of the officers toward King. Bringing in a series of experts who testified to the high-stake risks for those in law enforcement and then located these risks within the still images from the tape, the defense was able to convince the members of the jury that King was a serious threat to the officers' safety and that they had operated within the realm of proper police procedure. When asked by one of the prosecutors, "You can't look at the video and say that every one of those blows is reasonable, can you?" Officer Powell replied, "Oh I can if I put my perceptions in."[5] Another exclaimed that "Rodney King, in the very beginning, in the first six frames of this incident, went from the ground, to a charge. And what Sergeant Koon will tell you, [is that] this is his rendition of what he saw. This is how he perceived it."[6]

The final verdict in many ways hinged on the narratives each side used to frame the video and its images. And, as poet Elizabeth Alexander decried in her essay "Can You Be BLACK and Look at This?" the success of the defense's narrative often hinged on the deployment of brutal racial tropes and anxieties. King, they suggested, was a "buffed-out" "probable ex-con," a "bear-like wounded animal," "aggressive," "combative," and "a monster."[7] Preying on long-standing local anxieties about race and the Los Angeles Police Department, the attorneys for the accused officers framed their interpretation of the evidence to fit their narrative. In the end, rather than see the videotape as White had hoped, as showing "conclusively what happened that night" and to "believe . . . [their] own eyes," the jurors, many of whom shared the same cultural filters as the accused officers, saw the tape as part of a broader narrative of the dangers of policing and rendered a verdict of not guilty.

The tape seemed to contain "proof" of an extended beating of a seemingly defenseless man; the video instead was used to exonerate the officers at their trial. In many ways it was the technology, in particular the ability to blow up the images and isolate the events into stills, that changed the nature of the evidence. Technology aimed at making thing *more* visible—that is, it allowed the attorneys for the defendants to treat each frame as its own discrete story and disrupted the flow of the multiple hits contained on the tape. Defendant Stacey C. Koon later exclaimed, "If we had our way, we'd go down to Dodger Stadium and rip off that big-screen Mitsubishi and bring it into the courtroom and say, 'Hey, folks, you're in for the show of your life. . . . Because when this tape gets blown up it's awesome."[8] The uses of Holliday's videotape at the officers' criminal trial not only demonstrated the ways in which technologies of vision can shape our understandings of what and how we see what is before our eyes, it showed how the same visual evidence can be manipulated to tell very different stories. By blowing up and freezing the frames, the actions of the four officers on trial, as well as King's own movements, were—at least in the eyes of the jurors—disconnected from the rest of the tape as well as from the fraught history of race relations in the United States.

The King case set the stage for a narrative that allowed unchecked police brutality against people of color to become, if not normalized, then legally acceptable. Today, with the proliferation of recording devices on cell phones, and now even watches, similar events continue to be caught on camera at a regular pace. From the dashcam footage of the routine traffic stop of Philando Castile in 2016 to the video of the shooting of Stephon Clark in his backyard in 2018—which ultimately led to both individuals' deaths but, as in the King case, helped to exonerate the officers and justify state violence—visual evidence seems to have lost its power to convict, or even, in some cases, just to persuade.

Poet Claudia Rankine also marks the verdict in the Rodney King trial as a turning point:

> I know when Rodney King's jury came back and said that despite the video, the police had done nothing wrong, that was a moment for me. I literally burst into tears. I had this weird feeling walking around the streets of New York, that I didn't know who these people were. All of a sudden I felt like an alien. I felt like, holy shit, I am walking around, and all of these people, white people, are okay with my black body being beaten and kicked, even when they're seeing the violence actually happen and don't have to rely on hearsay. . . . That was really a crisis moment for me. You just feel like, okay, you need to start paying attention. It's the same line, from Rodney King to Michael Brown. It's a continuum.[9]

Taking a cue from Rankine, who records a growing list of men, women, and children killed by police in each reprint of her 2014 prose poem *Citizen*, in this project I hope to harness the power of the visual to combat attempts at narrative erasure.[10] The names Rankine cites on her ongoing list have been expunged in multiple ways. Murdered and with no convictions against the perpetrators, their lives seem not to matter in a legal context; there has been no justice or official ramification for those who killed Tamir Rice, or Walter Scott, or Freddie Gray. Their deaths have been erased from the record. Yet by writing their names in her book, Rankine has memorialized the victims' lives in typeface. She has materialized their bodies on the page. At the same time, those names get lighter as the list proceeds, rendering the men, women, and children simultaneously absent and yet still present. They continue to haunt us. Rankine's text fades at the bottom of the page, but it has not disappeared. Seeing still matters.

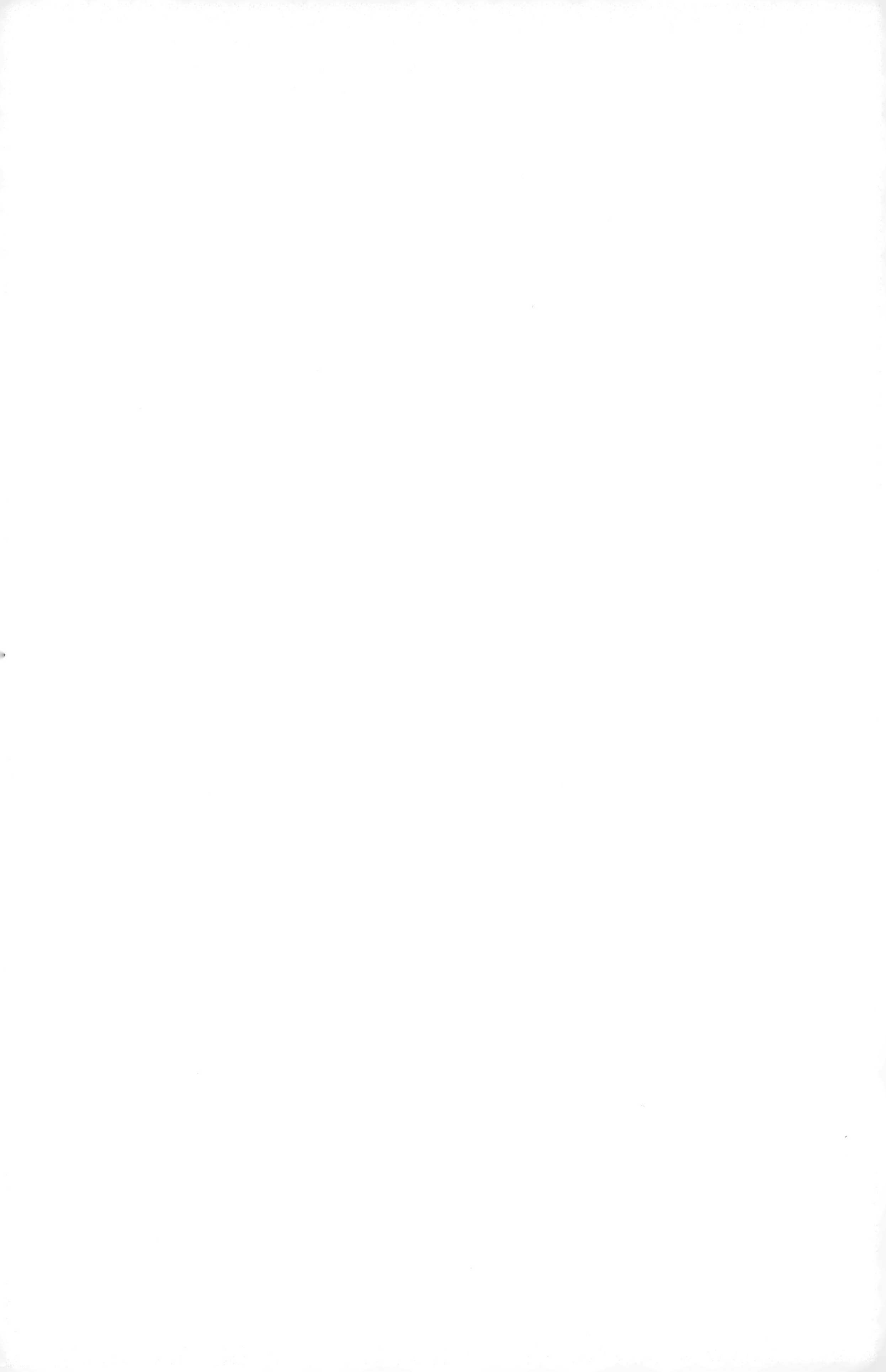

Introduction
Making Sense of What We See

La Historia Universal de las Cosas de Nueva España (*The General History of the Things of New Spain*), best known as the Florentine Codex, is a twelve-volume illustrated account of the Spanish conquistador Hernán Cortés's defeat of the Aztec ruler Moctezuma II in Mēxihco-Tenōchtitlan (current-day Mexico City). It was written and illustrated by native Nahua students of the Franciscan missionary Father Bernardino de Sahagún, who was sent to the Americas in 1529, eight years after the conquest. The events recounted took place between February 1519 and August 1521, yet the work was created over a span of thirty years following the Spanish victory and was in the possession of the Medici family in Florence, Italy, by 1588. Sahagún's goals for the project were multifold: to create a visual translation of the Aztec language, Nahuatl; to describe Aztec religion, beliefs, practices, and gods, and to record the history of the indigenous people before and after their encounter with the Spaniards. His was a proselytizing mission at least partly in the service of the Spanish empire. Sent to New Spain by the Catholic Church to "detect the sickness of idolatry," he believed that to convert the native peoples to Christianity, he first needed to understand their world and their belief systems. Sahagún was both distressed and impressed by Aztec culture, writing in the prologue to book 1 of the codex that the Mexicans "are considered as barbarians, as a people at the lowest level of perfection, when in reality . . . in matters of good conduct they surpass many other nations which have great confidence in their administrations."[1] Moreover, he continued, "whatever it may be that they were in times past, we now see through

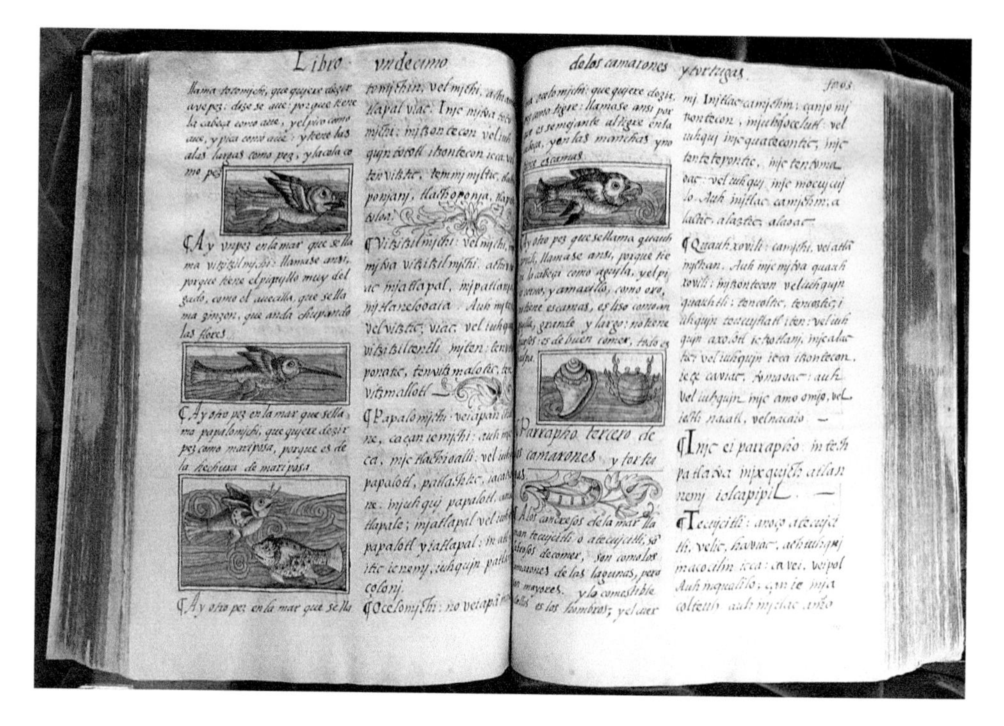

Fig. 1 Fray Bernardino de Sahagún, *General History of the Things of New Spain: The Florentine Codex*, introduction, indexes, book 1. Medicea Laurenziana Library. Image courtesy of the World Digital Library.

experience that they are capable in all the crafts, and they practice them. They are also capable in learning all the liberal arts and sacred theology. . . . They are no less capable of our Christianity; besides, they have been duly indoctrinated therein."[2] Sahagún saw the natives as literally "salvageable," and his multifaceted account reflects this deep belief.

To gather information, Sahagún deployed a research methodology akin to modern anthropological fieldwork. He systematically interviewed groups of native peoples from what is now central Mexico and enlisted his students at the College of Santa Cruz in Tlatelolco, the first European school of higher learning in the Americas, to record their answers in a pictorial form of writing that they then phonetically transcribed into Latin, to which he added his own Spanish translations. He explained, "And they, being knowledgeable in the Latin language, inform us of the properties of the words, the properties of their manner of speech. And they correct for us the incongruities we express in the sermons or write in the catechisms. And whatever is to be rendered in their language, if it is not written congruently in the Latin language, in Spanish, and in their language, cannot be free of defect."[3] The Mesoamerican codex tradition dates back to the ancient Maya. The earliest works were created on long sheets of bark cloth and consisted of images and pictograms not meant to precisely symbolize spoken language. Most pre-Columbian works on paper were destroyed by Catholic priests and conquistadors who, as part of their conversion and conquest efforts, wanted to erase the visual record of the preconquest past. Yet shortly following the Spanish victory, at the bequest of Charles V, the Holy Roman Emperor and King of Spain, Spanish priests and emissaries began recording events and information in this hybrid form to send back to Europe.[4] The earliest, the Codex Mendoza (named for Don Antonio de Mendoza, the Viceroy of New Spain, who commissioned it), contains an illustrated history of the Aztec people and an inventory of Aztec daily life. The work, however, never made it to Spain since the ship carrying it was attacked by French pirates, and it remained in France in obscurity for the next four hundred years. Thus Sahagún's work is often credited with being the earliest account of Aztec history and culture written for a Spanish audience rather than for an indigenous one.[5]

Pairing image with text (and translation), Sahagún and his informants presented both a textual and pictorial narrative that accommodated a range of worldviews within the larger history of Spanish conquest and religious conversion. Through twelve volumes and 2,468 rich and detailed images, the codex tells multiple stories: of everyday life in Tenochtitlan, of Aztec religion and ritual, of war and conquest (see fig. 1). Among other things that the manuscript asserts was that Cortés was able to easily defeat the powerful Moctezuma, an accomplished astronomer and astrologer, in part because Moctezuma recently had witnessed eight omens that had come to him in a dream, suggesting the end of his reign—including the return to earth of the red-feathered deity Quetzalcoatl, whom he interpreted as rematerialized in the body of the red-haired Cortés. In book 12, chapter 16, for example, Moctezuma greets Cortés with the following speech:

> O our lord. . . . Thou hast come to arrive on earth. Thou hast come to govern thy city of Mexico; thou hast come to descend upon thy mat, upon thy seat, which for a moment I have watched for thee, which I have guarded for thee. . . . I by no means merely dream, I do not merely see in a dream, I do not see in my sleep; I do not merely dream that I see thee, that I look unto thy face. I have been afflicted for some time. I have gazed at the unknown place whence thou hast come from among the clouds, from among the mists. And so, this. The rulers departed maintaining that you would come to visit thy city, that thou wouldst come to descend upon thy mat, upon thy seat. And now that hath been fulfilled; thou hast come. . . . Peace be with thee. Rest thyself. Visit thy palace. Rest thy body. May peace be with our lords.[6]

Sahagún's biases are clear in the images of the encounter that present Moctezuma in native dress, his naked belly protruding over a scanty loincloth, his oversized hand raised in awkward salute (see fig. 2). Moctezuma wears a richly patterned cape and a headdress. The Spaniards, in contrast, are depicted in full

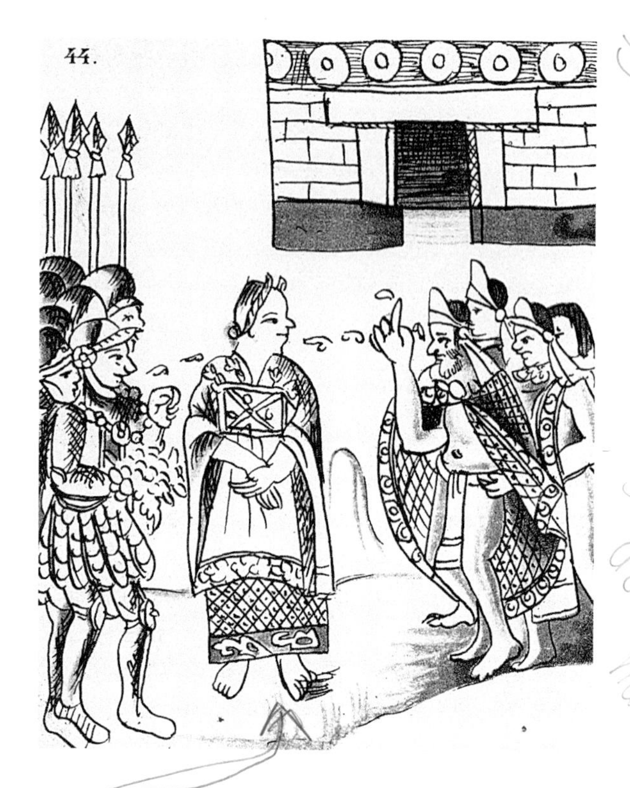

Fig. 2
Fray Bernardino de Sahagún, *General History of the Things of New Spain*, Cortés and Moctezuma meet, introduction, indexes, book 12. Medicea Laurenziana Library. Image courtesy of the World Digital Library.

armor, with long metal bayonets pointing skyward. In the middle is Malinche, the native slave Cortés took as a lover and translator.[7] Also dressed in richly patterned robes, she mediates between the two groups. But unlike Moctezuma, Malinche (who was converted to Catholicism shortly after Cortés enslaved her) is fully dressed, with her hands primly crossed in front of her. This visual representation would register differently with contemporary indigenous and European audiences. To European viewers, Moctezuma seems foreign and exotic while Malinche and the Spanish soldiers appear more civilized and disciplined. Although Moctezuma's lack of dress marks him as less refined to European audiences, to native viewers and artists, his nakedness would likely be of little consequence; one look at his magnificent cape and they would know he was important. Similarly, the language used in the text follows the Nahua convention of deploying couplets that differ just slightly, such as "thy mat / thy seat" and "from among the clouds / from among the mist," as a means of calling attention to the importance of the story. Yet by linking Cortés and his conquistadors to his departed ancestors, as seen in dreams and arriving from "among the clouds, from among the mists," the text posits to Spanish viewers that through both image and text, Moctezuma saw not what was in front of him, but what he already believed.[8]

Today we know that while Moctezuma did indeed believe in astrological omens—which included, among other things, a column of fire streaking across the sky, a lightning bolt that would destroy the temple of Xiuhtecuhtli (the god of fire), and a woman weeping in the middle of the night, as well as the return to earth of the feathered deity, Quetzalcoatl—we also know that Moctezuma's belief in visions was not the primary reason why Cortés and his small band of conquistadors were able to defeat the mighty Aztecs with seeming ease. Nevertheless, Sahagún's narrative frame continues to provide an explanation for what happened: Moctezuma was superstitious and he mistook the Spaniards with their gunpowder, cannons, and braying horses as the ancient gods returning to the earth as foretold by signs he read in the stars. Therefore, instead of unleashing his mighty army on the early Spanish explorers and perhaps changing the course of history, he welcomed them to his palace and gave them gifts of gold and other treasure. Sahagún, too, believed in the power of prophecy and used it as part of his proselytizing mission to warn against the dangers of believing in pagan auguries. As anthropologist Susan D. Gillespie explains, "the existence of signs sent by God was integral to medieval Christianity" and Catholic priests and missionaries, including Sahagún, regularly interpreted God's intentions through omens of their own. Gillespie argues that those who believed that "Cortés was fulfilling the will of God in bringing Christendom to the new world would have expected such omens and portents to be sent."[9] Thus, in this story, Sahagún also saw what he already believed.

Moreover, while Moctezuma did indeed believe in portents and signs, the story is more complicated than Sahagún and his students would have us understand. Composed thirty years after the events took place, Sahagún's native sources would not have been among those who had such intimate access to Moctezuma's personal reactions to the invasion. Instead, as Inga Clendinnen writes, this account "bears the hallmarks of a post-Conquest scapegoating of a leader who had indeed admitted the Spaniards to his city in life, and was so made to bear the weight of the unforeseeable consequences in death."[10] The scapegoating of Moctezuma, as well as the veneration of Cortés as an exemplary military leader, was deployed by all sides of this conquest narrative, Spanish as well as native.[11] Placing blame on Moctezuma for his belief in omens and dreams offers a viable explanation for the Spanish victory. It also provides a moral lesson. By portraying Moctezuma as overwhelmed by fear brought on by the appearance of Cortés, his soldiers, and their columns of fire and beset by superstitions and pagan beliefs, the codex places the blame on Moctezuma's belief in visions and his misinterpretation of visual signs, rather than on the gunpowder, horsepower, and germs that the Spanish brought with them.[12]

How the codex made its way to Italy is unclear; however, by 1588 the multivolume manuscript was part of the Medici collections in Florence. Upon first hearing of the project, King Phillip II called for Sahagún to stop production and instructed his officers to "seize those books, without any original or copy remaining," and "not allow any person to write things having to do with the superstitions and the way of life of the native, in any language."[13] Apparently

Sahagún did not receive these instructions (or chose to ignore them) and continued his work, which was smuggled out of the Americas upon completion. Scholars speculate that the work made its way via Madrid to Rome, where it was bound in multiple leather volumes, given as a wedding gift to Grand Duke Francisco de Medici in 1578, and then placed in the family's Laurentian Library. The library—commissioned by Clement VII, the Medici pope, in 1523 (and designed by Michelangelo)—was built to showcase the family's growing collection of books and manuscripts, as well as to display the vast works of science and art that they had begun to commission and assemble as a means of demonstrating that they were no longer merely successful bankers and merchants but also important members of the Renaissance intelligentsia.[14] Thus objects such as the codex served as material evidence of the Medici family's position as custodians and purveyors of new global forms of knowledge through the ownership and display of things.

Renaissance scholars and missionaries repeatedly used objects such as the Florentine Codex, which involved the painstaking cataloging of the known world as *las cosas*, or things, as a means of asserting new ways of understanding the universe. Through them they stressed the importance of measured thought over pagan belief and direct observation over mythology and the (mis)interpretation of signs as a means of distinguishing between the work of their God and the false prodigies of demons, witches, and other forms of pagan idolatry. The production and circulation of objects such as the Florentine Codex, I would argue, also marks a key moment in the transformation of the nature of vision and the advent of a new form of spectator, removed from the events of the story but in search of information grounded in experience—often the encountering of foreign and exotic objects. It signals a more modern way of seeing as tied directly to notions of evidence and understanding as rooted in sensory perception of visual and material things.

The links between seeing and knowing date back to antiquity. Aristotle, in his circa 350 BCE treatise *De anima*, explicitly ties images to the "medium of thought," arguing that "the soul never thinks without an image."[15] For Aristotle, "no one can learn or understand anything in the absence of sense, and when the mind is actively aware of anything it is necessarily aware of it along with an image, *for images are like sensuous contents except in that they contain no matter.*"[16] Plato similarly asserted the primacy of sight as the noblest of the senses when he linked reason with the "eye of the soul."[17] The relationship between images and matter has been a source of philosophical debate for centuries. I am not going to engage these arguments in detail here, but I do want to highlight the centrality of this issue in the history of Western thought more broadly and visual culture studies more specifically. For example, in his foundational text *Ways of Seeing*, British cultural critic John Berger positioned sight as the privileged sense for making meaning of the world around us when he wrote, "But there is another sense in which seeing comes before words. It is seeing which establishes our place in the surrounding world; we explain that world with words but words can never undo the fact that we are surrounded with it."[18] Berger's materialist assertion that seeing precedes words continues to dominate much of the work done in visual culture studies.[19] We read texts, we look at images, we understand the past as well as our present primarily through sight. Yet as Hal Foster argues in the preface to his edited volume *Vision and Visuality*, seeing is always socially and culturally constructed:

> Although vision suggests sight as a physical operation, and visuality sight as a social fact, the two are not opposed as nature to culture: vision is social and historical too, and visuality involves the body and the psyche. Yet neither are they identical: here, the difference between the terms signals a difference within the visual—between the mechanism of sight and its historical techniques, between the datum of vision and its discursive determinations—a difference within the visual—a difference, many differences, among how we see, how we are able, allowed, or made to see, and how we see this seeing or the unseen therein.[20]

vision

Foster's important analysis of the relationship between vision and visuality continues to be key in delineating the field of visual studies. But, as Nicholas Mirzoeff more recently has pointed out, "visuality is an old word for an old project. It is not a trendy theory word meaning the totality of all visual images and devices, but is in fact an early nineteenth-century term meaning the visualization of history." Tracing the origins of the term back to Thomas Carlyle, Mirzoeff identifies what he calls a "complex of visuality" that involved practices of observation and control that range from the eighteenth-century plantation system to the current military-industrial complex. In all his examples he demonstrates how visuality acts as a tool for aestheticizing, and thus naturalizing, dominant and oppressive power structures and social orders. In response, Mirzoeff articulates a theory of what he calls *countervisuality* as "the assertion of the right to look, challenging the law that sustains visuality's authority in order to justify its own sense of 'right'" and to provide alternatives that imagine possible new worlds.[21]

The complex of visuality has been a masculinist endeavor for the most part, premised on systems of surveillance and oppression. In part my project is an intervention in these accounts. By focusing on objects of vision often excluded from master narratives—material artifacts and ways of seeing that are too easily dismissed as unimportant, strange, frightening, and even silly—I hope to make room for other voices and more inclusive ways of understanding the world. Objects of vision, as I hope to demonstrate, are not seen objectively—or simply for what they are—but are situated within a context of relationships, ideas, and

authors goal

cultures that shape what we see when we view these objects. Of particular interest to me are forms of ephemera, or, rather, objects of vision that are fantastic, wonderous, and often marginal to our understanding of historical moments. Following Avery Gordon, I am interested in images that haunt their subjects and thus defy easy classification and control. For Gordon, "haunting is a constituent element of modern social life. It is neither premodern superstition nor individual psychosis; it is a generalizable social phenomenon of great import."[22] By exploring the role of "visions," loosely defined, I hope to interrogate the relationship between visions and visuality to articulate a sensory history of seeing and its larger links to knowing.

I am using the concept of visions both literally and metaphorically to describe the myriad ways that we as spectators continue to envision ourselves as actors in daily life, as well as to include those things that have been revealed in dreams or reveries, ghostly presences captured on film, and messages sent by the gods. Visions are inherently sensory phenomena. They require interpretation and context to differentiate between what is visionary and what is madness; they frame our understanding of optical processes and apparatuses and underlie how we see and act in the world.

Perhaps it should not be surprising that René Descartes, the "father of modern philosophy" and a key theorist of vision, attributed his success to heavenly intervention. According to his first biographer, Adrien Baillet, on November 10, 1619, the evening of the Vigil of the Feast of St. Martin, Descartes had three dreams that he later described as "the most important thing in his life." Interpreting them as a sign from God that he had been given a divine order to establish an all-encompassing theory of human knowledge, these dreams formed the basis for his investigations into analytical geometry, optics, and the scientific method. Descartes took these visions so seriously that in thanksgiving for this divine intervention, he vowed to the Virgin Mary that he would make a pilgrimage and then journeyed to her shrine in Loreto, Italy, to offer prayers of gratitude. Although Descartes would later argue that dreaming was a form of deception, the tension between the generative potential of his visions and his general distrust of dreams speaks to what Stuart Dalton calls "the unresolved tension within Descartes's philosophy concerning images, vision and the visual."[23] Indeed, how to differentiate between God's will and "the work of an Evil Deceiver who is the god not of love and truth, but of deception, fear and madness,"[24] was a question that Descartes tried to make sense of for the rest of his life—and in many ways fueled the quest for disenchantment at the root of much of the modern Enlightenment project.[25]

Following scholars such as Jane Bennett and Philip Fisher, I aim to reclaim enchantment as part of a deliberate and ethical strategy of resistance and take seriously moments of sensory disruption that challenge the rational disavowal of seemingly magical and miraculous encounters.[26] Paying particular attention to the confluence of space, narrative, and technology in framing the idea of visions, I concentrate in this project on the idea of *making* visual sense, with an emphasis on the making. Inspired by the groundbreaking work of social historians such as E. P. Thompson for whom making is "an active process, which owes as much to agency as to conditioning,"[27] I treat the visual as a set of relationships much like Thompson does class: "as a social and cultural formation, arising from processes which can only be studied as they work themselves out over a considerable historical period."[28]

This is not a comprehensive history of vision nor of visual culture. We cannot isolate one sense on its own. Rather, a sensory history of ways of seeing must also take into consideration the other four senses as well.[29] In this book, by presenting a series of linked case studies that highlight moments of seeming disconnect between seeing and believing—hoaxes, miracles, spirit paintings, manipulated photographs, and holograms, to name just a few of my objects—I hope to make room for many of the things that are not a part of the modernist project of rationalism and scientific method. For example, belief, desire, affect, pleasure, and fear have all influenced how we have chosen to see things over time and provide a narrative that accounts for what Marc Bloch, paraphrasing the ancient Greek historian Herodotus, allows for "great and marvelous exploits . . . [that] should not lose their radiance,"[30] or what Carolyn Walker Bynum designates as "the special characteristic of the historian, a sense of wonder."[31]

Descartes identified "wonder" in 1649 as "a sudden surprise of the soul which makes it tend to consider attentively those objects which seem to it rare and extraordinary."[32] Centuries later, Bynum notes that "medieval philosophers and theologians emphasized wonder as a first step towards knowledge."[33] She writes, "If, to theologians, chroniclers, and preachers, the wonderful was indeed often the strange, the rare, and the inexplicable, it was never the *merely* strange or the *simply* inexplicable. It was the strange that mattered, that pointed beyond itself to meaning." Bynum encourages contemporary historians to continue to highlight wonder in their narratives, concluding that "the flat, generalizing, presentist view of the past encapsulates it and makes it boring, whereas amazement yearns toward an understanding, a significance, that is always just a little beyond both our theories and our fears."[34] For Descartes, wonderment was both a spiritual and a sensory process that takes place when

> the impression formed in the brain which represents the object as rare, and consequently worthy of close consideration; and then by the movement of the spirits, which are disposed by this impression, first, to rush towards the part of the brain where it is located in order to reinforce it and preserve it there, and, secondly, to flow from there into the muscles that serve to keep the sense-organs in the same state as they are now, so as to keep the original impression going (supposing it was formed by them in the first place).[35]

As with dreams, however, Descartes warned that wonder could also be deceptive. Figuring out how to differentiate between light and dark wonder—how to trust and then make meaning from his visions—was foundational to his thought. Moreover, for Descartes (and after), wonder increasingly has been tied to things—from the objects collected in Renaissance *wunderkammer* (or wonder cabinets) to the "marvelous possessions" encountered in colonial voyages of exploration that for Stephen Greenblatt encapsulate the awe many experienced in the new world, or, as in the case of the Florentine Codex, *las cosas de nueva España*. One of my goals for this project is to highlight the importance of the strange and the wonderful in understanding changing notions of vision and visual culture both within and outside the spectacle of the marketplace but also within different and often conflicting belief systems. This brings us back to the Florentine Codex and its circulation as a visual object across time and space.

The early history of the Florentine Codex corresponds to the emergence of the idea that objects—paintings, manuscripts, ethnographic matter, et cetera—have cultural value and thus can be displayed and collected for their intrinsic worth, as well as for what they reveal.[36] The Florentine Codex's desirability stemmed both from its status as a rare and unique object as well as from the information contained within its pages. In addition to being a dictionary of the Nahuatl language and a compendium of indigenous cosmology, history, and philosophy, included within the twelve volumes were encyclopedic descriptions of the flora and fauna of the new world, as well as their possible uses. Book 11, for example, contains over seven hundred meticulously illustrated entries of various plants, animals, and minerals—both real and imagined. Each is carefully numbered and is accompanied by details of their possible medicinal and other uses. The authority ascribed to the manuscript by European audiences stems largely from the provenance of the source material contained within: native informants. Many of them would not have been present at the events they recorded, yet because they could translate the story, in picture and in text, from Nahuatl into an account legible to Spanish Catholic audiences, they were considered credible sources. Sahagún verified the legitimacy of his approach, explaining, "Everything that we discussed was given to me by means of pictures, which was the writing they had used of old, and the grammarians explained them in their language, writing the explanation at the foot of the picture."[37]

Yet with its hand-drawn images and local sources of information, the Florentine Codex also runs counter to narratives of progress as rooted in more objective forms of observation and new forms of technology that began to emerge during this time.[38] During the Renaissance new technologies such as the microscope and telescope located knowledge in that which could be observed. Renaissance humanists such as Leonardo da Vinci argued that "nature is the source of all true knowledge" and that "if you find from your own experience that something is a fact and it contradicts what some authority has written down, then you must abandon the authority and base your reasoning on your own findings."[39] Nearly two hundred years later, John Locke argued in *An Essay Concerning Human Understanding* (1689) that all human knowledge is a posteriori, or derived from experience. Using the metaphor of the tabula rasa, or blank page, Locke posited that "the senses convey into the mind, I mean, they from external objects convey into the mind what produces there those perceptions. This great source of most of the ideas we have, depending wholly upon our senses, and derived by them to the understanding, I call 'sensation.'"[40] For Locke the acquisition of sensory experience took the form of a technology of vision: the camera obscura. Writing of the "dark room" Locke explains:

> External and internal sensation are the only passages I can find of knowledge to the understanding. These alone, as far as I can discover, are the windows by which light is let into this dark room. For me thinks the understanding is not much unlike a closet wholly shut from light, with only some little openings left to let in external visible resemblances, or ideas of things without: would the pictures coming into such a dark room but stay there, and lie so orderly as to be found upon occasion, it would very much resemble the understanding of a man, in reference to all objects of sight, and the ideas of them.[41]

For art historian Jonathan Crary, the camera obscura is the dominant metaphor for conceptualizing vision from the late sixteenth through the eighteenth centuries. He writes, "The camera obscura was not simply an inert and neutral piece of equipment or a set of technical premises to be tinkered upon and improved over the years." Rather, he argues, "it was embedded in a much larger and denser organization of knowledge and the observing subject." It became a model for ordering visions and structuring "how observation leads to truthful inferences about an external world."[42] Advances in optical apparatuses such as the camera obscura (and following it photography and digital imaging) contributed to the widespread belief that new forms of technology and advances in science could reveal new forms of truth.

With new ways of seeing came new ways of understanding.[43] Enlightenment-era thinkers created elaborate systems for the orderly display of knowledge into recognizable categories in an attempt to make sense of the world around them and to create seemingly objective forms of truth tied to visual objects. In 1735, for example, the Swedish botanist Carl Linnaeus organized the natural world into a hierarchical system of units consisting of eight taxa: domain, kingdom, phylum, class, order, family, genus, and species. Linnaeus's taxonomies, which are still used today, became the basis for identifying and sorting things into fixed scientific categories arranged on a flat, pictorial plane. Perhaps

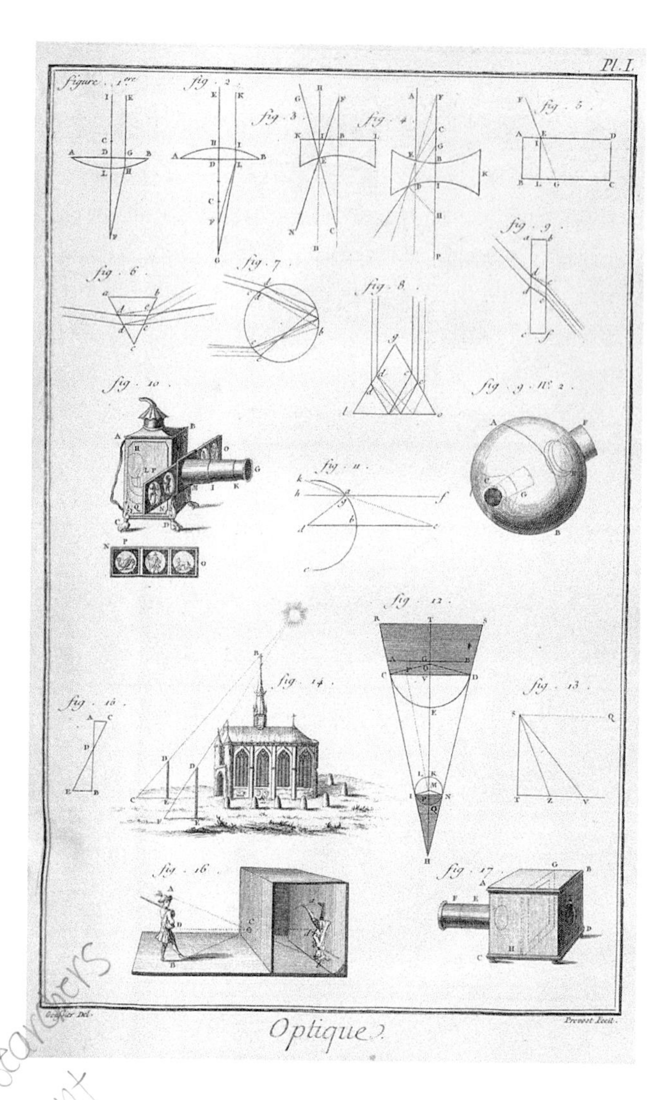

Fig. 3
SCIENCES. MATHÉMATIQUES. | *OPTIQUE*, entries in Jean le Rond d'Alembert and Denis Diderot, *Encyclopédie* (Paris: Briasson, 1751). Image courtesy of the ARTFL Project, Special Collections Research Center, University of Chicago Library.

the most ambitious Enlightenment project for organizing knowledge, however, was Denis Diderot's *Encyclopédie*. Created between 1751 and 1772 and collaboratively sourced from over 140 contributors, the twenty-eight-volume work was edited by Diderot and Jean de la Rond d'Alembert, who identified its two primary aims as "to set forth as well as possible the order and connection of the parts of human knowledge" and "to contain the general principles that form the basis of each science and each art, liberal or mechanical, and the most essential facts that make up the body and substance of each."[44]

Diderot, an avowed atheist, saw the *Encyclopédie* as a way to standardize the attainment of knowledge and secularize learning (and to move away from what he perceived as the stranglehold of the Jesuits, by whom he had been educated). His goal, he explained in an article about its production, was "to change the way people think" and "for people to be able to inform themselves and to know

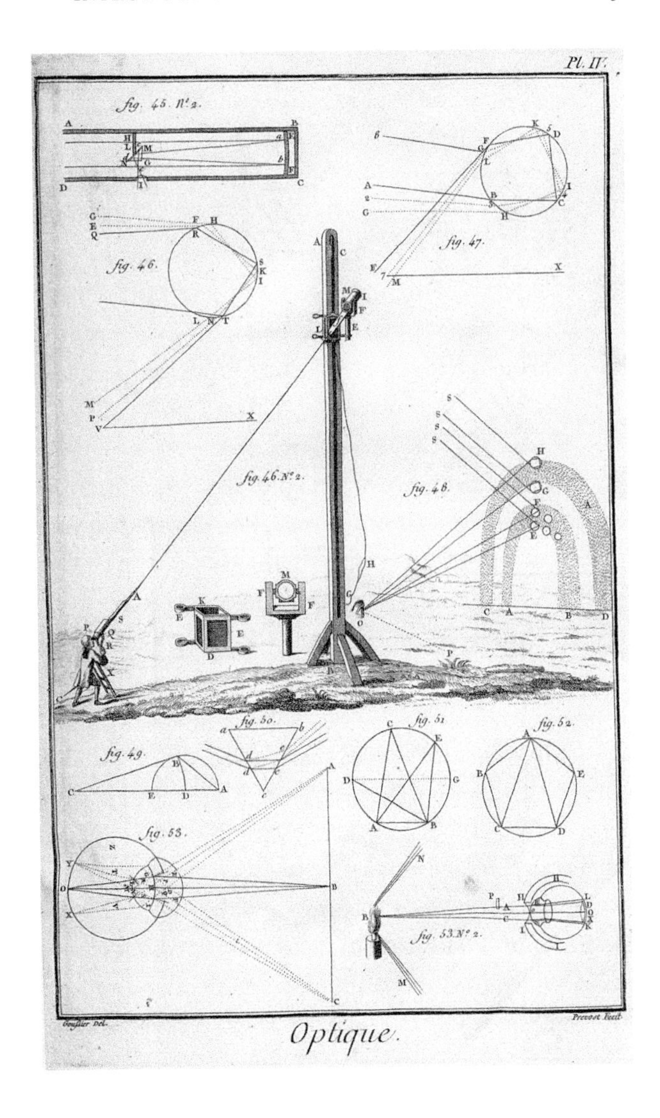

things."[45] One way that the authors of the *Encyclopédie* attempted to standardize knowledge was through the inclusion of elaborate technical images and mechanical diagrams. For example, the entry on "Optics" contained six plates that depicted new technologies of vision such as the telescope, the microscope, and various camera obscuras, as well as drawings that traced the principles of reflection and refraction of light in more mathematical terms (see fig. 3). By linking the drawings to scientific processes, they attempted to yoke fact to vision. For Diderot there were direct links between sight and insight, and both were rooted in the senses.

The importance of the senses was further highlighted in Bonaventure-Louis Prévost's engraving for the frontispiece of the work.[46] The image depicts a group of female figures representing Reason and Philosophy, Truth, and Imagination (see fig. 4).[47] Diderot described the scene as such:

> Beneath an Ionic Temple, the Sanctuary of Truth, one sees Truth enveloped in a veil and radiating light which parts the clouds and disperses them. To the right, Reason and Philosophy are busy, one in raising the veil from Truth, the other in tearing it away. At her feet, Theology, on her knees, receives the light from on high. In following this chain of figures, one finds on the same side Memory, Ancient and Modern History; History records the pomp and ceremony, and Time serves as its support. Below them are grouped Geometry, Astronomy, and Physics. The figures below this group represent Optics, Botany, Chemistry, and Agriculture. At the bottom are several Arts and Professions which derive from the Sciences. At the left of Truth, one sees Imagination, who positions herself to adorn and crown Truth. Below Imagination, the artist has placed the different Imitation: Music, Painting, Sculpture, and Architecture.

In this engraving, "Truth" is personified at the top of the frame as a radiant vision seated high in the clouds. Emanating light, she inspires the disciplines and attributes below her: Beauty, Reason, Geometry, Physics, Poetry, Painting, and Sculpture are all part of the same tableau. Alongside "Truth" sits "Imagination." By deploying a hierarchical structure with "Truth" at the top of the pyramid-like formation, joined just below by "Imagination," the image provides an alternative visual taxonomy in more narrative, allegorical form. It also harnesses the internal senses to the external senses as the foundation for the acquisition of knowledge.

In addition to the figurative image in the frontispiece, Diderot and d'Alembert attempted to further order their project through a series of schematic maps. These charts helped orient readers to the material within a Linnaean-like classification system. In so doing, these maps reduced vast amounts of information to a single, two-dimensional, hierarchically ordered schema. As with the frontispiece, Diderot amended his chart with a narrative "Detailed Explanation" in which he again linked human knowledge to the work of the senses, arguing:

> Physical beings act on the senses. The impressions of these beings stimulate perceptions of them in the understanding. The understanding is concerned with its perceptions in only three ways, according to its three principal faculties: memory, reason, and imagination. Either the understanding makes a pure and simple enumeration of its perceptions through memory, or it examines them, compares them, and digests them by means of reason; or it chooses to imitate them, and reproduce them through imagination. Whence results the apparently rather well-founded general distribution of human knowledge into *history*, which is related to *memory*; into *philosophy*, which emanates from *reason*; and into *poetry*, which arises from *imagination*.

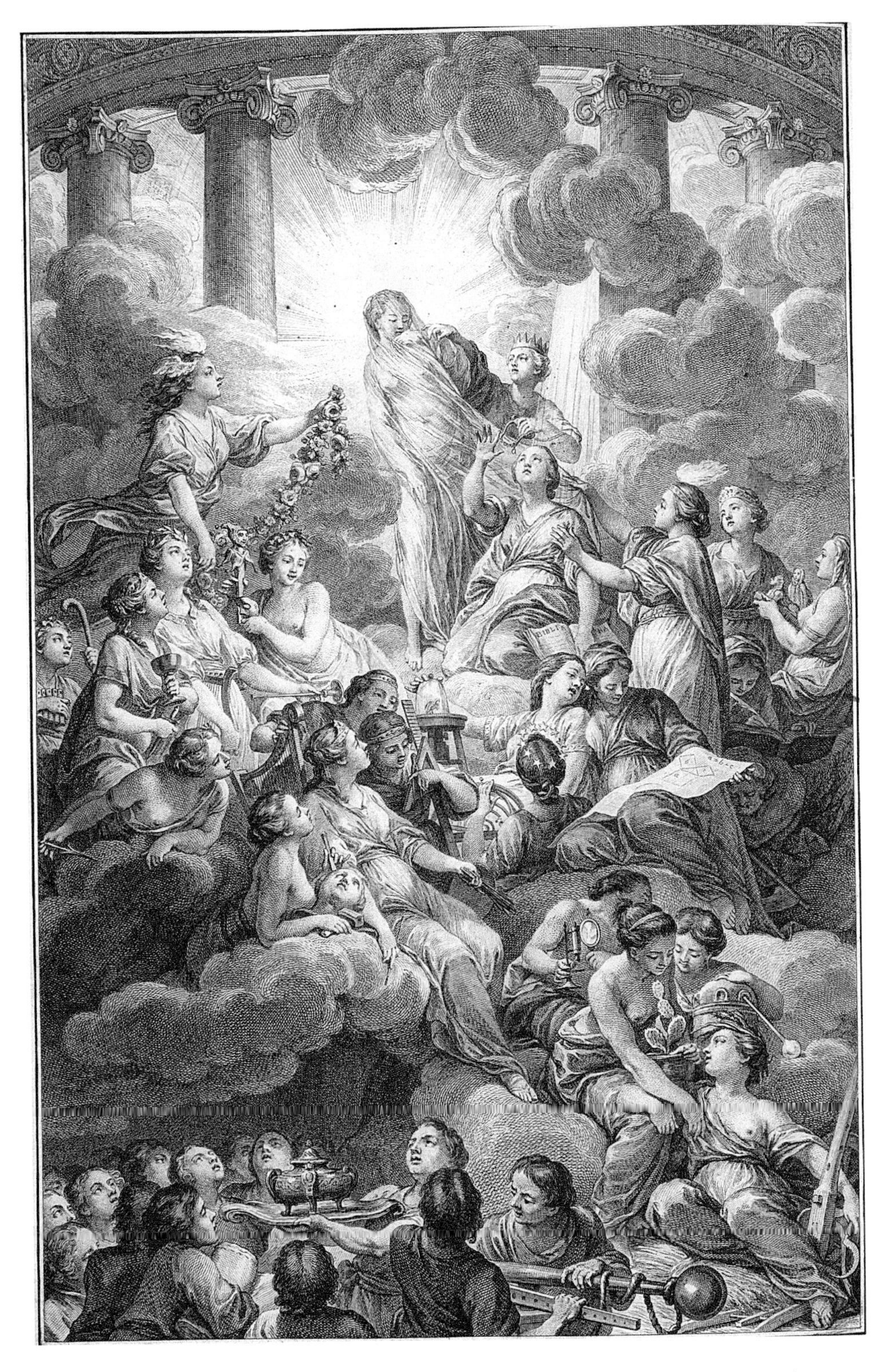

Fig. 4 Frontispiece to Jean le Rond d'Alembert and Denis Diderot, *Encyclopédie* (Paris: Briasson, 1751). Image courtesy of the ARTFL Project, Special Collections Research Center, University of Chicago Library.

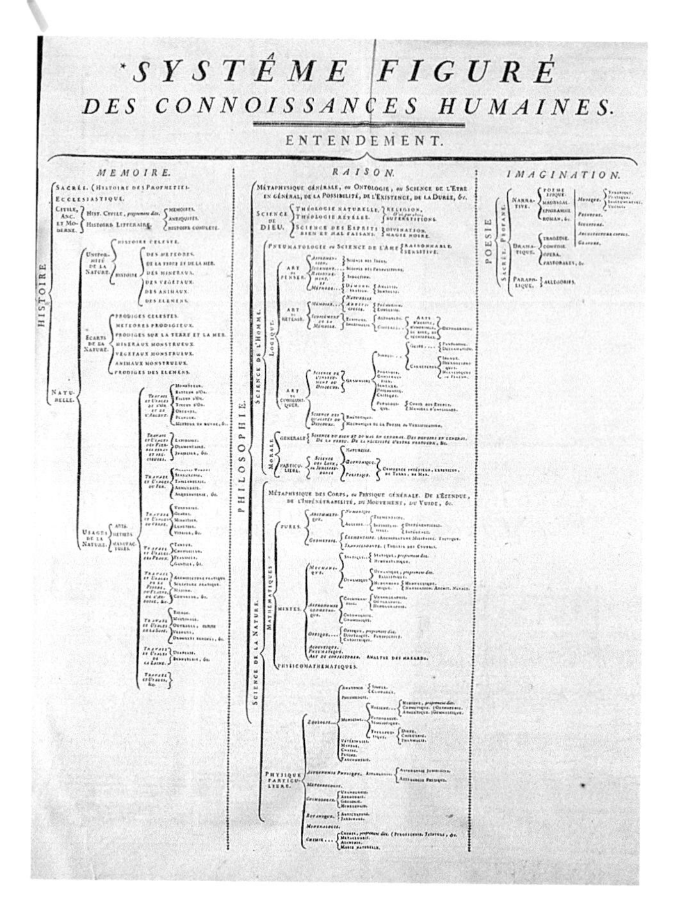

Fig. 5
"Système Figuré des Connaissances Humaines" (The figurative system of organization of human knowledge), chart from the 1752 edition of Jean le Rond d'Alembert and Denis Diderot, *Encyclopédie* (Paris: Briasson, 1752). Image courtesy of the ARTFL Project, Special Collections Research Center, University of Chicago Library.

Once again Diderot stressed the importance of imagination, together with reason and memory, in stimulating understanding. By highlighting the importance of various "perceptions" alongside the seemingly objective display of information contained in the *Encyclopédie,* he made room for different visions as well as visualizations of knowledge to coexist in the pages of the multivolume text (see fig. 5).

In a supplement to the *Encyclopédie,* the editors included a woodcut by Chrétien Frederic Guillaume Roth illustrating their map as a "tree of knowledge" whose three main branches were memory and history, reason and philosophy, and imagination and poetry, thus formally visualizing their plan in organic form for readers of the text. The fruit of this tree took the form of small orbs of varying sizes, each representing all the "domains of science known to man and featured in the encyclopedia."[48] Roth's encyclopedic tree presented knowledge as exhaustive and hierarchically dense, but also as mappable and thus attainable (see fig. 6). Moreover, by providing so many possibilities for the procurement of knowledge, this tree challenged the either/or scenario set forth in the Old Testament's tree of knowledge in which "the LORD God commanded the man, saying, 'You may surely eat of every tree of the garden, but of the tree of the knowledge of good

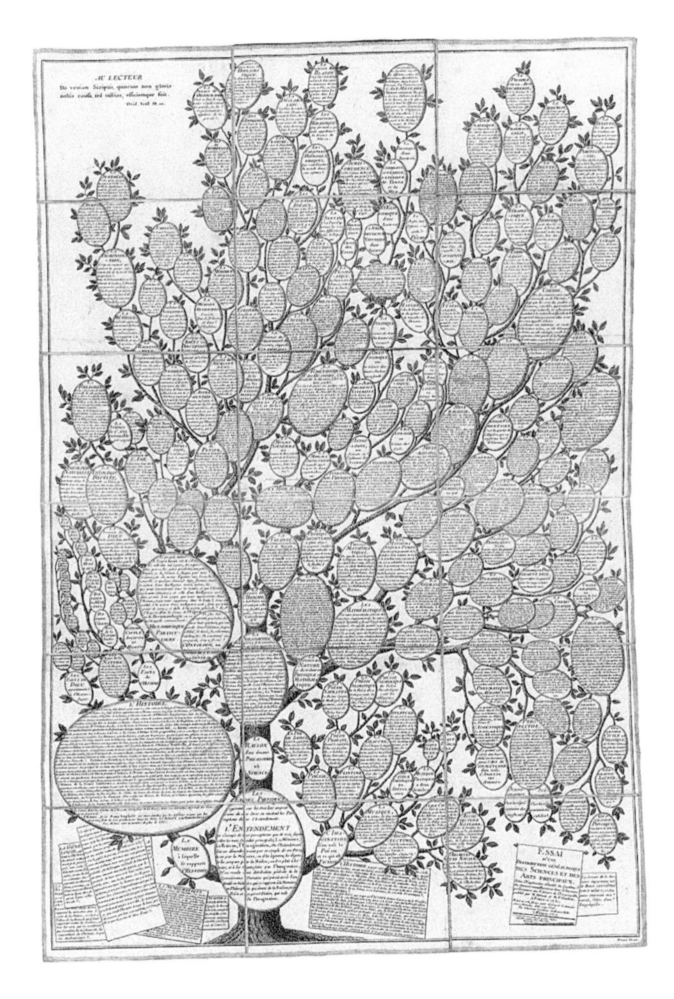

Fig. 6
F. G. Roth, *Explication détaillée du systeme des Connoissances Humaines tirée du Discours Préliminaire du Tome I. de l'Encyclopédie Publiée par Mr. Diderot et Mr. d'Alembert à Paris pour Servir à l'Usage de l'Arbre Encyclopédique*. Image courtesy of the ARTFL Project, Special Collections Research Center, University of Chicago Library.

and evil you shall not eat, for in the day that you eat of it you shall surely die'" (Gen. 2:16–17). Instead, Roth's encyclopedic tree contained multiple branches and no evil agents in masquerade—there was no threat of death (nor any expulsion from paradise) as a result of partaking of their trees of knowledge and no possibility of mistaking the messenger as an evil vision.

Over three hundred years later, Michel Foucault argued that the quest for disciplinary order as embodied in the *Encyclopédie* was one of the hallmarks of what he called the classical episteme, or the historical a priori that grounds knowledge and its discourses within a particular epoch. Characterized by the systematic ordering of difference along taxonomic criteria, the classical episteme fell between the Renaissance quest for resemblance and similitude and the modern epoch. In many ways Foucault underscores the absurdity at the root in encyclopedic thinking by quoting a passage from Jorge Luis Borges's description of "a certain Chinese encyclopedia" in the preface to his text: "It is written that animals are divided into: (a) those that belong to the Emperor, (b) embalmed ones,

(c) those that are trained, (d) suckling pigs, (e) mermaids, (f) fabulous ones, (g) stray dogs, (h) those that are included in this classification, (i) those that tremble as if they were mad, (j) innumerable ones, (k) those drawn with a very fine camel's-hair brush, (l) others, (m) those that have just broken a flower vase, (n) those that resemble flies from a distance."[49] Nevertheless, despite the seeming futility of objectively and exhaustively placing ideas and things into legible categories, the impulse to catalog people, things, and ideas persists across epochs and epistemes.

Perhaps nowhere have knowledge and vision been knit together through the display of people, things, and ideas more than in the encyclopedic museum.[50] Institutions such as the British Museum in London, the Louvre in Paris, and the Smithsonian Institution in Washington, DC, emerged as Enlightenment establishments whose purpose was to advance the belief that the world was knowable and could be understood through the organization and seemingly rational display of things and ideas, often in the name of colonial agendas and national sovereignty. The British Museum was founded in 1753 by an act of Parliament in response to the bequest by the naturalist and physician Sir Hans Sloane. Sloane, an enthusiastic collector who had amassed over seventy-one thousand objects—including books, manuscripts, ethnographic material, natural specimens, and antiquities (e.g., coins and medals, prints and drawings)—bequeathed all these to King George II in exchange for a £22,000 payment to his heirs. Included in his bequest, which he meticulously cataloged in forty-six volumes, were "the saw of a sawfish," "the shoes of a grown-up Chinese woman which were no bigger than those of a child of 2 or 3 in Sweden," "a striped donkey from the Cape of Good Hope," "the stuffed skin of a rattlesnake," "the headdress of a West Indian King made out of red feathers," "all sorts of Roman and other antiquities," and many other *cosas* that recall the Florentine Codex, as well as Borges's nonsensical taxonomies.[51]

In accordance with Sloane's philosophy, the museum's founding credo was that "all Arts and Science have a Connexion [*sic*] with each other, and Discoveries in Natural Philosophy and other branches of speculative Knowledge for the Advancement and Improvement whereof said Museum or Collection was intended, do and may in many instances give Help and success to the most useful Experiments and Inventions."[52] As Alan Trachtenberg has noted, museums are the "'seat of the muses,' a place of making as well as showing."[53] But what exactly are they making? Often divorced from their original uses and contexts, many of the objects on display in the hallowed halls the British Museum's galleries—the Elgin Marbles from the Parthenon, casting stones from the Great Pyramid of Giza, Buddhist reliefs from the Amaravati Stupa in India—act as wonderous emblems of the country's massive colonial footprint and imperial power. Brought back to London and displayed alongside others of their kind—antiquities, decorative arts, African arts, and so forth—they create and then solidify categories of display across the collections and set a template for the other encyclopedic museums that soon followed.

The Louvre, which displays over 350,000 objects from the prehistoric to the present, was established in Paris, France, in 1793. The Hermitage, founded in 1754 by Catherine the Great, opened to the public in Saint Petersburg, Russia, in 1852. Its collections contain over three million items, including the largest collection of paintings in the world. In 1846 the Smithsonian Institution was founded as the National Museum of the United States to promote "the increase and diffusion of knowledge." Its guiding directive, as the naturalist G. Browne Goode explained, was that "to see is to know."[54] All of these institutions deployed exhibition strategies similar to those established at the British Museum in the eighteenth century. Two centuries later, they all still have as their mission to promote an understanding of the world through cross-cultural encounter as rooted in the categorical display of things, or *las cosas*. Yet the histories of their acquisition haunt their exhibition and add to the sense of wonder and strangeness that often surrounds their display.

As with the Medici centuries earlier, as private wealth increased in the nineteenth and early twentieth centuries, the ownership of rare and exotic objects and original works of art also became a mark of individual taste.[55] The ability to differentiate between original works and copies became one way of demonstrating an individual's status at the turn of the twentieth century as economic elites tried to distinguish themselves from the masses in increasingly stratified Western societies through defining the objects and venues of high culture. Museums quickly evolved into sites of cultural hegemony. This, coupled with new and better techniques of reproduction, furthered the distinction—as well as the perceived importance of the difference—between originals and copies, hoaxes and real events, as I will outline in the pages that follow.

Perhaps no one has been more responsible for articulating changing attitudes surrounding issues of authenticity in the twentieth century than the German theorist Walter Benjamin, who lamented the historical conditions that led to this shift in his much-cited work "The Work of Art in the Age of Its Mechanical Reproducibility."[56] For Benjamin, changes in conceptions of art parallel changes in economic structures and are rooted in and deeply shaped by sensory perspectives. But, for Benjamin, sensory perspective is neither completely biological nor natural; it is also historical. As he explains, the "earliest artworks originated in the service of rituals." For Benjamin, the "here and now of the original," or what he calls the object's aura, "underlines the concept of its authenticity, and on the latter in turn is founded the idea of a tradition which has passed the object down as the same, identical thing to the present day."[57] Take the case of the Florentine Codex, for example. As I stated earlier, neither the native informants who compiled the work nor the Spanish priests who commissioned it were present at the events being recounted; moreover, we now know that much of the story told in its images and text may not be factually true—yet the Codex's presence in time and place, sixteenth-century Mexico, has bestowed on it a form of temporal authenticity and provides a version of truth that may run counter to the sources of knowledge it initially was meant to contain.

Interestingly, as Miriam Hansen notes, Benjamin's first conceptualization of the concept of the aura takes place in a dreamlike state brought on by his experiments with hashish. Thus rather than see it only as an aesthetic category, Hanson links the concept of the aura more directly to the dream worlds that preoccupied Benjamin in many of his other writings—it is significant, I think, that it came to him as a vision.[58] Benjamin's focus on the aura, "a strange tissue of space and time: the unique apparition of a distance, however near it may be," has come to dominate much critical discourse surrounding the status of objects, or *cosas*, in the twentieth century.[59] And while the work needs to be understood within his own poetic form of Marxist philosophy and should be situated within the context of the spread of fascism in Europe in the years before the Second World War, Benjamin's entreaty that "for the first time in world history, technological reproducibility emancipates the work of art from its parasitic subservience to ritual" and his admonition that "the work reproduced becomes the reproduction of a work designed for reproducibility," is key to understanding not only the continued veneration of original art works in the nineteenth and twentieth centuries—it is also key to understanding the late twentieth-century development of more postmodern conceptions of artistic value and aesthetic worth, divorced from historical referent and rooted in spectacle and simulation.[60]

As in the case of the Holliday video with which I begin this project, the ways we frame objects of vision have enabled multiple ways of seeing over time and across media. That is the subject of this project. I have organized the book into four chapters. They do not proceed in a neat chronological fashion, and there is often overlap between them. Some of my subjects are well trod, others are more obscure. I have tried through all my examples, however, to identify and describe what I see as key ways of seeing to understand how we make sense of the world around us. Chapter 1 explores the persistence of what I am calling miraculous vision by looking at instances of divine encounter that can transfer across mediums through replication and reproduction. Chapter 2 looks at the centrality of technological vision in the context of nineteenth-century visual hoaxes. Chapter 3 details the emergence of camera vision and indexical sight through an examination of the material culture of the Spiritualist movement. Chapter 4 investigates the development of the pseudo-event and the emergence of postmodern ways of seeing. I conclude with a short consideration of virtual modes of seeing to complicate notions of authenticity as tied to visual truth.

At the heart of all these visions, or ways of seeing, is a desire for individual agency. The ability to inspect and explore, to challenge or confirm beliefs, to justify the wonderous and impossible, to take an active role in the creation and negotiation of meaning, have given tremendous import to these various forms of vision and their ability to endure. Vision remains the currency of contemporary claims to truth. Advances in technology allow us to see the invisible: fetal heartbeats, seismic activity, cell mutations, virtual space. Yet in an age when experience is so intensely mediated by visual records, the centuries-old realization that knowledge gained through sight is inherently fallible takes on troubling new dimensions. Nevertheless, images and other forms of visual evidence continue to be foundational to understanding the world around us. This disconnect between seeing, knowing, and believing is not new. On the contrary, as I hope to demonstrate, it has persisted across centuries, continents, and media forms and is often legitimized by visual evidence that in many cases directly contradicts what seems to be real. Yet in all the cases I detail below, as silly as some of them may seem to us today, the visions referenced and the stories they tell continue to matter.

CHAPTER 1

The Persistence of Miraculous Vision

A small painting housed in one of the upper rooms in the museum of the Cathedral of Sainte-Anne-de-Beaupré, a few miles north of Quebec City, depicts a scene that reportedly took place in 1650, someplace on the Saint Lawrence River (see fig. 7). According to legend, a group of Breton sailors were caught in a ferocious storm. In their moment of crisis, they prayed to Saint Anne, the patron saint of sailors and the patroness of Brittany (their homeland in France), to save them from the harrowing wind and angry waves—promising to build a shrine to her should they survive the tempest. In the top corner of the image is Saint Anne. Seated in a cloudlike pod and attended by angels, she hovers miraculously over the boat, which seems about to capsize in the turbulent waters. Yet despite the chaos of the moment we see in the image, tragedy allegedly was averted and, with the help of Saint Anne's divine intercession, "morning dawned, and to their great astonishment, [the sailors] found themselves on the bank of the river at Beaupré. They landed and erected a little shrine in honor of good St. Anne, their deliverer.[1]

A similar canvas, titled *Aparición de Nuestra Señora de Guadalupe al Pastor Gil Cordero* (*Apparition of Our Lady of Guadalupe with Pastor Gil Cordero*), hangs in the museum of the Cathedral to the Virgin of Guadalupe in Extremadura, Spain (see fig. 8). This small painting portrays an encounter between a young Spanish cowherd named Gil Cordero and the Virgin Mary, which purportedly took place in 712 CE while Cordero was looking for a cow that had wandered away from his pack. After three days of searching for the lost animal, Cordero found it lying prone and seemingly dead atop a pile of rocks hidden in the forest. Desiring to salvage the hide, he made a cross-like incision in the animal's chest. According to lore, it was at this moment that the Virgin appeared and instructed him to revisit the site with the village priest to excavate a small statue that had been buried there to hide it from Muslim invaders centuries earlier. Cordero

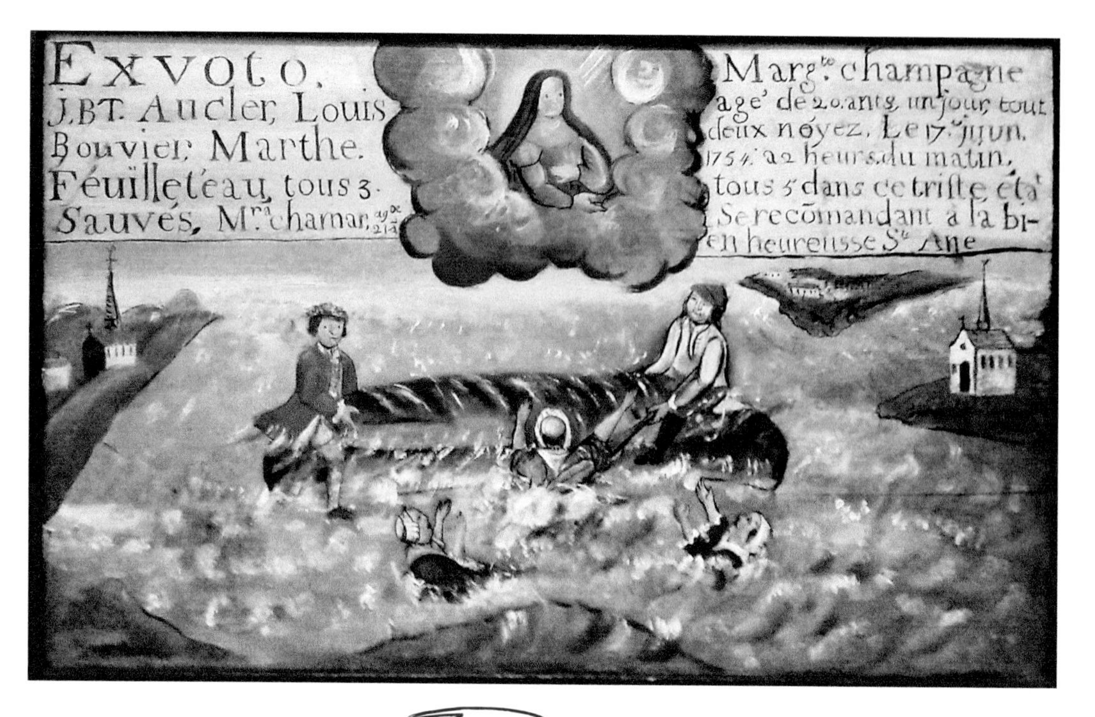

Fig. 7 Ex-voto painting depicting Saint Anne saving the Breton sailors. Museum of the Basilica of Sainte-Anne-de-Beaupré, Quebec, Canada. Photo by author.

returned with a contingent from the church and unearthed "a marvelous statue that was an image of Mary, and built a shrine in the mountains."[2]

Much like in the painting of Saint Anne and the Breton sailors, in this pictorial recounting of the divine encounter between Cordero and the Virgin, Mary sits atop a heavenly cloud, surrounded by angels and cherubs, as she seems to speak to the young man. In both instances, the picture plane of the painting is divided into two distinct spheres. The top segment signifies the heavenly domain, home to Saint Anne and the Virgin Mary, while the bottom of the work denotes the earthly realm, inhabited by the human interlocutors and messengers. Yet the dividing line between the space of the divine and the space of the mortals is not fixed in these works. Saint Anne crosses her arms above the struggling ship, as if she is about to reach out of the clouds to calm the turbulent waves, and Mary's gaze and outstretched hand point toward the young cowherd in a painted form of direct address.

I begin this chapter with these two examples of Catholic ex-voto painting as examples of what I am calling miraculous vision. From the Latin *ex voto suscepto*, meaning "from the vow made," ex-votos are small vernacular offerings placed in a church or shrine as acts of thanks for miracles received. Ex-votos can take the form of painted accounts such as those I have just described or they can be small objects that in some way encapsulate the miraculous event being recorded (a tin

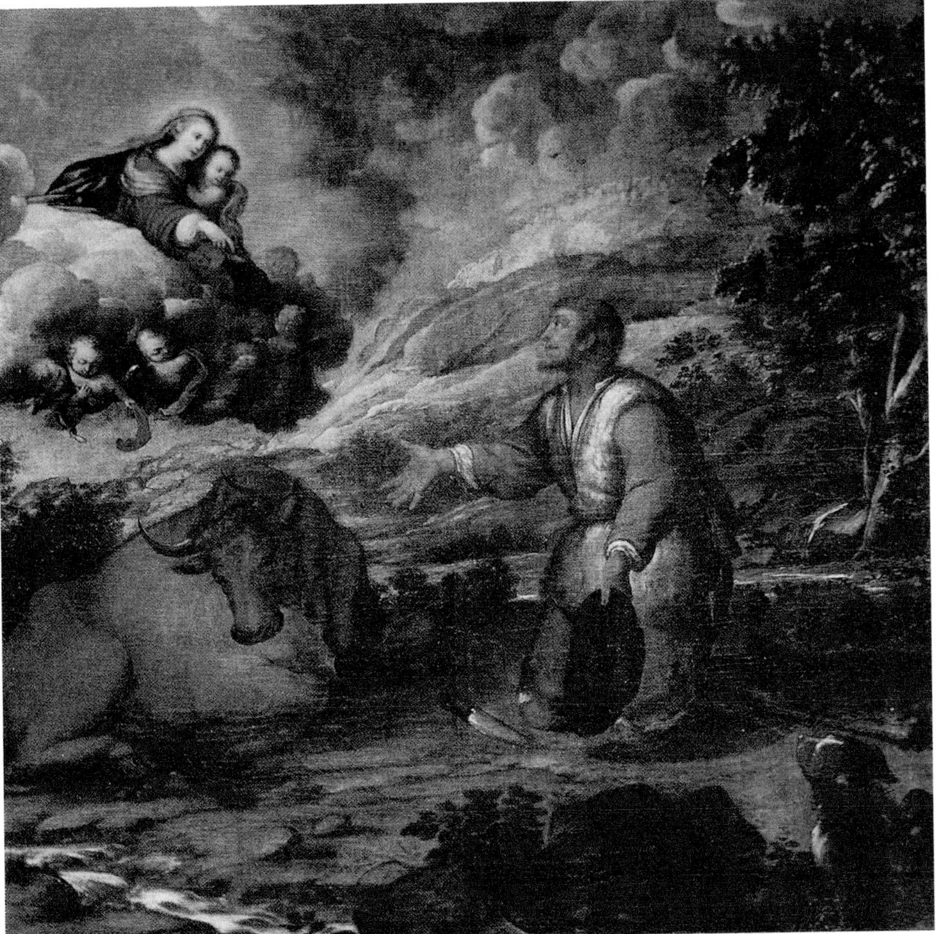

Fig. 8 *Aparición de Nuestra Señora de Guadalupe al Pastor Gil Cordero*. Oil on canvas. Image from Sebastián García Rodríguez and Francisco Tejada Vizuete, *Camarín de Guadalupe: Historia y esplendor* (Guadalupe: Ediciones Guadalupe, 1996).

pendant with a portrait of a loved one, a discarded crutch or brace, a carved body part made of metal, wood, or wax). Often the works are anonymous, depicting incidents and outcomes known only to the supplicants making the gift. Other times they contain or are accompanied by detailed textual accounts of the favors asked and received with names, dates, and times described in various levels of detail. Ex-votos are also offered in thanksgiving for unexpected miracles. They are public affirmations of the presence of the divine in the lives of the faithful, in particular in the lives of the poor and dispossessed. In all instances, they are material professions of faith, testimonials that the events described—as fantastic as they may seem—actually happened.[3]

Aside from their significance as examples of divine encounter, the two images with which I begin this chapter are interesting to me for other reasons as well.

Both Saint Anne and the Virgin of Guadalupe have maintained their status as cult figures across time and space—and the places associated with their miraculous acts, from first-century Europe to the present-day Americas, have become sites of continued pilgrimage and devotion. As sites of pilgrimage, they collapse physical and temporal borders (between heaven and earth, past and present). They function on multiple levels and rest on a number of paradoxes rooted in objects of vision and particular ways of seeing. In the case of the two ex-voto paintings I have just described, for example, their sacred status derives from their distinct associations with miraculous events that reportedly occurred at specific moments in the past. In this way they are static testimonials, visual accounts of the individual miracles recounted on their canvases. But they are simultaneously dynamic. Their power can be transferred through engagement not just with the original image or site, but also, as we will see, with its reproductions and surrogates—past, present, and future. Miraculous vision can travel backward and forward in time, not just with the original beholder but also with those who encounter its traces later and who believe in the transformative powers of the visions referenced in the images or sites contained within them. Despite advances in scientific understandings of vision and new technologies for seeing over the past three centuries, miraculous vision, as I will demonstrate, persists to this day. The belief in miraculous vision frequently defies logic and rests in hope and persistent, if often blind, faith. Yet miraculous vision has its own logic, and even laws, that enable it to endure over time and to persevere in the face of repeated challenges to its power.

The custom of bestowing gifts to gods or spirits as an act of thanksgiving goes back to ancient Mesopotamia and Egypt. The Etruscans placed offerings, called *donaria*, on the walls of their temples, next to statues of divinities or outside adjacent to sacred trees and plants as tributes to their gods. The ancient Greeks also regularly imbued representations of their gods—who walked freely among them on earth—as well as the sites where they worshiped them, with divine powers. Erich Auerbach in *Mimesis*, his groundbreaking study of Western literature, for example, identifies what he considers to be "the basic impulse of the Homeric style: to represent phenomena in a fully externalized form, visible and palpable in all their parts, and completely fixed in their spatial and temporal relations."[4] The panoply of ancient gods and their attributes—love, wisdom, hubris, war—regularly took material form, conjoining visions of the physical and spiritual on the earthly realm. The idea of a duality of vision was first articulated by Plato, who in his famous allegory of the cave in the *Republic* differentiated between what he termed the visible world and the intelligible world. He explained the distinction in spatial terms, through the metaphor of a divided line:

> Now take a line which has been cut into two unequal parts, and divide each of them again in the same proportion and suppose the two main

> divisions to answer, one to the visible and the other to the intelligible, and then compare the subdivisions in respect of their clearness and want of clearness, and you will find that the first section in the sphere of the visible consists of images. And by images, I mean, in the first place, shadows, and in the second place, reflections in water and in solid, smooth and polished bodies and the like. . . . Imagine, now, the other section, of which this is only the resemblance, to include the animals which we see, and everything that grows or is made.[5]

According to Martin Jay, Plato's distinctions between the visible and the intelligible world paralleled ancient understandings of how light works, in particular the perceived difference between lumen (an inner light that radiates outward) and lux (its real-world result), and complemented emerging concepts of vision as rooted in notions of either speculation (what the mind sees) or observation (what the eye sees).[6] Aristotle further elaborated on his teacher's distinction between what the mind sees and what the eye sees in his treatment of what he called the internal senses, in particular the imagination, which he described as "that in virtue of which an image occurs in us."[7]

For early Christian thinkers, Jay argues, "the contrast between a higher *lumen* and inferior *lux* was often redescribed into religious terms." Light, perceived as divine lux rather than perceived lumen, came to "symbolize a harmony between the mathematical regularities in optics and God's will."[8] Saint Augustine, following both Plato and Aristotle, conceived of sight as a process of extramission whereby rays of light "shine through the eyes and touch whatever we see." Augustine identified three types of vision—corporeal, intellectual, and spiritual—and differentiated between what he called the "eye of the body" and the "eye of the mind," both of which he grounded in the senses as guided by faith. Writing in *De Trinitate* in 400 CE, he argued, "If we at any time try to distinguish internal spiritual things more subtly and describe them more easily, we must take examples from external things to illustrate them. Now the outer person, gifted with the bodily senses, perceives bodies." Yet, he continued, "this bodily sense is actually five senses: sight, hearing, smell, taste, and touch. But it is difficult and unnecessary to ask all the senses about what we are looking for."[9] Like Aristotle, Augustine also distinguished between internal and external senses and included imagination among the four internal senses, joined by common sense, judgment, and memory in the "storehouse of forms received through sense." Yet Augustine privileged sight, or "the testimony of the eyes," over all other senses because, he argued, "this sense far exceeds the rest, and although it is a different kind of vision, it is close to spiritual vision."[10]

Saint John of Damascus further elaborated on the idea of spiritual vision as something more than physical vision in his 726 CE defense of idols, "Apologia Against Those Who Decry Holy Images," one of three treaties he wrote in response to the Byzantine Emperor Leo III's order for the destruction of all religious images, or icons, earlier that year. Saint John of Damascus defended the existence of icons, positing that "an image is a likeness of the original with a certain difference, for it is not an exact reproduction of the original. Thus, the Son is the living, substantial, unchangeable Image of the invisible God." Moreover, he continued, "an image is expressive of something in the future, mystically shadowing forth what is to happen."[11]

Responding to the iconoclast charge that "Satan misled men, so that they worshipped the creature instead of the Creator. The Law of Moses and the Prophets cooperated to remove this ruin. . . . But the previously mentioned demiurge of evil . . . gradually brought back idolatry under the appearance of Christianity,"[12] Saint John of Damascus claimed instead that he did not worship matter, "but rather the creator of matter, declaring, "But I also venerate the matter through which salvation came to me, as if filled with divine energy and grace." For him, this included "the wood of the Cross," the "ink and holy book of the Gospels," and sacred paintings and sculpture. In linking symbolic objects with divine energy and grace he set the stage for the veneration of spiritual images as embodying sacred properties and the process of viewing them as transformative sensory experiences, or what I am calling miraculous vision. He explained, "When we set up an image of Christ on any place, we appeal to the senses, and indeed we sanctify the sense of sight, which is the highest among the perceptive senses."[13]

But how to determine which images had sacred powers? How to authenticate the presence of the divine and differentiate miraculous images from the false terrors of demons or witches? For Saint Augustine, all of nature was a miracle since it represented the will of God realized: "For how can anything done by the will of God be contrary to nature, when the will of so great a creator constitutes the nature of each created thing?"[14] Following Augustine, Saint Thomas Aquinas explained, "The word miracle is derived from admiration, which arises when an effect is manifest, whereas its cause is hidden. . . . Now a miracle is so called as being full of wonder; as having a cause absolutely hidden from all: and this cause is God. Wherefore those things which God does outside those causes which we know, are called miracles."[15] For Aquinas, the processes through which the hidden becomes visible is proof of God's presence. This mindset took hold during the Middle Ages, as historian Lorraine Daston has noted, when miraculous encounters moved from private devotional occurrences to public events. Daston writes that God began to perform "miracles for an audience, which credits them in proportion to the wonder they excite, which wonder in turn measures the magnitude of the audience's ignorance. Miracles convert and convince by their psychological effects; they are God's oratory."[16] Yet like the iconoclasts before them who warned of the power of idols and wary clerics who decried black magic and the threats of witchcraft and evil visions, the need arose for believers to differentiate between types of visions to gauge the authenticity of miraculous encounters and to safeguard against the trickery of false gods or demons.

As a result, the Catholic Church set up standards for evaluating miraculous images. In 1582, for example, the Archbishop of Bologna distinguished between what he considered "sacred" and "holy" images. An image is sacred, he wrote, "if it enters into contact with the body, or with the face or with other parts of our Lord or one of his saints." Images were holy, he continued, "that would be made by a holy person, like those by St. Luke," or "because it was made in a miraculous manner . . . that is not made by the hand of man, but invisibly, by the work of God, or by other similar means," or "when God has performed manifest signs and miracles in that image . . . or through them."[17] By differentiating between images that were sacred and images that were holy, the archbishop provided a classification system, a prototaxonomy, for the seemingly unscientific organization of miraculous events and images.

According to the historian Richard Trexler, the widespread belief in the transformative and holy power of images took hold more popularly during the Italian Renaissance and continued into the sixteenth and seventeenth centuries. Images became animate. The Renaissance humanist Leon Battista Alberti alleged that it was natural to kiss and talk to images, "to cry with the crier, laugh with the laugher, sorrow with the sorrower." Similarly, the art historian Vasari spoke of the affective power of images "more real than life itself," and Leonardo da Vinci declared, "Write up the name of God in one place and place his figure over against it and you will see what will be more revered."[18] Specifically, Trexler locates Renaissance Florence as the site where miracles regularly began to take material form: "Florentines witnessed or discussed miracles involving images etched on wood, canvas, stone and coins, representing the names or figures of Christian and pagan deities." At the same time that artists and philosophers were reworking man's relationship to the universe and scientists were charting the heavens using new optical technologies, Florence was also "filled with thousands upon thousands of potential miracle-workers, powerful, intimate vessels of love and hate, spiritual ancestors dynamically affecting the civic cosmos."[19] With the preponderance of new religious rituals that arose around different representations of the Virgin Mary in particular, Florence became a fertile site for the cult of the Virgin in the fourteenth and fifteenth centuries.[20] For devotees, Mary's representation contained her heavenly powers and visitors flocked to the various shrines across the city to behold her likeness in the hopes of witnessing her divine favor through visual renderings. Florence thus became a site of pilgrimage and images of Mary became stand-ins for the holy mother herself.

Like ex-voto offerings and devotional images, religious pilgrimages operate as material as well as performative acts of faith. They are what the anthropologists Edith and Victor Turner call "kinetic rituals."[21] Pilgrimages link belief and desire to the experience of physically being in a hallowed space as well as to the feelings provoked before, during, and after the visit. Much as with the power of the image of the ex-voto, with the pilgrimage, the place—as well as the journey itself—takes on the attributes of the divine.[22] In all of these instances of miraculous encounter sacred objects and spaces operate both inside and outside of daily life. They are supernatural and extraordinary, yet they hold the power to transform the quotidian in both magical and mundane ways, in what Robert Orsi calls occasions of "lived religion."[23] With miraculous vision, both the beholder and the object beheld participate in an exchange of meaning that hangs on a number of seeming contradictions. The viewer must simultaneously suspend rational belief systems yet also maintain certainty in the authenticity of the object on display or the site in question and their transcendent powers. Moreover, and more pertinent to the notions of miraculous vision in this project, are the ways in which the meanings affixed to pilgrimage sites and sacred images remain static but also change over time—up to and including the present day.

The Basilica of Sainte-Anne-de-Beaupré, for example, became identified as a site of miracles from the moment of its earliest construction. The first church was built in its current location in the small town of Petit Cap, just north of Quebec City, in 1658. One of the construction workers on the site, a man named Louis Guimond, suffered from acute rheumatism and walked with the aid of a crutch. According to the *Jesuit Relations* journal, after placing just three stones on the shrine's foundation, Guimond was "suddenly cured" of all his ailments.[24] As word of this miracle spread, others came to visit the church hoping (and praying) to receive miracles of their own. But according to historian Mary Corley Dunn, the shrine had larger symbolic resonance for early French colonists. It marked the frontier between the seeming wilderness and civilization and acted as "a safe haven of sorts for the habitants of Petit-Cap," as relations between the French and their Iroquois neighbors deteriorated. Dunn argues that the miracles that took place should be "understood as strategies by which social bodies" defined colonial identities in opposition to both English Protestantism and Native American spiritual worldviews. In part, Dunn notes, "appropriation of symbols" by French colonists buttressed their faith in a world "governed by the inscrutable power of God rather than the predictable forces of nature."[25] Miracles marked the frontier between the seeming wilderness and civilization and acted as "a safe haven of sorts for the habitants of Petit Cap," as relations between the French and their Iroquois neighbors deteriorated.[26]

The shrine at Sainte-Anne-de-Beaupré fulfils a number of narrative and performative functions and operates simultaneously on individual and communal, official as well as vernacular levels—and all of these factors contributed to the reputation of the church as a site of pilgrimage. As a result of its increasing popularity, the building underwent several additions, becoming a basilica in 1876. In March 1922, a fire destroyed the church and, after substantial renovation, it reopened in the fall of 1931. Today, the Basilica of Sainte-Anne-de-Beaupré is the

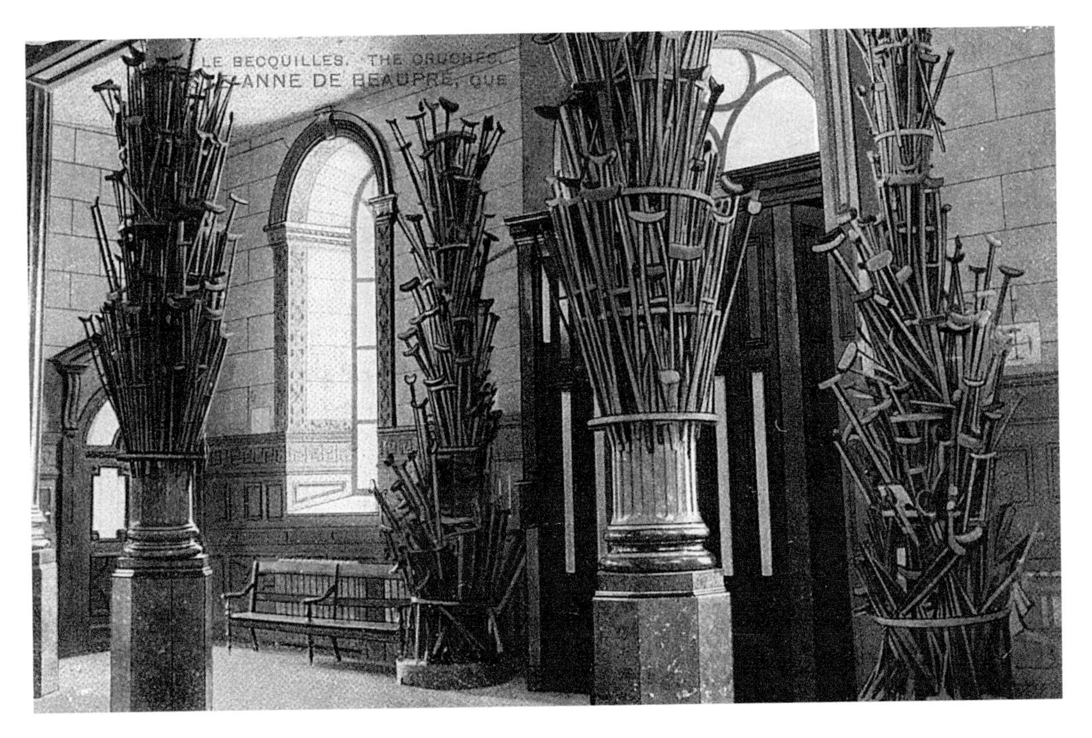

Fig. 9 The crutches. Basilica of Sainte-Anne-de-Beaupré, Quebec, Canada, about 1910. Photomechanical print. © McCord Museum. P-0000.1204.1.

second largest pilgrimage site in North America, drawing an estimated million visitors every year.[27]

At first sight the church looks much like many other majestic Catholic cathedrals with its vaulted ceilings and stained-glass windows. Yet upon closer inspection, an impressive number of crutches, canes, and braces line the walls and church galleries. Writing of his visit to the church in 1850, Henry David Thoreau described seeing crutches that had been "suspended on the walls, some for grown persons, some for children which it was to be inferred so many sick had been able to dispense with" (see fig. 9).[28] The collection of discarded crutches grew, year after year, until at one point they seemed to fill almost every bare wall space. Today these ex-voto offerings are integrated into the church design and fully cover two large support pillars at the back of the church as well as a small chapel adjacent to the basilica (see fig. 10). The site also has a separate history museum that displays many other objects left by devotees as offerings of thanks or appeal: wedding dresses, baby cradles, as well as the painting—and others like it—that I described at the start of this chapter.

At the front of the church, atop a marble pedestal, sits a devotional statue of Saint Anne that was brought to Beaupré in 1670 from the cathedral in Carcassonne, France, by Francis-Xavier de Montmorency-Laval, the first bishop of Quebec and the father of the Canadian church. Carved from a single piece of

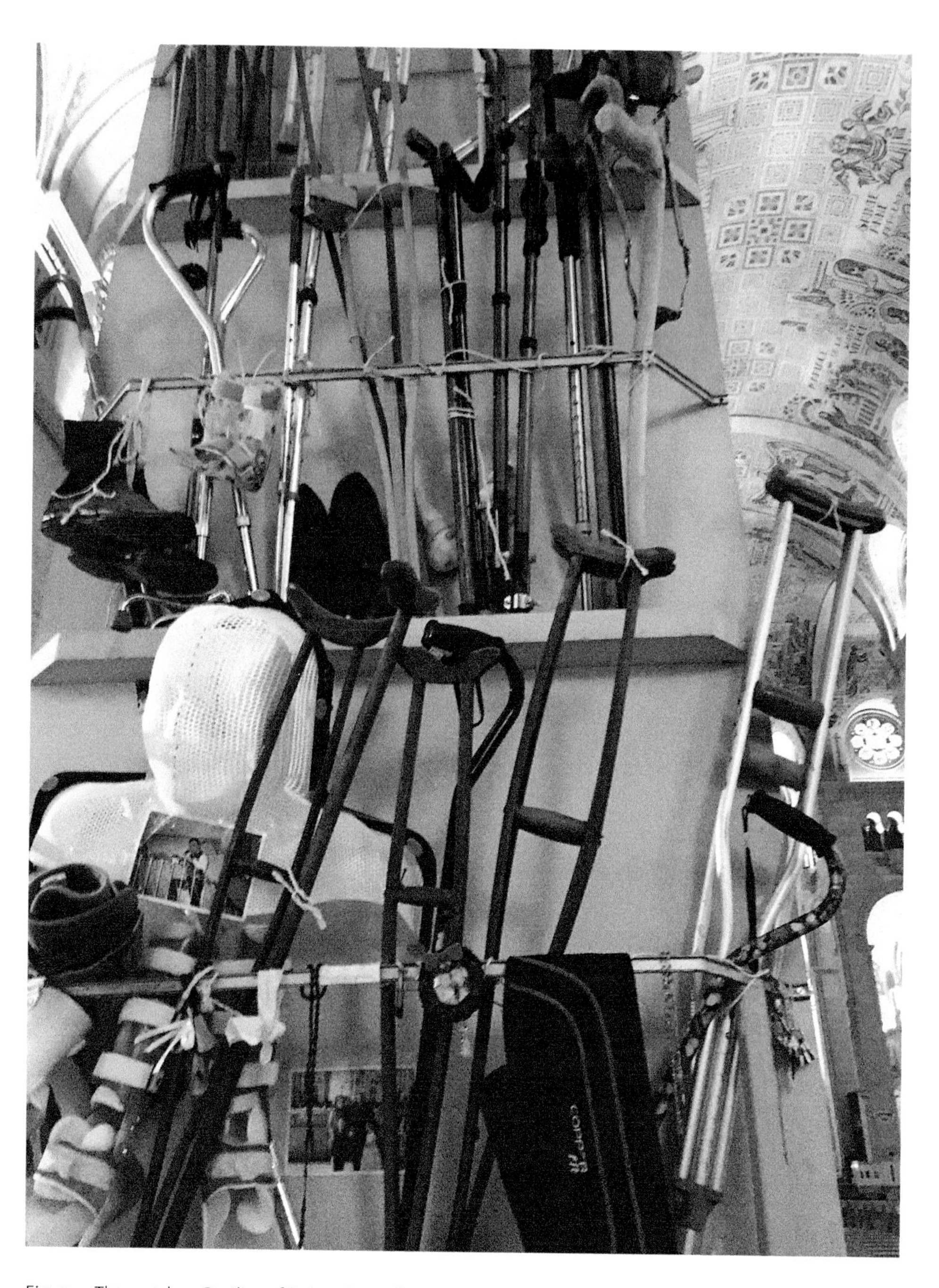

Fig. 10 The crutches. Basilica of Sainte-Anne-de-Beaupré, Quebec, Canada, 2016. Photo by author.

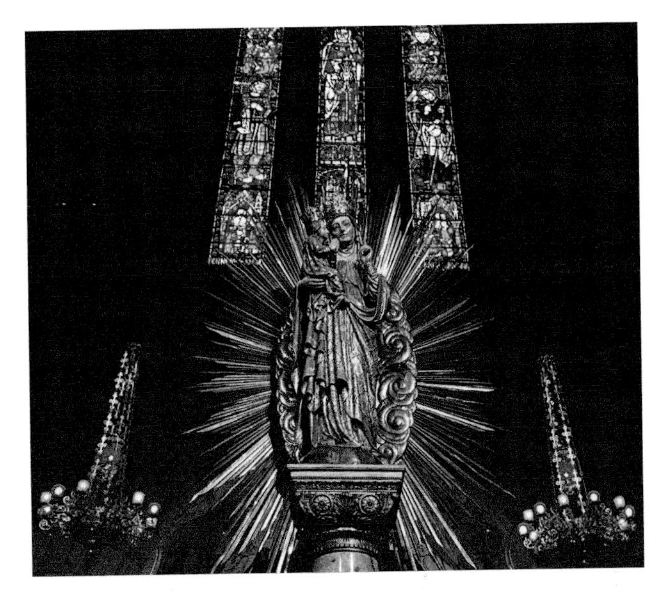

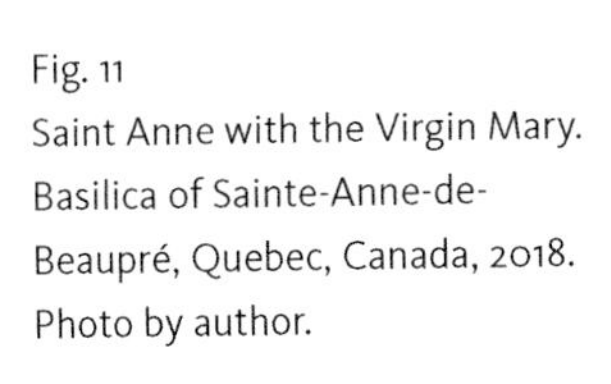

Fig. 11
Saint Anne with the Virgin Mary. Basilica of Sainte-Anne-de-Beaupré, Quebec, Canada, 2018. Photo by author.

oak, the colorful wooden statue depicts Saint Anne holding her child, the Virgin Mary (see fig. 11). Both wear sumptuous-looking gowns, jewel-studded crowns, and are enveloped by a golden halo. This statue, which miraculously survived a devastating fire in 1922, is the object of many a pilgrim's visit. There they place offerings and ex-votos, light candles, and pray for intervention. But Saint Anne is not the only sacred figure represented on the altar in the basilica. Hanging adjacent to the main altar, directly behind the miraculous statue of Saint Anne, is a large painting of Saint Kateri Tekakwitha, also known as Lily of the Mohawks (see fig. 12). A smaller chapel located on the lower level of the church also contains images of scenes from Kateri's life. Kateri's repeated inclusion in the sacred spaces of Saint Anne is significant, especially when one considers Dunn's claim that the church functioned historically as a sacred refuge from native threats.

Kateri Tekakwitha was born in 1656 to a Mohawk father and an Algonquin mother who had converted to Catholicism, in what is now Fonda, New York, about twenty miles north of present-day Albany. As a child, Kateri contracted smallpox in an epidemic that killed her parents and siblings. Later Christian accounts of her life read her survival as an act of "divine grace that enabled her to renounce all attachments to the flesh and embrace the state for which she was destined." Covered in scars and very ill, she went to live first with her uncle and, ultimately, after repeatedly rejecting the marriage arrangements that he had set up (and being accused of sorcery), she joined a group of Jesuit missionaries in what is now Kahnawake, Quebec, where she resided until her death at the age of twenty-four. According to one of her Jesuit biographers, Kateri "burned with an intense desire to embrace the Christian faith" and committed to a regular

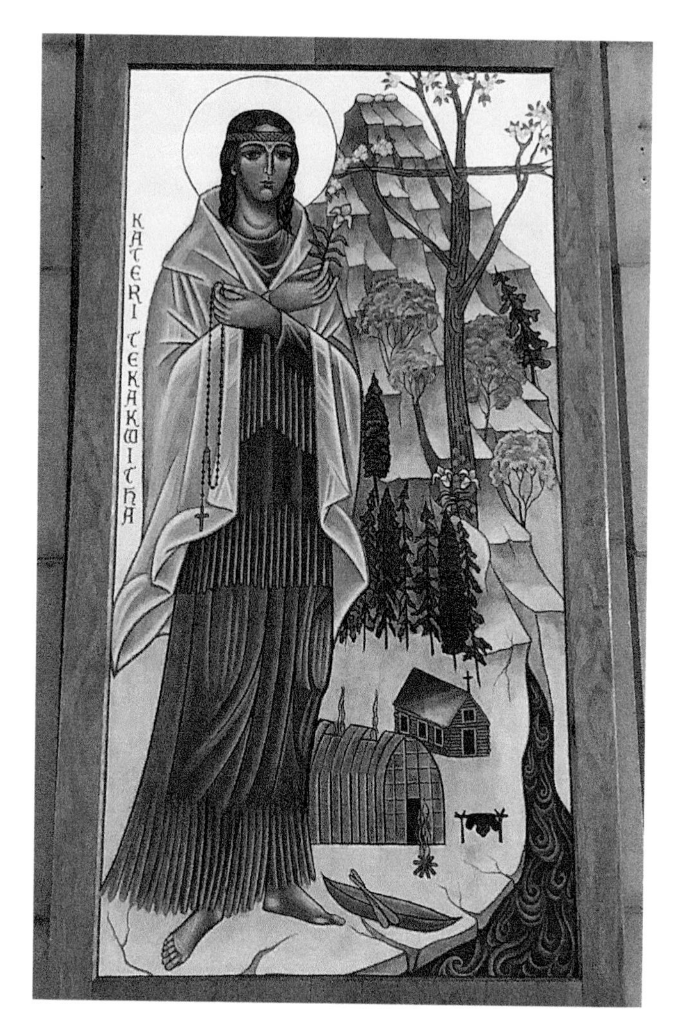

Fig. 12
Kateri Tekakwitha painting on the altar. Basilica of Sainte-Anne-de-Beaupré, Quebec, Canada, 2018. Photo by author.

practice of bodily mortification that included extreme fasting, self-flagellation with a metal-spiked belt, and sleeping on a thorn-filled bed to demonstrate her fidelity to Christ. Finally, on the Feast of the Annunciation in 1679, she took religious orders, claiming that "I have consecrated myself entirely to Jesus, son of Mary. I have chosen him for my husband and He alone will take me for wife."[29]

Kateri's devotion became legendary and her piety and religious zeal soon received credit for a number of seemingly miraculous acts. According to one Jesuit account, on her deathbed, after proclaiming her love to Jesus, "the pock marks from smallpox completely vanished and her face shone with radiant loveliness." Immediately following her death, both Native American and European settlers began praying for her heavenly intercession and "several people, including a priest who attended Kateri during her final illness, reported that she had appeared to them and many healing miracles were attributed to her."[30] The list of miracles increased and she was anointed to sainthood in 2012.

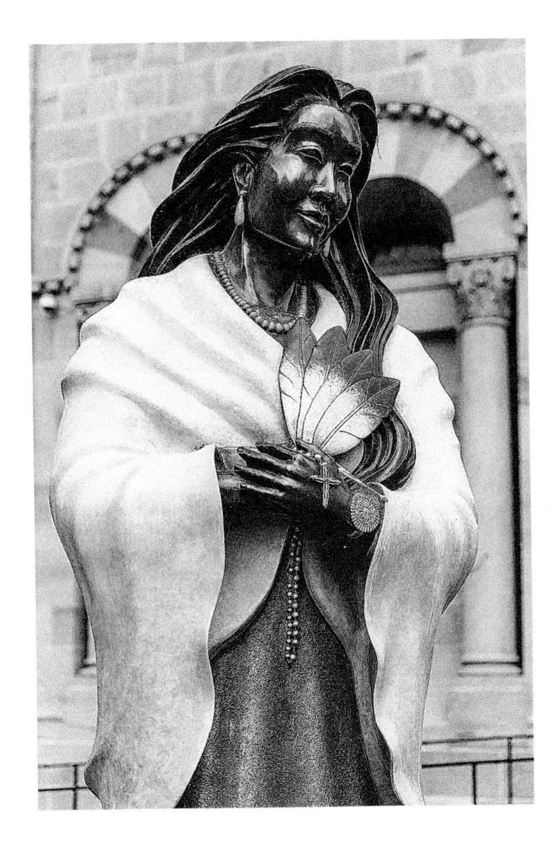

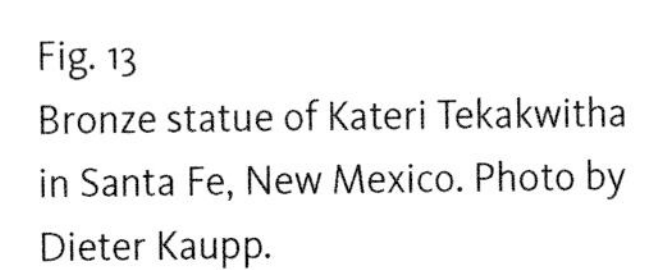
Fig. 13
Bronze statue of Kateri Tekakwitha in Santa Fe, New Mexico. Photo by Dieter Kaupp.

Stories of Native American converts to Catholicism are not unique during this time period. The story of Kateri is important for her status as the first Native American saint, but also for the ways in which her figure has evolved over time to become an emblem of both Native and female empowerment—from northern Quebec to the American Southwest—in concert with Catholic dogma. Today, in addition to her presence at Sainte-Anne-de-Beaupré, there is a shrine to Kateri in her birthplace of Fonda, New York, and another just outside of Montreal in Kahnawake, Quebec. Statues of Kateri appear in Catholic churches on Native American reservations across North America, often dressed in the local fashion, and pan-tribal sodalities known as Kateri Circles or Tekakwitha Conferences exist across the United States as "the Voice, Presence and Identity of Indigenous Catholics of North America under the protection and inspiration of Saint Kateri Tekakwitha" (see fig. 13).[31]

In her ethnographic study of contemporary devotion to Kateri, Paula Elizabeth Holmes traces what she calls the "repatriation of Kateri through narratives as told through her Pueblo women devotees" who continue to find (often miraculous) inspiration in her likeness. Through these women's counter-hagiographical accounts of her life and influence, Holmes argues that Kateri "is translated from a historically silent figure, bordered by colonial Jesuit categories, into a multivalent intertribal Catholic symbol—a reclaimed Indian Saint of creative and heroic character."[32] Similarly, in their 2016 volume on *Native North American Art*, Janet Catherine Berlo and Ruth Phillips include the work of the art collective AbTeC (Aboriginal Territories in Cyberspace), a collaboration between contemporary media artists Jason Edward Lewis and Skawennati Fragnito, who feature Kateri in an episode of their multipart *TimeTraveller* series. In the fifth installment, one of the main characters, a contemporary Mohawk woman named Katherine, returns to 1680 while doing research for an art history project. Here she encounters Kateri with the missionaries in Kahnawake. In their exchange, Kateri expresses her desire to establish an order for Iroquois girls who, like her, "detest men" and "don't want to marry." Kateri wants to create "a place to practice our ceremonies in peace" and "tap into the spiritual power of Sky Woman" and the Virgin Mary, both of whom, she asserts, bore children "without a man." On her deathbed, this Kateri expresses certainty that Sky World and heaven are the same. As she dies, her pocked skin magically clears and she emanates rays of light and the scent of flowers, leading witness to claim the presence of a miracle.[33]

Through this virtual encounter, *TimeTraveller* syncretizes Native and Catholic cosmologies. The Iroquois goddess Sky Woman, who fell from the celestial Sky World to find earth, communes with the Virgin Mary in an otherworldly realm in which indigenous and Christian paradises overlap in this twenty-first-century art project. Kateri's image maintains her miraculous powers across time, space, and media platforms—from seventeenth-century Quebec to contemporary cyberspace—uniting often divergent worldviews and ways of seeing with her divine presence regardless of the form she takes.

Nowhere, however, do we see the transition of a European deity into a Native American force more clearly than in the many iterations of the Virgin of Guadalupe. Today, her image—perched atop a crescent moon cradled by an angel, with her golden halo and blue mantle surrounded by stars—is one of the most recognizable religious symbols across the globe. Known widely as the patroness and protector of the Americas after her miraculous appearance to the Nahuatl-speaking peasant Juan Diego Cuauhtlatoatzin in the hills outside of Tenochtitlan in 1531, the Virgin of Guadalupe has her roots in the encounter between the Virgin Mary and the cowherd Gil Cordero that I referenced at the start of this chapter. Yet the story of the original icon dates back even further to the Moorish occupation of the Iberian Peninsula in the eighth century.

According to legend, the small black wooden statue unearthed by Gil Cordero was said to be carved by Luke the Evangelist and given as a gift by the Archbishop of Seville to Pope Gregory I. It was buried by practicing Christians in the hills of Extremadura in the seventh century to protect it from Moorish invasion and unearthed six hundred years later after a vision of Mary appeared to Cordero and instructed him of its whereabouts. Much like the shrine to Saint Anne, devotees soon built a church at the site of her appearance that began to draw visitors regularly to its doors in the hopes of their own divine interventions.

Among those who made regular visits to the shrine in Extremadura, Spain, was Queen Isabella. Indeed, she and King Ferdinand met twice there with Christopher Columbus to discuss and then authorize his voyages under their flag. Columbus became a devotee of this Marian apparition and the associated site and revisited Extremadura upon his return from his explorations to thank the Virgin for his safe passage to and from the "new world."

Hernán Cortés was also dedicated to this particular iteration of the Virgin Mary. He carried a small statue of her with him for divine protection and brought prints containing her likeness with him on his travels to the Americas for use in his conversion efforts. His soldier Bernal Diaz del Castillo's narrative of the conquest of what is now Mexico is filled with references to Cortés and his army disseminating crosses and images of the Virgin Mary on their march from what is now Veracruz to Mexico City. According to del Castillo:

> He [Cortés] then presented them with the image of the Virgin Mary and a cross, which he desired them to put up instead. These would prove a blessing to them at all times, make their seeds grow and preserve their souls from eternal perdition. This and many other things respecting our holy religion, Cortes explained to them in a very excellent manner. . . . He then ordered a quantity of lime to be collected, which is here in abundance, and with the assistance of the Indian masons a very pretty altar was constructed, on which we placed the image of the holy Virgin.[34]

For Cortés and other Spanish conquistadors, images of the cross and of the Virgin were key tools for both their proselytizing and colonization campaigns. They would often build Catholic churches on the same sites as preconquest temples to ease in the evangelization process, visually substituting one set of icons for another to help with conversion, harnessing the power of miraculous vision in the service of empire. We can see this clearly in the case of the Mexican iteration of the story of the Virgin of Guadalupe, who first appeared on December 8, 1531, in the hills just north of Mexico City.

Like her Spanish counterpart, the new world Guadalupe appeared as a vision, in this case to an indigenous convert named Juan Diego while he was on his way to mass. According to the official Catholic Church account, she addressed him in the Aztec language of Nahuatl:

> My dear little son, I love you. I desire you to know who I am. I am the ever-virgin Mary, Mother of the true God who gives life and maintains its existence. He created all things. He is in all places. He is Lord of Heaven and Earth. I desire a church in this place where your people may experience my compassion. All those who sincerely ask my help in their work and in their sorrows will know my Mother's Heart in this

> place. Here I will see their tears; I will console them and they will be at peace. So run now to Tenochtitlan and tell the Bishop all that you have seen and heard.[35]

Juan Diego brought her appeal directly to the archbishop, Juan de Zumarraga, who rejected his petition on two separate occasions. Finally, after the archbishop asked for proof of her existence, the Virgin instructed Juan Diego to pick the roses that had miraculously appeared in a barren stretch of land and carry them in his *tilma,* or cloak, to present as verification. According to legend, when Juan Diego opened his *tilma* to present the miraculous flowers to the archbishop, not only did an abundance of roses spill out from it, but the Virgin's image was transferred to the cloth of the cactus-fiber cloak. The archbishop acknowledged the miracle and called for the creation of a church on the site she had chosen. Despite Juan Diego's repeated insistence that he had seen her likeness, it was only with the miraculous appearance of her portrait, imprinted on the coat, that convinced the archbishop of the validity of his claims. Her image thus substantiated her presence.

Today millions flock to the hills of Mexico City to pay tribute to Juan Diego's *tilma*, which hangs above the altar of the National Shrine and Basilica of Guadalupe. The Basilica of Guadalupe is the oldest and largest pilgrimage site in North America and the second largest Catholic devotional site in the world (next to the Vatican). Because of spatial constraints, and also because the old basilica is sinking, a new church was constructed between 1974 and 1976. The architect, Pedro Ramírez Vásquez, constructed the new space in the round so that the image of the Virgin would be visible from every seat in the church. A moving sidewalk runs in both directions underneath the altar, providing visitors the opportunity to view the miraculous image without disrupting the masses that run throughout the day in the space above (see fig. 14).

In his 1958 study of the Virgin of Guadalupe, Eric Wolf designates her as a "Master symbol," or something that "enshrines the hopes and aspirations of an entire society." For Wolf, "the Guadalupe symbol thus links together family, politics and religion; colonial past and independent present; Indian and Mexican. It reflects the salient social relationships of Mexican life, and embodies the emotions which they generate. It provides a cultural idiom through which the tenor and emotions of these relationships can be expressed. It is, ultimately, a way of talking about Mexico: a 'collective representation' of Mexican society."[36] More recently, art historian Jeannette Favrot Peterson has contested Wolf's reading of the Virgin of Guadalupe as "an unchanging single Master symbol," arguing instead that this iteration of the Virgin has had "extraordinary staying power, based, paradoxically, on both her constancy and her flexibility to meet the shifting social, religious, and political needs of a heterodox society to the present day."[37] Nevertheless, for both scholars, it is the Virgin's image that continues to

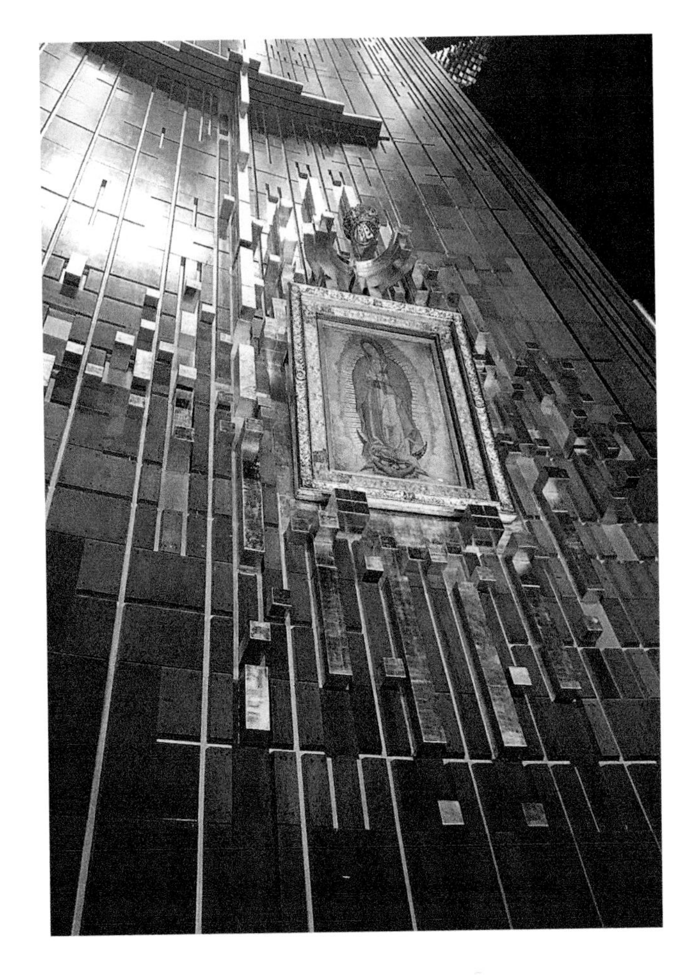

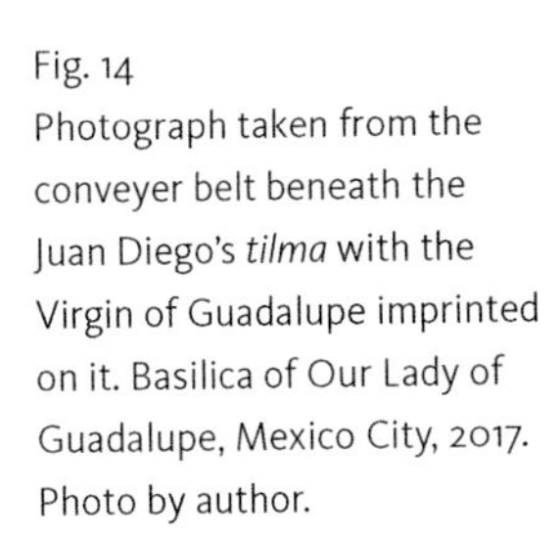

Fig. 14
Photograph taken from the conveyer belt beneath the Juan Diego's *tilma* with the Virgin of Guadalupe imprinted on it. Basilica of Our Lady of Guadalupe, Mexico City, 2017. Photo by author.

contain her miraculous powers. Each iteration of her portrait contains the same potential divine authority as the original as she moves across time and space.

Indeed, the forms of and reasons for the Virgin of Guadalupe's popularity have changed over time. In sixteenth-century Mexico, devotion to the Virgin of Guadalupe closely resembled that of the Aztec fertility goddess Tonantzin, also known by her Nahuatl name Coatlaxopeuh, or "our sacred mother." When the Virgin identified herself to Juan Diego—as well as to his uncle, whom she cured miraculously from his deathbed—she addressed them in Nahuatl, not Spanish. The poet and scholar Gloria Anzaldúa contends that Guadalupe's indigenous origins were in large part linguistic, since the pronunciation of the two names is similar. Because of this, she argues that the Spanish saw her as parallel to "the dark Virgin, *Guadalupe,* patroness of West Central Spain."[38] Anzaldúa includes Coatlaxopeuh and Coatlicue as variants of her name, thereby linking the Virgin to a range of other Mesoamerican fertility goddesses as well. For Irene Lara, Tonantzin, Coatlicue, and Cihuacoatl are "among a group of indigenous goddesses who were demonized by Christianity." She reads Tonantzin in

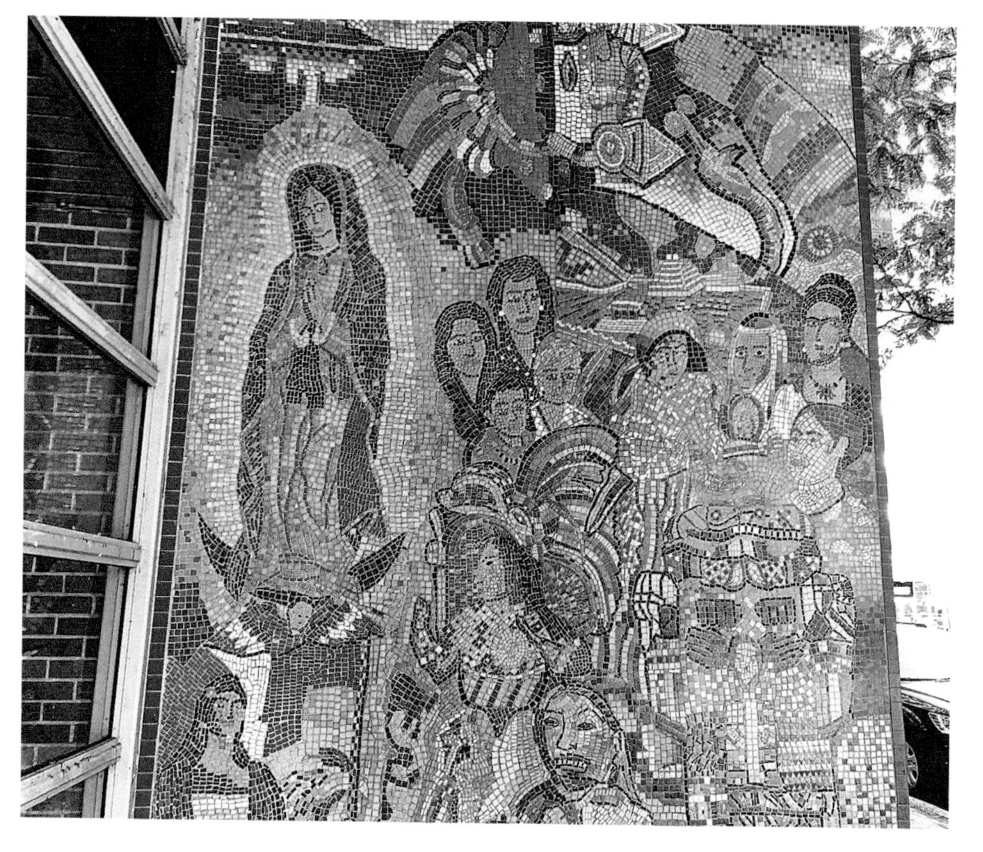

Fig. 15 Mosaic image featuring the Virgin of Guadalupe. Pilsen subway station, Chicago, 2017. Photo by author.

particular as "Guadalupe bruja-ized (witched)." Indeed, the hill on which the Virgin appeared to Juan Diego was the location of an Aztec shrine dedicated to Tonantzin, to whom regular offerings were made hundreds of years before the arrival of the Spaniards.[39] Thus the substitution of one fertility goddess for another allowed for the seemingly seamless syncretism of the two worldviews under the auspices of miraculous vision.

Guadalupe gained a wider following in the seventeenth century and, according to Peterson, can "best be understood in the context of class distinctions, which were largely based on skin color."[40] She became a creole Madonna with brown skin and black hair and began to work miracles for all classes of Mexicans—native, Spanish, and mestizo. Fidelity to her image continued to grow across Mexico and spread into South America in the seventeenth, eighteenth, and nineteenth centuries. Her likeness was appropriated by revolutionaries in the Mexican Revolution and embraced by the artists of the Mexican mural renaissance in the early twentieth century as an emblem of native identity and pride. Today, the Virgin of Guadalupe continues to serve a representation of Mexican and Mexican American empowerment and her portrait can be found in murals and folk art across the United States and Mexico (see fig. 15). Like Kateri, the Virgin of Guadalupe acts both as a symbol of colonial oppression and as one of contemporary liberation. She carries with her the often-violent history of Catholic indoctrination and European settlement, but her likeness also acts as an indigenous touchstone, a means of claiming space for native voices and female empowerment in oppressive patriarchal arenas.

This ambiguity, as well as longevity, is key to the idea of miraculous vision that I mentioned at the start of this chapter. Miraculous vision exists in the spaces between the viewer and their objects of vision. When imbued with divine meaning these objects of vision are capable of generating transformative sensory experiences for viewers across time. Miraculous vision can move across mediums through replication and reproduction, thus becoming not only transhistorical but also transmaterial. As the many incarnations of the Virgin of Guadalupe over the past two thousand years demonstrate—she began as an Islamic idol, became a black Madonna revered by agents of the Spanish Empire, and is now the ubiquitous brown-skinned patron saint of the Americas, with lasting Mesoamerican and well as Spanish colonial associations—disparate viewers have been able to reconcile her image with often contradictory messages and meanings. Moreover, the persistence of miraculous vision across space and time, as the histories of Kateri and the Virgin of Guadalupe demonstrate, challenges the evolutionary histories of ocular-centrism that privilege links between new technologies of seeing and rational thought that I discussed in the introduction to this project.

Indeed, the same moment that Trexler designates as marking the popular explosion of the belief in the miraculous powers of visual talismans—Renaissance Florence—also saw a tremendous number of scientific breakthroughs in technologies of vision. Inventions such as the camera obscura and optical lenses led to a break between medieval ways of seeing and the more perspectival-space-based Renaissance ideal that now dominates visual discourse in both science and art. As I discussed in the introduction, Jonathan Crary has delineated a genealogy of technologically enhanced vision "in which photography, and eventually cinema, are simply later instances of an ongoing deployment of perspectival space and perception," to explain later, nineteenth-century modernist ruptures with this way of seeing the world. For Crary, "problems of vision, then as now, were fundamentally questions about the body and the operation of social power."[41] Crary links technologies "for imposing visual attentiveness, rationalizing sensation, and managing perception" to new ways of ordering knowledge and information during the Renaissance and after. For empirical humanists, observation became the foundation for knowledge and truth.[42]

When it comes to miraculous vision, however, technological veracity does not always quell belief. Take, for example, the case of the Santa Sindon, or the Shroud of Turin.[43] According to the gospel of Luke, following Jesus's crucifixion Joseph of Arimathea "went to Pilate and asked for the body of Jesus. Then he took it down and wrapped it in a linen shroud, and laid him in a rock-hewn tomb, where no one had ever yet been laid" (24:52, 53). The gospels of Mark and John tell a similar story, adding that when the apostles returned to the tomb two days later, the rocks had been moved and the body was gone but the linen wrap remained: "Then Simon Peter came, following him [John], and went into the tomb; he saw the linen cloths lying, and the napkin, which had been on his head, not lying with the linen cloths but rolled up in a place by itself" (John 20:6, 7).

What happened next remains a subject of intense debate. Biblical scholars posit that the cloth moved from Edessa (now Şanliurfa in Turkey) to Constantinople (now Istanbul) in 944 CE. A burial cloth, which some think may have been the shroud, was among the possessions of the Byzantine emperor, but it disappeared in 1204 when Constantinople was attacked. In 1354 a piece of linen identified as Christ's shroud appeared in the possessions of the French knight, Geoffroi de Charnay, seigneur de Lirey, who most likely acquired it during the Crusades. Upon his death, de Charnay's granddaughter purportedly gave it to a member of the royal House of Savoy. In 1502 this cloth was displayed on the altar in the Sainte-Chapelle, Paris, and in 1503 it was shown at the palace of Philibert the Handsome in Bourg-en-Bresse, Flanders, where, according to Peter Geimer, "it was dipped in boiling oil, thrust into the fire, and rubbed down several times to test its authenticity—the impressions and images proved impossible to efface or remove."[44]

The shroud's legitimacy has been in question since the cloth first went on exhibition in 1389. Upon viewing it, the local Bishop of Troyes declared it a fraud, "cunningly painted, the truth being attested by the artist who painted it," whom he identified as a local thief. Yet soon after the bishop condemned it, Clement VII, the Avignon antipope, while not authenticating it outright, condoned it as an object of devotion to be venerated as an "image or representation" of the true shroud. When the Savoy capital moved to Turin in northern Italy in 1578, the cloth was relocated to the royal chapel of the Cathedral of Saint John the Baptist, where it has been ever since. In 1898 as part of a royal ceremony the cloth was brought out of storage for the first time in years and displayed on the altar of the cathedral. Secondo Pia, a lawyer and amateur photographer (and also the mayor of the nearby town Asti), was commissioned to photograph the relic to mark the event.

Pia did his work at night so as not to interfere with the vast crowds who made their way from near and far to witness the sacred cloth. To fully capture the work, he set up a special platform in front of the altar that he illuminated with arc lights. On the night of May 28, 1898, he successfully shot two images on glass plates. When he later developed the plates in his darkroom, Pia was amazed: "Ensconced in my chamber, entirely focused on my work, I felt a powerful shock when, during the development process, I saw the Holy Face gradually emerge on the plate."[45] According to Geimer:

> The image in the developer bath was subject to a peculiar inversion that would prove pivotal to the subsequent history of the shroud: the development of the negative had produced not a negative but a positive image, in which what were dark markings on the shroud appeared as the bright lineaments of a body. In the upper part of the picture, a human face and hair can be seen; folded hands appear near the center.

Pia hypothesized that the image on the cloth was actually a negative and thus the image he captured was a positive image: "The miracle of photography now took possession of the shroud in its entirety . . . the shroud itself became a photograph. Its history begins with this moment."[46]

Pia's assertion that "the shroud itself became a photograph" does indeed mark a key moment in the shroud's history. By claiming a physical referent for the impression on the fabric as a type of protophotographic image, he changed the narrative of the shroud's provenance from one born of a miraculous encounter to one rooted in what Tom Gunning calls the "truth claims" of photography, which for Gunning stem primarily from what the American mathematician and philosopher Charles Sanders Peirce called "indexicality."[47]

For Peirce the world of appearances consisted entirely of signs, or "qualities, relations, features, items, events, states, regularities, habits, laws, and so on that have meanings, significances, or interpretations."[48] Peirce distinguished between what he considered to be three different kinds of signs: the icon, the index, and the symbol, making clear that each category contained elements of the other two. Icons, for example, have specific physical properties in common with the thing being represented—maps, portraits, diagrams, and so forth. Indexes are directly influenced by their objects but are not a part of them; weather vanes, for example, represent the direction of the wind, smoke suggests the presence of fire. For Peirce, the index represents its object independently of the object itself. He explained, "The index is physically connected with its object; they make an organic pair; but the interpreting mind has nothing to do with this connection, except remaking it, after it is established."[49] Symbols are more complicated since they have culturally based relationships with their objects and often bear no physical resemblance to them: for example, numbers and alphabets.[50] I will discuss the indexical nature of photographs in more detail in chapter 3. What is significant here is that by claiming the shroud as a protophotograph, Pia legitimizes the image on the fabric as evidence of a bodily presence (see fig. 16).

Years later, the French art historian Georges Didi-Huberman called the shroud an "index of an absent wound." Media scholar Mary Anne Doane writes of Didi-Huberman's analysis that it marks "the transformation of the index into an icon via a photographic technology with all the sacred connotations attached to iconology." For the faithful, Doane argues, "there is a certain inescapabilty of the iconic, which is willed into existence through a technology whose objectivity

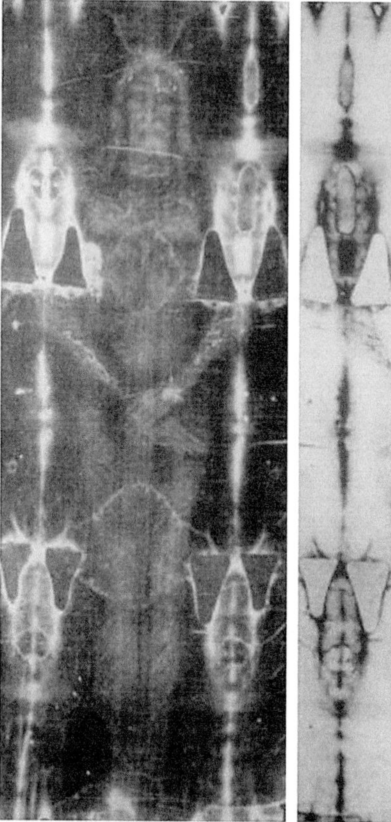
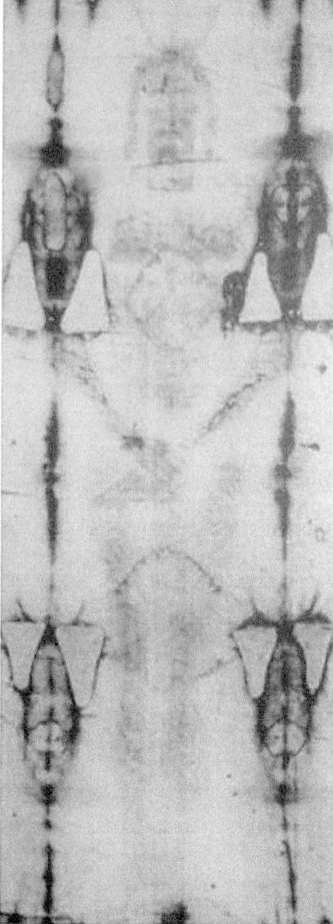

Fig. 16
Turin shroud, negative and positive. Photo: The History Collection / Alamy Stock Photo.

and authenticity seem incontestable."[51] Yet many believers have refused to make this semiotic move. Rather, they continue to see the impression on the cloth as indexically marked. They hold fast to the idea that this image arose from a miraculous encounter as a means of substantiating the truth claims of the shroud as a one-to-one trace of the once-present body of the crucified Christ. As such they continue to perform experiments using increasingly sophisticated science to validate their beliefs.

In 1969 Cardinal Michele Pellegrino granted permission to the Shroud of Turin Research Project (STURP), an international collective of scientists, to conduct "a scientific examination" of the cloth. The committee convened in 1973 and then again in 1978 and 1983 as advances in radiocarbon dating technology improved. In October 1987 the Pontifical Custodian of the Shroud, Archbishop of Turin Anastasio Ballestrero, acting on instructions from the Holy See, selected three laboratories (at the Universities of Arizona, Oxford, and Zurich) to oversee the testing. Under the direction of the British Museum, STURP set up four accelerator-mass-spectrometry techniques (AMS) and two small gas-counter radiocarbon laboratories. Using optical microscopy, scientists in the three labs examined the pollen grains in the fabric and classified them to the genus and species levels to determine the geographic areas in which the corresponding plants and fibers would have been originally located. They also performed DNA analyses on the biological sources of the dust particles ("this included the pollen grains, as well as cell debris and other minuscule organic specimens, such as plant-derived fibers and blood-like clots") corresponding to the face, hands, glute area, and feet of the body-like image reflected on the cloth. In addition, they performed radiocarbon dating on the lateral edge of the cloth. According to their findings, which they published in a variety of scientific journals including *Nature*:

> To identify plant taxonomic entities and human genetic lineages, universal plant DNA sequences, including nuclear rDNA intergenic transcribed spacers (ITS) and chloroplast DNA (cpDNA) barcodes, and human mitochondrial DNA (mtDNA) target regions were amplified and sequenced. This allowed the identification of DNA sources from a wide range of plant species and human mitogenomes belonging to numerous haplogroups. The overall findings were then evaluated to determine whether the geographic areas of origin and distribution of detected plant cpDNA species and human mtDNA haplogroups might provide novel clues concerning the origin of the Turin Shroud.[52]

Their conclusions yielded "a calibrated calendar age range with at least 95 percent confidence for the linen of the Shroud of Turin of 1260–1390 CE (rounded down/up to nearest 10 year). These results therefore provide conclusive evidence that the linen of the Shroud of Turin is mediaeval" and thus not from the biblical time of Jesus's crucifixion.[53]

Nevertheless, despite the conclusions from STURP, in 2005 Raymond Rogers, a retired chemist from Los Alamos National Laboratory in New Mexico, challenged the labs' findings, suggesting that the material used in the 1988 radiocarbon analysis was cut from a swatch of fabric that was woven into the shroud by medieval nuns who patched the holes and stitched the shroud to a reinforcing material known as the Holland cloth. "The radiocarbon sample has completely different chemical properties than the main part of the shroud relic," he argued in a paper published in the journal *Thermochimica Acta*, "an International Journal Concerned with All Aspects of Thermoanalytical and Calorimetric Methods and Their Application to Experimental Chemistry, Physics, Biology and Engineering." Instead, Rogers claimed that the original shroud is between 1,300 and 3,000 years old. More recently, an international team of scientists and others who call themselves the Yahoo Shroud Science Group assert that the idea that the shroud supports "the Resurrection of Jesus of Nazareth [and] cannot be rejected." In a similar vein, the Italian chemist Giulio Fanti of the University of Padua argues that "the image might have been burnt into the upper layers of the cloth by a burst of 'radiant energy'—bright light, ultraviolet light, X-rays or streams of fundamental particles—emanating from the body itself." Fanti cites Luke 9:29 as proof: "As he was praying, the appearance of his face changed, and his clothes became as bright as a flash of lightning."[54]

Regardless of the veracity of repeated scientific reports that discredit the possibility that this piece of fabric is old enough to be the cloth in which Jesus of Nazareth was wrapped after his death, pilgrims continue to make their way to Turin to pay homage to the object, which is now hidden from view for conservation reasons. For many, following the Avignon anti-pope, just the suggestion of its presence as the "image or representation" of the true shroud is enough to satisfy their desire for miraculous encounter. Pushing against ongoing scientific-based efforts to prove its existence are other forms of knowing through visual encounter. Indeed, as the many crutches, braces, and other ex-voto offerings that line the columns of the majestic Cathedral of Sainte-Anne-de-Beaupré in northern Quebec and the crowded conveyer belt running continuously beneath the altar of the Virgin of Guadalupe in Mexico City demonstrate, despite centuries of technological breakthroughs and scientific advances, the links between seeing and believing continues to be ambiguous. When it comes to miracles and miraculous vision, people still see what they want to believe.

CHAPTER 2

Technological Vision

Hoaxes and the Desire to Believe

Over the course of six days in August 1835, the *New York Sun* ran a series of articles divulging "recent discoveries in Astronomy which will build an imperishable monument to the age in which we live and confer upon the present generation of the human race a proud distinction through all future time."[1] On the front page of the paper, under the tantalizing headline "Great Astronomical Discoveries Lately Made by Sir John Herschel, L.L.D., F.R.S., &c. at the Cape of Good Hope," the *Sun* made reference to an article from the *Edinburgh Journal of Science* that claimed that Herschel, the son of the esteemed astronomer Sir John Herschel Sr. had recently discovered life on the moon. In six serialized front-page installments, the paper laid out a rambling seventeen-thousand-word narrative detailing discovery after magnificent discovery, each day promising that the following day "revelations more stupendous than those already made would soon be disclosed." Fantastic drawings of the moonscape with colossal waterfalls, lunar pools, and lush vegetation accompanied later installments of the text, filling out many of the amazing particulars for avid readers and adjacent bystanders as the story unfolded in the pages of the penny press (see figs. 17 and 18).

Thanks in large part to the *Sun*'s novel mode of distribution—newsboys who hawked the daily paper on city streets and in public spaces across the city—all New Yorkers, even those who did not read the *Sun*, were soon made aware of Herschel's lunar discoveries. And although the entire account was ultimately revealed to be an elaborate hoax, the moon story became one of the first full-blown media sensations, simultaneously engaging multiple senses—sight, sound,

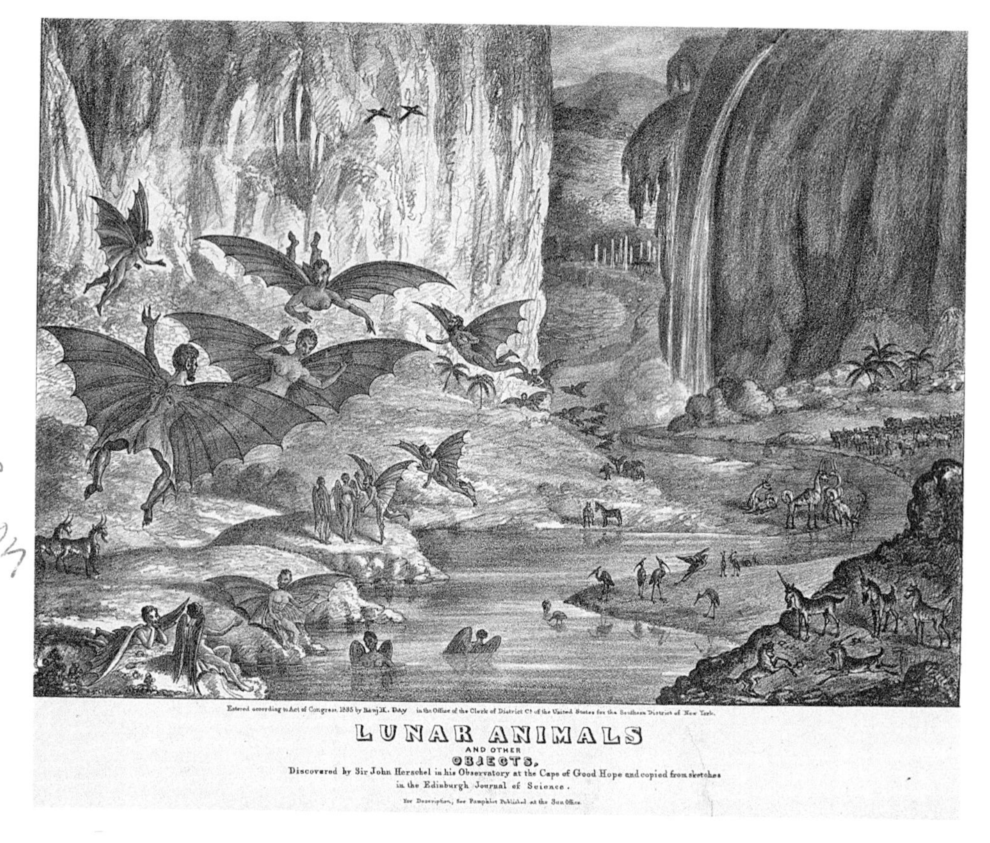

Fig. 17 Lunar animals and other objects discovered by Sir John Herschel in his observatory at the Cape of Good Hope and copied from sketches in the *Edinburgh Journal of Science*. Courtesy of the Library of Congress.

and even touch—and stimulating the collective imagination. Through a combination of dramatic narrative flourish and just enough detail to seem possible, the piece provided a much-needed diversion from the escalating pressures over what historian David Grimsted has identified as increased "ethnic hatreds; religious animosities; class tensions; racial prejudice; economic grievances; moral fears over drinking, gaming, and prostitution; political struggles; [and] the albatross of slavery" that marked the period.[2] In this context, the idea of life on the moon, no matter how improbable, was a welcome distraction from pervasive fears of social disintegration running rampant across America in 1835.

At the center of these "stupendous discoveries" was Herschel's telescope, which the paper described as "an object-glass of twenty-four feet in diameter; just six times the size of his venerable father's." The "weight of this ponderous lens," it continued, "was 14,826 lbs., or nearly seven tons after being polished; and its estimated magnifying power 42,000 times," thereby making it "capable of representing objects in our lunar satellite of little more than eighteen inches in diameter." Thus this literal object of vision was able to reveal even more spectacular lunar objects through its optical gaze. For the bulk of the first day's story,

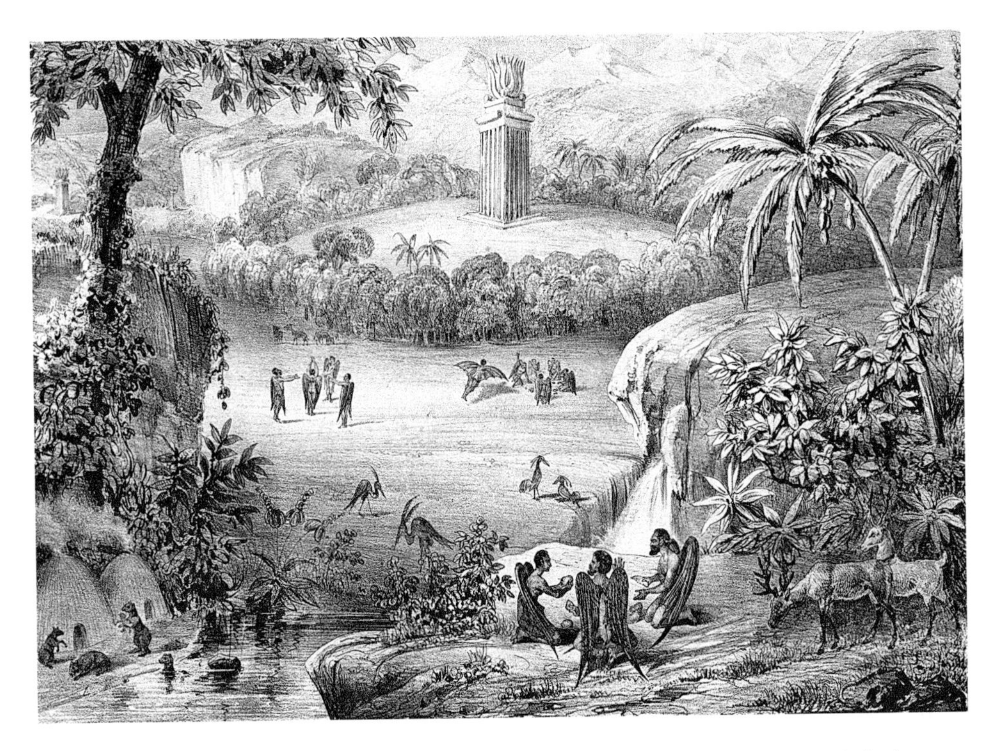

Fig. 18 Lunar temples. Lithograph depicting the Sapphire Temple discovered by Sir John Herschel in his observatory at the Cape of Good Hope and copied from sketches in the *Edinburgh Journal of Science*. Courtesy of the Library of Congress.

the paper recounted in painstaking and often monotonous detail the specifics of Herschel's lens for an attentive New York public.

The first few decades of the nineteenth century were full of techno-wonders. Steam engines had transformed transportation; in New York large-scale infrastructure projects such as the Erie Canal connected New York City to the western part of the state, opening up trade to the Great Lakes and beyond; new developments in the cotton gin and the commercial printing press heralded major changes in industry and urbanization; and breakthroughs in optical technologies allowed microscopes to reveal entire worlds within a drop of water. For many, therefore, it was not outside the realm of possibility that Herschel, who according to the piece had been "nursed and cradled in the observatory, and a practical astronomer from his boyhood," would be able to obtain his "distinct view of objects in the moon, fully equal to that which the naked eye commands of terrestrial objects at the distance of a hundred yards . . . and by what order of things." The text combined a mix of basic scientific information and hyperbolic flourish as it described to the *Sun*'s readership the ways in which the telescope functioned. A combination of pseudoscience and narrative embellishment contributed to the success of the story, which prominent New York diarist Philip Hone embraced, noting that even "if it is a fable, the manner of its relation with all its scientific details, names of persons employed and the beauty of its glowing descriptions, will give this ingenious history a place with *Gulliver's Travels* and *Robinson Crusoe*."[3]

Although subsequent entries revealed much more spectacular developments, the narrative adhered to a rational, Enlightenment-like pattern of description such as those I outlined in the introduction: lush portrayals of the flora and fauna of the moonscape in encyclopedia-like detail; the presence of bat-like men, in an evolutionary move predating Darwin's *On the Origin of Species;* as well as illustrations of the built environment that included places of worship. Nevertheless, I would argue that it was the lengthy textual legitimation of the telescope that acted as a crucial frame for the story's success. In the first part of the lead article, for example, the piece contextualized Herschel's efforts by outlining why others previously had failed to observe the planetary landscape, explaining to the lay public, "The law of optics, that an object becomes dim in proportion as it is magnified, seemed, from its exemplification in this powerful telescope, to form an insuperable boundary to further discoveries in our solar system." Moreover, it continued further down the page:

> unless the sun could be prevailed upon to extend a more liberal allowance of light to these bodies, and they be induced to transfer it, for the generous gratification of our curiosity, what adequate substitute could be obtained? Telescopes do not create light, they cannot even transmit unimpaired that which they receive. That anything further could be derived from human skill in the construction of instruments, the labors of his illustrious predecessors, and his own, left the son of Herschel no reason to hope.

The article placed Herschel within a long genealogy of well-known (as well as some lesser-known) scientists who had tried but failed in the past to observe the moon with a telescopic eye. This list included "Huygens, Fontana, Gregory, Newton, Hadley, Bird, Short, Dolland, Herschel [Sr.], and many others, all practical opticians, [who] had resorted to every material in any wise adapted to the composition either of lenses or reflectors, and had exhausted every law of vision which study had developed and demonstrated." As an added dramatic embellishment, the piece depicted the travails of the senior Herschel's last unsuccessful attempts to reach the moon with his lens:

> In the construction of his last amazing specula, Sir John Herschel had selected the most approved amalgams that the advanced stage of metallic chemistry had combined; and had watched their growing brightness under the hands of the artificer with more anxious hope than ever lover watched the eye of his mistress; and he had nothing further to expect

> than they had accomplished. He had the satisfaction to know that if he could leap astride a cannon ball, and travel upon its wings of fury for the respectable period of several millions of years, he would not obtain a more enlarged view of the distant stars than he could now possess in a few minutes of time; and that it would require an ultra-railroad speed of fifty miles an hour, for nearly the live-long year, to secure him a more favorable inspection of the gentle luminary of night.

Through trial and error, the story continued, the determined younger Herschel had perfected "his venerable father's" project. The next few paragraphs described in meticulous detail exactly how he did this and included his collaborators and suppliers to lend another level of credibility to the account. For example, it explained that in "casting this ponderous mass, he selected the large glass-house of Messrs. Hartly and Grant, (the brother of our invaluable friend Dr. Grant) at Dumbarton." It continued, "The material chosen was an amalgamation of two parts of the best crown with one of flint glass, the use of which, in separate lenses, constituted the great achromatic discovery of Dolland."

The piece outlined Herschel's successes, as well as his setbacks along the way: "Notwithstanding this failure, a new glass was more carefully cast on the 27th of the same month, which upon being opened during the first week of February, was found to be immaculately perfect, with the exception of two slight flaws so near the line of its circumference that they would be covered by the copper ring in which it was designed to be enclosed." And finally, it celebrated his ingenuity and ultimate achievement, a nearly seven-ton lens

> with an estimated magnifying power 42,000 times. It was therefore presumed to be capable of representing objects in our lunar satellite of little more than eighteen inches in diameter, providing its focal image of them could be rendered distinct by the transfusion of article light. It was not, however, upon the mere illuminating power of the hydro-oxygen microscope, as applied to the focal pictures of this lens, that the younger Herschel depended for the realization of his ambitious theories and hopes. He calculated largely upon the almost unlimited applicability of this instrument as a second magnifier, which would supersede the use, and infinitely transcend the powers of the highest magnifiers in reflecting telescopes.

Although tedious in places, the detailed description of the telescope's construction—the glass and metal used, the fabricators selected, the complex processes of assembling it—created a sense of materiality for the imaginary object. In so doing, these mechanical and scientific details conferred a technological legitimacy to the scientific fantasies that unfolded throughout the rest of the story.

The bestowal of legitimacy through the scientific frame is what I am calling technological vision. Herschel had created a device that could see the seemingly impossible; thus, by this logic, the impossible was not only imaginable, it was visible and therefore verifiable with the right tools. Merely the prospect of observation was enough to convince the reading public that the unfathomable—life on the moon—could be real.

Herschel's "hydro-oxygen microscope" with its "second magnifier" lens was crucial to this enterprise. By 1835 telescopes had been providing access to the firmament for over two hundred years and Herschel's ostensible embellishments were just the latest in a series of optical transformations that shaped not only ideas of life in the skies but also conceptions of life on earth. The first telescope was developed by German eyeglass maker Hans Lippershey in 1608, who, after watching two children play with the glasses in his store, inserted a tube between two lenses to magnify distances up to three times. His invention, which he called a *kijker* (or "looker" in Dutch) lay the groundwork for Galileo's design the following year. Galileo improved upon Lippershey's *kijker* and created a lens that could magnify objects up to twenty times. With this telescope, he was able to view the moon. He also discovered the four satellites of Jupiter, observed a supernova, and discovered sunspots. Moreover, with the help of his telescope, Galileo was able to substantiate Copernicus's theory that the earth and other planets revolve around the sun, disproving the geocentric notion that the sun revolved around the earth, thereby decentering the earth as the center of the universe (and causing a number of scientific as well as philosophical earthquakes, as it were).

Galileo was followed by Johannes Kepler, who in 1611 conceived of a telescope with convex objective and convex eyepiece lenses, and Christiaan Huygens, who by 1655 corrected the optical distortion that refracting telescopes such as Galileo's and Kepler's encountered. After much experimentation, Huygens discovered that image alteration could be cut by building lenses with much longer focal lengths. His resulting tubeless telescopes, which ranged from twelve to twenty-four feet in length, were capable of seeing great distances with less distortion. Isaac Newton built on these improvements to correct the chromatic aberration, or the fringes of color, that often surrounded bright objects—such as stars and planets—as seen through glass lenses, by taking the lens out of the telescope and replacing the primary lens with a round, polished, metal mirror.

Telescopic improvements continued throughout the seventeenth and eighteenth centuries, and the inventors' names as well as their innovations were detailed both in scientific treatises and in more popular publications. As I mentioned in the introduction, Diderot's *Encyclopédie* contained a number of plates devoted to optics and optical devices linking the attainment of knowledge to new advances in technologies of vision (see fig. 3). Such popular knowledge fueled larger debates and speculation regarding the place of humans in the universe. Just two years earlier, for example, the *Sun*'s own publisher, Benjamin

Day, had written an article in which he lamented the possibility that one would ever be able to see the moon through a telescopic lens:

> Some of the German astronomers gave out a few years since that they had discovered cities and regular fortifications in the moon. This we may doubt without fear of being skeptical, but is recorded in works of credit that a lunar volcano was seen at midday with the naked eye in the streets of London. It is now ascertained that no telescope can be made in the present state of science or art, which will enable us in the way of further discoveries to "Pluck bright honor from the pale-faced moon."

Thus the descriptions of Herschel's optical advances would have been met with great interest from the lay public. Indeed, as Timothy Reiss suggests in his 1982 study *The Discourse of Modernism*, throughout the seventeenth and eighteenth centuries the telescope functioned as a key example of "modern technological thinking." Using Galileo as his example, Reiss argues that the telescope acted as "an intermediary between the human mind and the material world before it, the object of its attracting gaze."[4] The expanding limits and possibilities of technological vision—both real and imagined—were key to changing notions of what it meant to be modern at this time. Whereas miraculous vision requires faith in the symbolic import embodied by the object of vision, technological vision seems to work in an almost opposite process. As I explained in the introduction, enlightenment technologies such as the microscope and telescope located a form of truth, and hence knowledge, in that which could be observed. The detailed description of Herschel's lens afforded readers access to the possibility of wonderous encounter within a rational, scientific frame.

Moreover, the emerging proliferation of daily newspapers transformed information into a consumable, material good. News became tactile. It was vetted by editors, printed on paper, and circulated across space and time, lending a validity to the stories published in the increasingly sensational penny press. Even those who doubted the ultimate veracity of the *Sun*'s account were willing to go along with the premise that the paper was reporting a story. Nevertheless, from the very first installment there were those who doubted the report; the most vociferous debunker was James Gordon Bennett, the publisher of the *Sun*'s biggest competitor, the *New York Herald*, who pointed out that the *Edinburgh Journal of Science* had ceased publication two years before and correctly attributed the story to the *Sun* reporter Richard Adams Locke. Bennett's dismantling of the story, however, was in large part motivated by financial competition rather than by concerns over accuracy of reportage. Similarly, other skeptical readers, such as the New York businessman Michael Floy, who publicly critiqued the story, did so not on ethical grounds but rather for failing to be scientifically viable. As Floy commented in his published diary on August 30, 1835:

> The author of these wonders says that an enormous lens of 30 feet diameter was constructed. He thought that would be a big enough lie in all conscience, but he should have said a lens of 100 feet diameter, as it is shown by writers on optics that such a diameter would be required to ascertain if any inhabitants in the Moon. Why not a make a good lie at once? But it is utterly impossible to construct a lens of half that diameter, and therefore we may despair of ever ascertaining whether the moon be inhabited.[5]

Even so, despite increasing doubt by informed readers regarding the reliability of the report, the *Sun* held fast to its charade and maintained the tenor of the story. Rather than admit to any duplicity in tricking its readers, the paper ultimately concluded the series with the unfortunate news that the telescope had been destroyed as a result of worker negligence combined with the power of the sun. Reporting that "the great lens, which was usually lowered during the day, and placed horizontally, had, it is true, been lowered as usual, but had been inconsiderately left in a perpendicular position." With the narrative embellishments of an adventure story or a travel monologue, it continued that "shortly after sunrise the next morning, Dr. Herschel and his assistants . . . were awakened by the loud shouts of some Dutch farmers and domesticated Hottentotts (who were passing with their oxen to agricultural labor), that the 'big house' was on fire!" Dr. Herschel leaped out of bed from his brief slumbers, and, sure enough, saw his observatory enveloped in a cloud of smoke"; the telescope, as well as "clump of trees standing in a line with them," had burned to the ground.

Through its serialized moon story, with its narrative cliff-hangers and elaborate descriptions of the extraterrestrial landscape, the *Sun* skirted the line between providing accurate information and spectacular entertainment. The images added to the sensational nature of the story, but, as fantastic as they may seem to us today, they also helped to concretize the news by providing visualizations of the information contained within the text. In one illustration, winged creatures—bearded men and voluptuous, bare-breasted women—lounge on rocks, swim in lunar pools, and fly through the air in front of majestic waterfalls. Animals with one horn resembling mythic unicorns graze nearby. Another image depicts a group of these bat-like humanoids with their arms raised in the air—seeming to worship in front of a massive lunar temple. In the foreground of this image, a group of the bat creatures share a meal over what appears to be a fire, testifying to their evolved status. Nearby bipedal beaver-like animals move in and out of huts. The images give visual form to the details in the larger narrative. In so doing, they became part of the evidence that helped to substantiate the hoax while simultaneously entertaining readers with their whimsical and fantastic nature.

This was not an unusual strategy for papers at the time. As Mario Castagnaro has observed in his analysis of the event, "The early nineteenth century was a culture of curiosity, one in which readers did not have clear-cut expectations about truth and fiction and the two usually blended together on newspaper pages; credibility was not the chief reason people picked up newspapers."[6] Technical detail was a staple of both popular and high literature as well. From Melville's cetological documentation of whales, to the myriad "how-to manuals" that flooded the marketplace, the American public enthusiastically consumed information as a form of entertainment. Indeed, even after the entire event was revealed as a hoax, people continued to follow the story. Popular songs and a variety of plays were performed on the subject in New York City and beyond. Moreover, the story continued to be reprinted, not only across the United States but also in England, Germany, and Italy. One of the most popular reprints was the 1836 *Altre scoverte fatte nella luna dal Sigr. Herschel* by Leopoldo Galluzzo. This Italian version included several new details as well as a gorgeous set of color lithographs. Along with depictions of the winged humanoid creatures and bipedal beavers, the Italian edition also featured a group of nineteenth-century missionaries who traveled to the moon via hot air balloon on a fact-finding and proselytizing quest (see fig. 19). Like the *Sun*'s moon story, these reprints adhered to the literary conventions of popular genres such as science fiction and adventure as well as to the more specialized and academic language of science and philosophy. In all these accounts, the telescope was key to this success since it allowed for these discourses to converge around issues of truth in observation.

I begin this chapter with an account of the moon hoax for a number of reasons; as I discussed in the introduction, the early nineteenth century marked the emergence of a new way of thinking about subjectivity in relation to new technologies of observation and objects of vision. Speaking of the moment just before the advent of photography in 1839, Jonathan Crary identifies a rupture with Renaissance and more classical models of vision that was "inseparable from a massive reorganization of knowledge and social practices that modified in myriad ways the productive, cognitive, and desiring capacities of the human subject."[7] Hoaxes, particularly those dependent on new technologies or advances in speculative observation such as the one perpetuated by the *Sun*, were a key part of this reconfiguration of knowledge in that they engaged the public directly in the establishment of boundaries of discernible truth. They also, I would argue, allowed for a sort of techno-optimism to emerge that sanctioned the possibility of new forms of vision that could substantiate the existence of new worlds and wonderful things. Herschel's purported telescope, as an optical technology full of scientific promise, was key to the hoax, but the spectacular nature of the story, in particular the sense of wonder it evoked (life on the moon!), also played an integral part in its successful dissemination.

Edgar Allan Poe, who had attempted his own moon hoax a few months before in his essay "The Unparalleled Adventure of One Hans Pfaall," published in the *Southern Literary Messenger*, begrudgingly wrote of the *Sun's* story, "The hoax

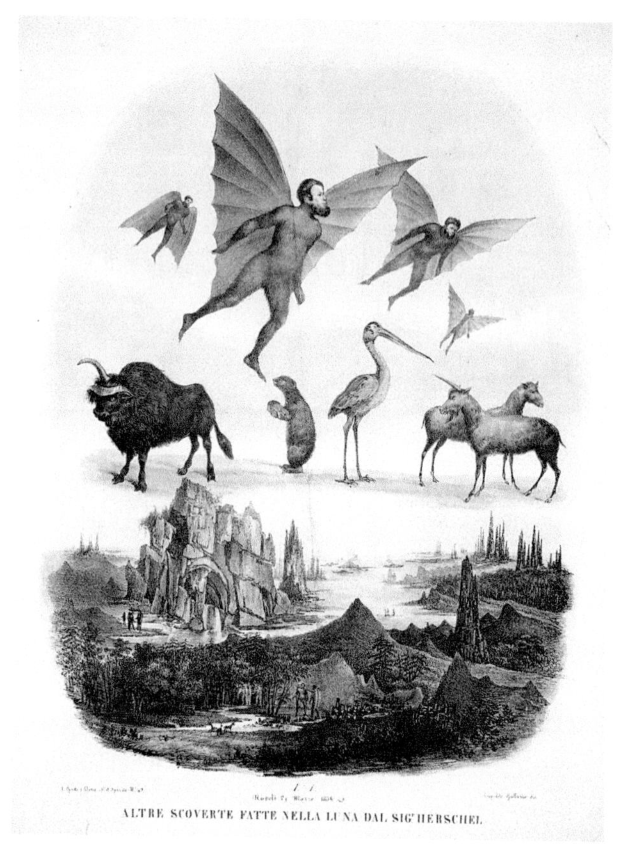

Fig. 19
Leopoldo Galluzzo, *Altre scoverte fatte nella luna dal Sigr. Herschel* (Naples: L. Gatti e Dura, 1836). The translated caption reads, "This portfolio of hand-tinted lithographs purports to illustrate the 'discovery of life on the moon.'" Smithsonian Institution Image Collection, SIL-SIL7-281-01_edit.

was circulated to an immense extent, was translated into various languages—was even made the subject of (quizzical) discussion in astronomical societies . . . and was, upon the whole, decidedly the greatest hit in the way of sensation—of merely popular sensation—ever made by any similar fiction either in America or in Europe."[8] While Poe was in part miffed that he was not the author of the successful deception, he was correct about the sensory impact of the media event. The 1835 moon hoax was indeed sensational in that it simultaneously engaged multiple senses in the hot, crowded, tense city that summer. Newsboys yelled the headlines from street corners, and their imperatives to "read all about it" shared sonic space with the day-to-day activities of urban dwellers from all walks of life. The story quickly spread across the world, captivating readers' imaginations and pushing the limits of their credulity. Merely the evocation of extraterrestrial life fueled a widespread sense of amazement among skeptics and believers alike. Indeed, just the suggestion of visualizing the awesome and the wonderful and their attendant sensory awe belied the optimism at the center of modern thought in the eighteenth and nineteenth century. With the proper technology, it seemed that anything could be observed and thus experienced.

Hoaxes, especially those that rested on the confluence of new technologies of vision, played a crucial role in reconfiguring what was real and what was possible in the modern age. As new paradigms of knowledge challenged previous epistemological truths, hoaxes became tools for both reinforcing and challenging the status quo and making sense of changing conceptions of the physical and spiritual worlds. Often there were anti-religious dimensions to these projects. For example, when Locke finally admitted that he was the author of the moon stories for the *Sun*, he claimed he did it as a satire aimed at those who exchanged religious explanation for science. It should come as no surprise, then, that one of the only architectural forms that Locke included on his lunar landscape was a majestic temple for the bat-like creatures to worship their God. On the story's fifth day he described in detail "a magnificent work of art. It was a temple . . . which, when consecrated to the Creator is devotion of the loftiest order; for it exhibits his attributes purely free from the masquerade, attire, and blasphemous caricature of controversial creeds, and has the seal and signature of his own hand to sanction its aspirations." For Locke, the continued replacement of unhindered religious thought for more empirical logic had led to an "imaginative school of philosophy that substituted airy fancies, pleasing to religion, for hard fact." In particular Locke took issue with the Scottish minister Thomas Dick, popularly known as the "Christian Philosopher," whose recent best-selling books *The Philosophy of Religion, or an Illustration of the Moral Laws of the Universe* (1830) and *The Christian Philosopher, or the Connection of Science with Religion* (1833) combined Christian theology with empirical science to chart the solar system and beyond.[9]

In a chapter titled "Illustrations of the Omnipotence of the Deity," for example, Dick credited God with creating the Milky Way, the planets, and their moons, and forecast life elsewhere in the universe:

> How great must be the power of that Being who commanded it to spring from nothing into existence, who measureth the ocean in the hollow of his hand, who weigheth the mountains in scales, and hangeth the earth upon nothing! . . . His energy extends to the utmost limits of the planetary system—to the planet . . . which revolves at the distance of 1,800 millions of miles from his surface, and there he dispenses light, and colour, and comfort, to all the beings connected with that far-distant orb, and to all the moons which roll around it.[10]

For Locke, pronouncements such as Dick's were dangerous "theological and devotional encroachments upon the legitimate province of science" and the purported impetus for his satirical treatment of the lunar discoveries, or so he claimed.

Similarly, another notorious nineteenth-century American hoax, the excavation of the Cardiff Giant, was also conceived as a challenge to religious fundamentalism and its encroachments on the legitimate province of science. Like the moon hoax, the story of the Cardiff Giant was rooted in the sensory experience of a seemingly fantastic object. It, too, pitted sacred and scientific modes of ocular experience against one another in the name of truth and progress to ultimately reveal the dangers of blind faith and the specious manipulations of scholarship using new technologies of vision.

In 1869, two workers on William "Stub" Newell's farm in Cardiff, New York, uncovered what they thought was "some old Indian" while digging a well on the property. Word soon spread about a fossilized body, which measured over ten feet long, weighed close to three thousand pounds, and had a discernable skeleton and genitalia (see fig. 20). Debates soon raged over the origin of the colossus. Some thought it was a petrified man; others a seventeenth-century statue used by Jesuits in the area to convert the local natives; and a vocal group, who came to be known as the "petrifactionists," designated it one of the giants mentioned in the Bible. Citing Genesis 6:4, "There were giants in the earth in those days," these biblical literalists celebrated the discovery of a prehistoric biblical fossil in the heart of New York State, an area so steeped in religious fundamentalism that it was known as the "Burned-Over District" for the many evangelical movements that "burned" through it in the mid-nineteenth century.[11]

Almost immediately after news of the discovery of the "giant," visitors began flocking to Newell's farm to marvel at this fantastic thing. Newell, an enterprising businessman, erected a tent over the excavation site and charged viewers twenty-five cents a head to view the body for up to fifteen minutes at a time, a sum he increased two days later to fifty cents a head. Andrew White, the president and one of the founders of nearby Cornell University, made the trip to see the figure and described the carnivalesque scene thus: "The roads were crowded with buggies, carriages, and even omnibuses from the city, and with lumber wagons from the farms—all laden with passengers." Similarly, a Philadelphia newspaper quoted a neighbor of Newell's as saying that Newell's farm had become a major attraction: "It has been visited today by hundreds from the surrounding country and examined by physicians, and they assert positively that it must have been once a living giant." The neighbor endorsed the petrifactionists' view that the recovered body was indeed a biblical relic, exclaiming, "The veins, eyeballs, muscles, tendons of the heel, and cords of the neck are all very fully exhibited. Many theories are advanced as to where he lived and how he came there. . . . It certainly is one of the connecting links between the past and present races, and of great value." Two days later, however, the same paper ran a different account, copied from the *Syracuse Standard* under the headline "The Giant Pronounced a Statue." Referring to an examination by the Columbia University–educated geologist Dr. John F. Boynton, the article explained that "the doctor made a most thorough examination of the discovery, digging under it in order to examine its back, and after mature deliberation pronounced it to be a statue of a Caucasian. The features are finely cut and are in perfect harmony."[12] Boynton, an early associate of Joseph Smith and a former apostle of the Mormon Church (he was

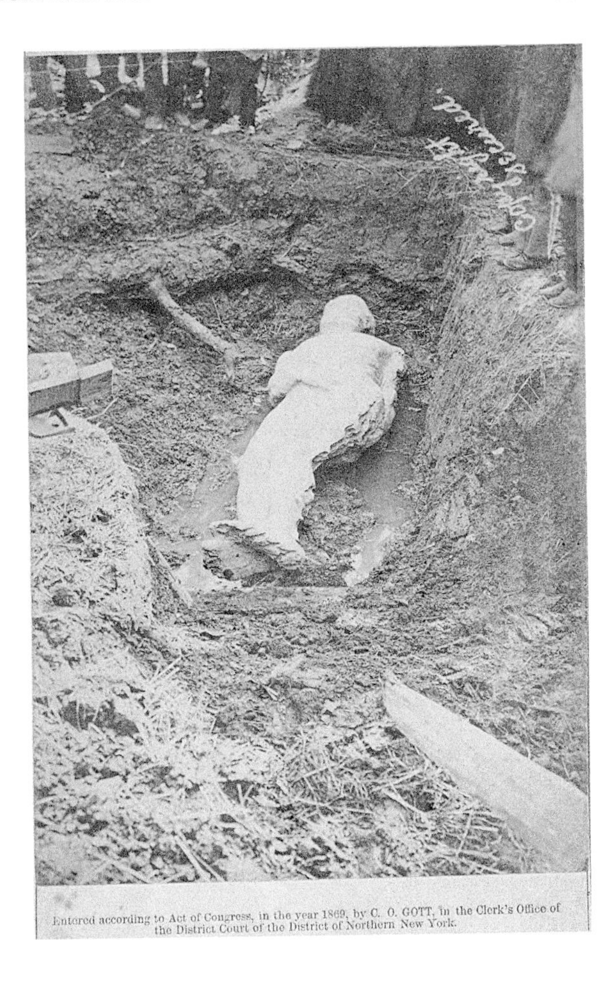

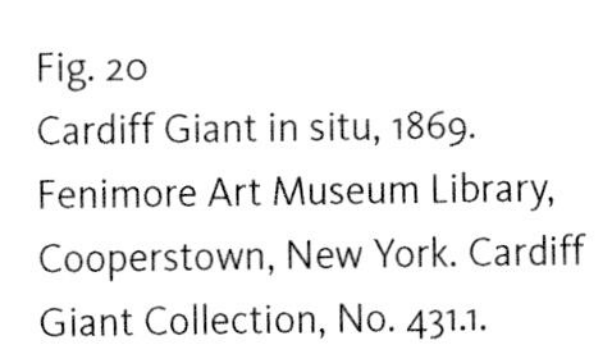
Fig. 20
Cardiff Giant in situ, 1869. Fenimore Art Museum Library, Cooperstown, New York. Cardiff Giant Collection, No. 431.1.

excommunicated in 1837 for apostasy), instead put forth the theory that the statue had been created by Jesuit missionaries during the seventeenth century as a proselytizing device.

In truth, the figure was neither a fossilized giant nor a Jesuit devotional tool; rather, it was a recent statue commissioned by Newell's brother-in-law, a successful tobacconist named George Hull. A devoted atheist, Hull reportedly had argued with a revivalist Methodist minister while collecting a debt in Iowa a few years earlier. Asking "why people would believe those remarkable stories in the Bible about giants," he explained, "Suddenly I thought of making a stone giant and passing it off as a petrified man." Convinced that he needed to execute his project far away from his home in central New York, he purchased a five-ton block of gypsum in Montana, explaining to the quarry owner that he wanted to create a large-scale statue of Abraham Lincoln. He had the block delivered to a German stonecutter in Chicago named Edward Burghardt, whom he swore to secrecy. Burghardt used Hull as a model, which he executed on a bigger scale. To age the piece, he experimented with stains and acids to make the giant's exterior look worn and repeatedly poked the body with steel knitting needles to give the

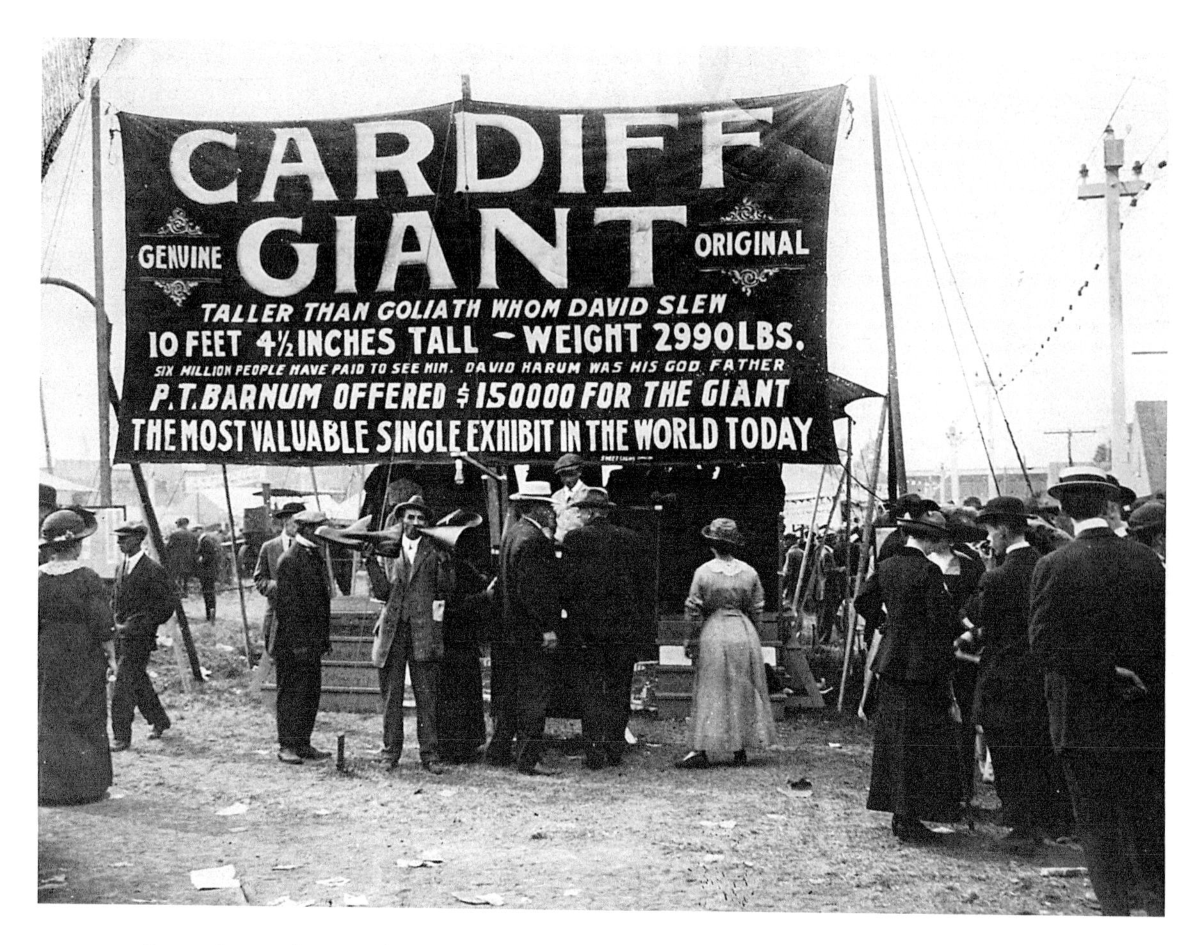

Fig. 21 Banner advertising the Cardiff Giant, 1869. Courtesy of the Farmers' Museum. Fenimore Art Museum Library, Cooperstown, New York. Cardiff Giant Collection, No. 431.1.

appearance of petrified skin. Hull then secretly shipped the work to the village of Cardiff, just south of Syracuse, where he buried it on Newell's farm. The following year, in October 1869, acting on instructions from Hull, Newell hired two workmen to dig a well in the spot where the statue had been buried.

The giant was an immediate sensation. The following day the *Syracuse Daily Standard* revealed the discovery, the authentication of which it credited to the emerging study of geology, writing that "geology is quite a new science. It depends on observation and all that it teaches us is that a Fossil Giant never was discovered until William C. Newell dug his well at Cardiff."[13] Papers in New York City and Boston picked up the story and immediately sent reporters to upstate New York to witness firsthand the remarkable specimen. Visitors came from all over to observe the wonder: scientists, missionaries, the curious public, all wanted to be amateur geologists and see for themselves the awesome discovery on Newell's farm (see fig. 21).

Advances in material science, in particular geology, were key to this hoax. Geology is the scientific study of the origin, history, and structure of the earth. Although Aristotle had made numerous observations about geographical change in the fourth century BCE, and Pliny the Elder made important strides in metallurgy and the study of fossils in the first century CE, it was not until the late eighteenth century that Scottish scientist James Hutton used chemistry to develop a theory for how the layers of the earth's surface had formed and evolved. Hutton argued against the prevailing theory of Neptunism (which posited that the earth emerged from a large body of water such as the ocean—or, allowing for biblical interpretations, a flood) and proposed instead that it had resulted from the gradual solidification of a molten mass at a slow rate over a tremendous period of time. This led him to the conclusion that the age of the earth was incalculable and thus could not possibly be explained within the timeline contained in the book of Genesis. Followers of Hutton, known as the Plutonists, believed that volcanic processes, not the biblical flood, were the source of the earth's creation. The discovery of the giant revived these debates, with both sides claiming victory in the unearthing of the colossal structure.

Writing in his 1904 autobiography, in a chapter titled "The Cardiff Giant: A Chapter in the History of Human Folly," Andrew White recounted overhearing how "a very excellent doctor of divinity, pastor of one of the largest churches in Syracuse," declared upon viewing the "giant," "Is it not strange that any human being, after seeing this wonderfully preserved figure, can deny *the evidence of his senses*, and refuse to believe, what is so evidently the fact, that we have here a fossilized human being, perhaps one of the giants mentioned in Scripture?" White cited another visitor, "a bright-looking lady," as remarking, "Nothing in the world can ever make me believe that he was not once a living being. Why, you can see the veins in his legs." Another, a "prominent" western New York clergyman, publicly "declared with *ex cathedra* emphasis" that the giant "is not a thing contrived of man, but is the face of one who lived on the earth, the very image and child of God." And a writer from one of the most important daily papers of the region dwelled on the "majestic simplicity and grandeur of the figure," and added "that ninety-nine out of every hundred persons who have seen *this wonder* have become immediately and instantly impressed with the idea that they were in the presence of an *object not made by mortal hands*. . . . No piece of sculpture ever produced *the awe* inspired by this blackened form."[14]

The veracity of the giant itself was enhanced by both facial details and visible traces of veins and musculature, as well as the veneer of scientific legitimacy added by the nascent field of geology. Even educated viewers were convinced of its realness, and the hoax enabled many to confirm their religious beliefs within a seemingly scientific framework. White, however, took issue with those who found biblical truth in the experience and concluded that many people found a "joy in believing" in the marvel. He attributed the success of the hoax to a "peculiarly American superstition that the correctness of a belief is decided by the number of people who can be induced to adopt it—that truth is a matter of majorities."[15]

As with the moon hoax, the story of the Cardiff Giant simultaneously challenged and substantiated notions of the awesome and the wonderful as the foundations of rational truth. As Michael Petit argues in his analysis of the event, "Many spectators understood the giant within the framework of wonder, in which extraordinary objects that seemed to transcend the laws of nature were valued and deemed authentic for precisely that reason." For Petit, "Wonder as a source and sentiment of inquiry had been central to reforms in natural philosophy during the seventeenth century but had subsequently been expelled from the domain of proper science."[16] As White's cynical nod to the "joy in believing" makes clear, the Cardiff Giant incident fed a public desire for wonder, a form of experience rooted in the "evidence of the senses" and its accompanying feelings of reverence and awe.

It is important to note that the giant was "discovered" just ten years after Charles Darwin published the *On the Origin of Species*, further challenging the idea of biblical time and creationist origin stories. It was, in a sense, a literal godsend for those who wanted to believe that biblical giants had once walked the earth, since the fossilized object seemed to reconcile biblical time with a form of evolutionary theory. Hull of course knew this and spent considerable time and money to discredit this melding of pseudoscience and theology. He also got rich in the process. After making a significant profit from selling views of the body, Newell, acting on Hull's instructions, sold the figure to a conglomerate of wealthy businessmen from Syracuse for close to $40,000.

P. T. Barnum was among those who made the trip to Cardiff to view the giant. Upon witnessing the spectacle surrounding the event, he made an offer to buy the giant for a reported $60,000. Newell and Hull, however, had already sold it, and the conglomerate of new owners refused Barnum a share in their group. Undaunted, Barnum commissioned his own giant—his was made hastily and of wood—and exhibited it in his American Museum on the Bowery in New York City as "the real" giant, citing multiple sources who had declared the Cardiff Giant a fake. Soon Barnum's giant was attracting more visitors than the original, which prompted the new owners, led by businessman David Hannum, to sue Barnum for questioning their statue's authenticity. When the case came to trial, however, the judge called Hull to testify and he confessed the entire story of the hoax. The judge thus ruled that Barnum could not be sued for calling Hannum's giant a fake since it was never actually a genuine giant.

Barnum's interest in the giant should come as no surprise since he was crucial to the culture of hoaxes, or what poet Kevin Young calls "bunk," that marked the period both in the United States and abroad.[17] As historian Andie Toucher has argued, late nineteenth-century America was the "age of the fake." In part,

Toucher suggests, the austere culture of nineteenth-century letters and reform in the United States was not merely obsessed with what was real and true, but also the opposite—with what was fake and wonderous. This was the "high tide of America's romance with facts that the word *fake* itself emerged from netherworlds that had previously been its main habitat to become a part of the public discourse."[18]

Barnum and his notion of "humbug" were vital in the emergence of a public culture of hoaxing and faking. Hull went to great lengths to fabricate his giant in a way that made it look like a convincing fossil, and he substantiated his claims with the new science of geology. For Barnum, verisimilitude and scientific proof were not the goals—the possibility of realness was enough for his humbugs to succeed. Yet as I will elaborate in the next chapter, there was an ethics to his forms of deceit. Barnum was a hoaxer, not a fraud. Defining the difference in a speech to visitors to the Fairfield County Agricultural Fair in Stamford, Connecticut, in November 1854, Barnum explained that "humbug is generally defined as 'deceit or imposition.' A burglar who breaks into your house, a forger who cheats you of your property, or a rascal, is not a humbug, a humbug is an imposter; but in my opinion the true meaning of humbug is a management tact to take an old truth and put it in an attractive form."[19] Provoking some sort of sensory experience was a significant component of successful humbugs, which were often grounded in some form of corporeal phenomena, most usually having to do with sight. Barnum's biographer, the historian Neil Harris, refers to this strategy as Barnum's "operational aesthetic," which he defines as "an approach to experience that equated beauty with information and technique, accepting guile because it was more complicated than candor."[20] Barnum very consciously cultivated this type of response throughout his long professional life. He later reflected, "At the outset of my career I saw that everything depended upon getting people to think, and talk, and become curious and excited over and about 'rare spectacle.'"[21] The cultivation of the "rare spectacle" was key not just to Barnum's success; it was increasingly a facet of modern urban life, from New York to Paris, as I will discuss in the final chapter.

Barnum was the consummate showman. Born in 1810 in Bethel, Connecticut, he spent his early years working on his family farm but left to begin selling lottery tickets when he was just twelve years old. In 1835 he paid $1,000 to obtain the rights to exhibit Joice Heth, a woman he claimed to be the 161-year-old wet nurse of George Washington. Heth was blind and almost completely paralyzed when Barnum acquired her, yet she could still sing and talk and Barnum exhibited her nightly in the Broadway theater, Niblo's Garden, before sending her on a seven-month-long tour of the United States. As seen in figure 22, he advertised her as

> unquestionably the most astonishing and interesting curiosity in the World! She was the slave of Augustine Washington, (the father Gen.

> Washington) and was the first person who put clothes on the unconscious infant, who, in after days, led our heroic fathers on to glory, to victory, and freedom. To use her own language when speaking of the illustrious Father of this Country, "she raised" him.

Eric Lott claims that Heth earned Barnum $1,500 dollars a week, an enormous sum of money at the time. When Heth died, the coroner who examined her placed her age in the low seventies. Rather than fight this claim, Barnum put Heth's cadaver on display and the public flocked to see the body and substantiate the hoax for themselves.

Following on the success of Heth, Barnum secured the rights to Charles Sherwood Stratton, better known as General Tom Thumb, a five-year-old midget he successfully toured across the United States and Europe, where he appeared twice before Queen Victoria in England, as well as at the French royal court. In 1841, Barnum purchased Scudder's American Museum on Broadway in New York City. There he exhibited "500,000 natural and artificial curiosities from every corner of the globe."[22] One of the first curiosities he acquired was the "Feejee Mermaid," which he obtained from his associate Moses Kimball, the proprietor of the Boston Museum. As part of a widespread publicity campaign, Barnum fomented a type of "mermaid fever" by distributing flyers that featured a woodcut of a mermaid to newspapers across New York City, promising each editor that he had sole rights to the image. Each publisher, thinking they had an exclusive story, published the image on their front page; thus papering the entire city with the mermaid's depiction. The woodcut, which looked remarkably like a woman, bore no resemblance to the actual object on view in his museum, which Barnum later described as an "ugly, dried-up, black looking and diminutive specimen" (see figs. 23a–b). In truth, the Feejee Mermaid was a horrible-looking thing consisting of the head and arms of a monkey sewn to the body of a fish. Nevertheless, the public flocked to the museum to see the exhibit and willingly participate in Barnum's humbug.

Regarding the popularity of Barnum's museum, which sold more than thirty million tickets between 1842 and 1865, Neil Harris asks, "Why were Americans apparently so credulous, why could they be fooled so easily, why did they flock to see mermaids, woolly horses, and other anatomical monstrosities that seem in later days to be so patently false? Why did they accept commonplace objects—wooden legs, articles of clothing, minerals and weapons—as sacred relics associated with famous men and historic events?"[23] For Harris, part of the explanation has to do with a mixture of "competitive materialism" and a pervasive thirst for knowledge prevalent in the United States at this time. As the British visitor Edward Hingston noted on his tour of the United States, "Every American believes himself to be the repository of extensive information; within him is the pent-up source of knowledge; his amiable spirit of benevolence prompts him to let it flow forth

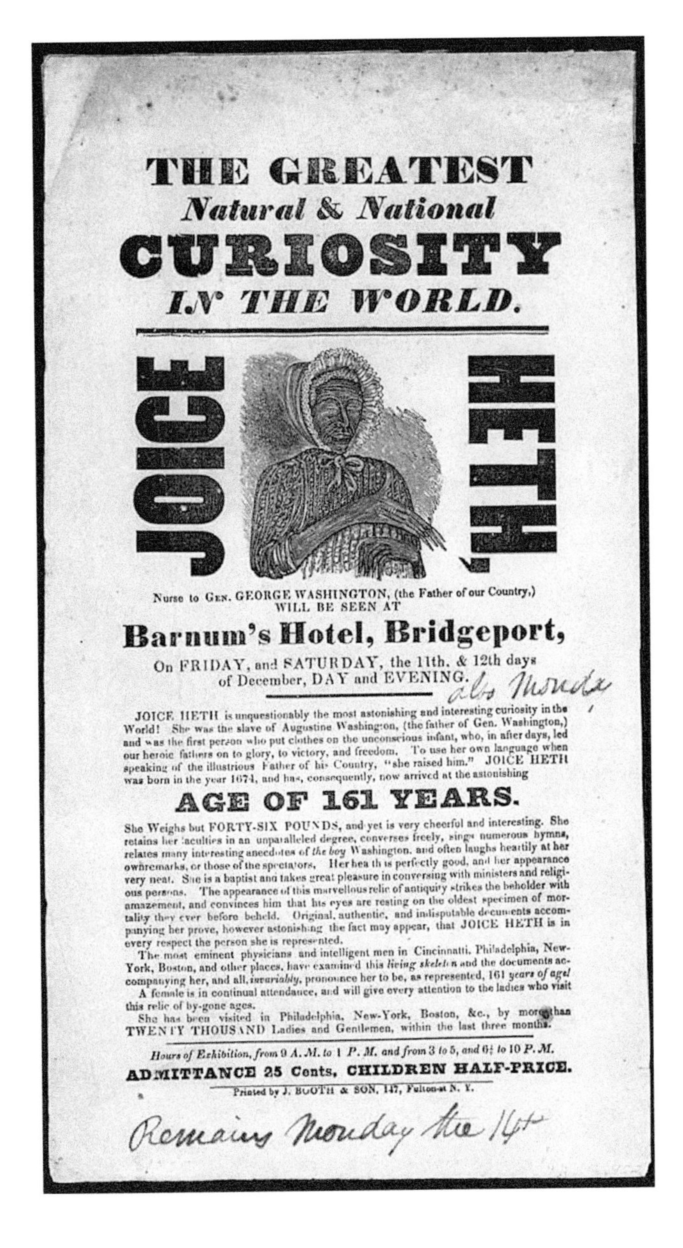

Fig. 22
P. T. Barnum, printed handbill, "The Greatest Natural & National Curiosity in the World," advertising Joice Heth. Photo: The History Collection / Alamy Stock Photo.

for the enlightenment of his benighted fellow-citizens, and the outer world of darkness generally."[24] Barnum's museum fed a public desire for information as rooted in the experience of material things. Witnessing these supposed freaks of nature—the 161-year-old Heth, the miniature man-child Tom Thumb, the Feejee Mermaid—fueled the market for sensory knowledge while also underscoring the "normalcy" of the viewer. With the world changing so quickly around them, visitors to the American Museum could take comfort in the knowledge that they did not resemble the oddities on display in Barnum's galleries. Moreover, Barnum's exhibits conditioned Americans to seek out knowledge for themselves

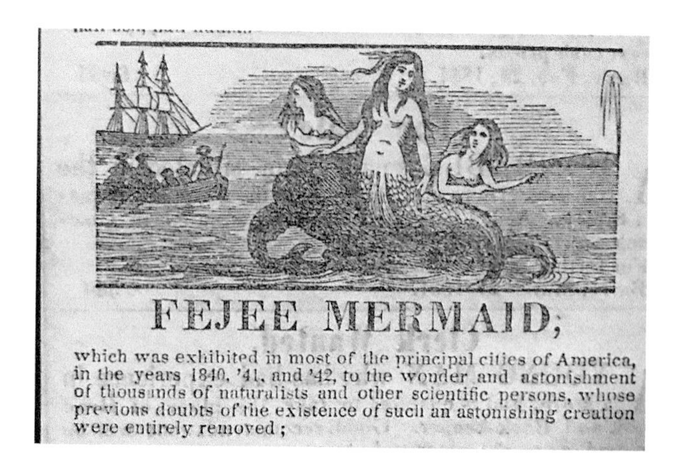

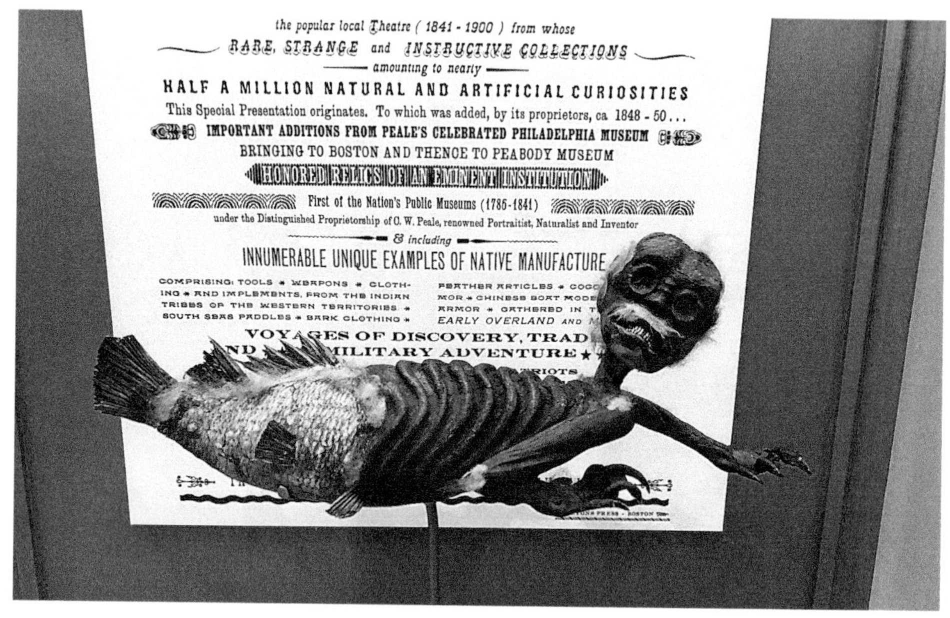

Fig. 23 (a) P. T. Barnum's advertisement for "The Mermaid, and Other Wonderful Specimens of the Animal Creation," 1842. Somers Historical Society, Somers, New York. Marc Hartzman Collection. (b) Barnum's actual mermaid in front of a reproduction of printed handbill. Peabody Museum, Harvard University. Photo by author.

and to delight in the process of distilling fact and truth from fantasy and fiction. As Harris argues, this "aesthetics of operations" substituted for a more spiritual engagement. Visitors found refuge from more existential dilemmas of their age and, for at least an afternoon, discovered for themselves something tangible and true—these wonders were hoaxes and they were not fools.[25]

Yet Barnum maintained the veneer of legitimacy by deploying many of the exhibition strategies I discussed in the introduction. He adhered to Linnaean taxonomies when possible and provided elaborate histories tracing his objects' provenance. Moreover, in 1843 Barnum purchased the competing Peale Museum, just down the street at 252 Broadway, for $7,000. The museum belonged to the sons of Charles Willson Peale who inherited the institution upon their father's death in 1827. Peale, a soldier in the Revolutionary War, is perhaps best remembered as a painter of American portraits, in particular those of George Washington, Benjamin Franklin, and Thomas Jefferson. A prolific artist who painted over a thousand works in his lifetime (including at least 771 oil portraits, 297 portrait miniatures, 29 landscape paintings, 11 still lifes, and 10 history paintings), Peale began displaying his paintings in his home in Philadelphia. In 1786, after running out of room in his house—and acting on the advice of his friend Benjamin Franklin, who had visited the British Museum in London and the Natural History Museum (Jardin du Roi) in Paris—Peale moved his paintings, along with many of his props, to a nearby exhibition space, which he called the Philadelphia Museum. Informed by the encyclopedic sentiments that I discussed in the introduction, Peale later moved his collection to the second floor of Independence Hall, physically cementing the link between his museum and American national identity.

Peale conceived of his museum as "a world in miniature." His ambition was to include examples from all areas of the animal, vegetable, and mineral kingdoms to create "a great national school of science, of reason and of morality." A quintessential Enlightenment thinker, Peale believed that the way to understand both God and human was through "natural religion"—the application of one's "right reason" to "observations of the world about [them]."[26] He tied all this to a patriotic sense of an emerging American identity. He worked closely with Thomas Jefferson and the explorers Meriwether Lewis and William Clark to procure distinctly American specimens for display in his galleries.

The impetus for his museum came from a gift Peale received in the early 1780s of fossilized mastodon bones that had been recovered at Big Bone Lick in Kentucky. Peale exhibited these bones alongside his paintings in his gallery. The bones were an immediate sensation and Peale set to work collecting other natural phenomena to show alongside his artwork, ultimately amassing thousands of specimens that he displayed using the classification system developed by Linnaeus less than thirty years earlier. Indeed, Peale was one of the first Americans to adopt the Linnaean taxonomies that organized plants and animals in a descending hierarchy of categories: kingdom, phylum, class, order, family, genus, and species. Indeed, each room in his museum contained a framed inventory of the genus and species of every object within it, each with a numerical association keyed to the case in which it was exhibited. To help explain this method to viewers he listed, over each case, the name of the object and its Linnaean designation in Latin, English, and French.

Peale's cabinet of curiosity–style museum taught the public how to see science within a decidedly American patriotic lens of progress. He depicted this process

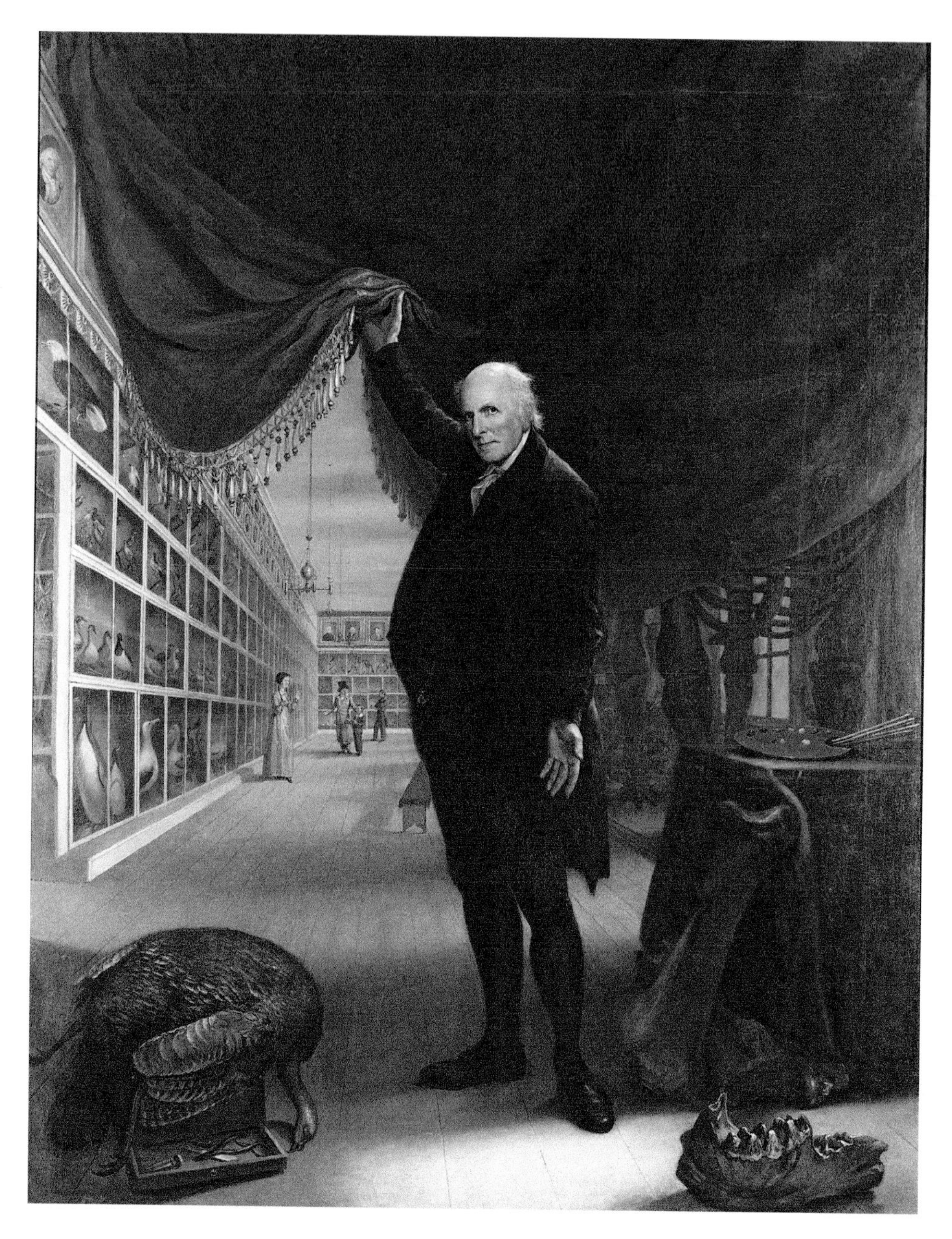

Fig. 24 Charles Willson Peale, *The Artist in His Museum*, 1822. Oil on canvas. Courtesy of the Pennsylvania Academy of Fine Art, Philadelphia. Gift of Mrs. Sarah Harrison (The Joseph Harrison, Jr. Collection).

in his 1822 self-portrait *The Artist in His Museum* (see fig. 24). The full-length work depicts the elderly Peale—he was eighty-one when he painted it—pulling back a red velvet curtain to reveal his gallery. The bones of a mastodon and the stuffed body of a taxidermized turkey frame each side of the artist's feet. His palette, with wet paint visible, lies atop a nearby table, thus signaling his dual passion for science and art. Likewise his gallery is marked by neatly organized rows of preserved animal specimens exhibited beneath a collection of his portraits, a mix here of scientists, presidents, and other American heroes. Hidden behind the curtain is the fully reconstructed skeleton of one of the mastodons that he helped to excavate (and document) twenty years earlier.

Peale paints himself in revolutionary dress. His britches and tights had long gone out of fashion by 1822, yet here remind the viewer of his participation in the war effort, as a solider and as a chronicler of an emerging American history. In the background of the painting, he depicts four visitors to the museum, all experiencing the space in different ways, ranging from quiet contemplation to active engagement. Although Peale's first goal was to educate the public on American flora and fauna, he was also a salesman and engaged in a number of sensational tactics—such as painting habitats for his animals, and using light and sound to augment his exhibits—to entertain his visitors, on whose repeated patronage his museum depended. As Alan Trachtenberg notes, by depicting himself at the foot of his painting, as if on the "proscenium of a stage—an effect produced also . . . by the curtain he lifts and by his theatrical gestures," Peale represents himself not just as "the artist" but also as "an impresario, a showman,"[27] thus raising the question: "Where exactly is this artist—in his museum, a place of rationalist enlightenment, or in a theater of illusions, of artful deception?"[28] And what does this tell us about the objects and images on display, here and elsewhere: Can we trust them as representations of reality? Or are they, too, part of a larger deception substantiated through new forms of technologically enhanced vision?

Despite his efforts to make his scientific and artistic displays more engaging, Peale could not compete with Barnum's more sensational tactics. After his death, his sons could not maintain his spaces (he had opened satellite museums in New York and Baltimore) and sold the New York museum to Barnum at a discounted price. Despite the proximity of the two spaces on lower Broadway in New York, Barnum did not combine the two institutions; instead, he kept Peale's museum as a seemingly competing venue. In truth, Peale's museum acted as a necessary foil to his more spectacular exhibition hall. Barnum explained, "I was still in show business, but in a settled, substantial phase of it, that invited industry and enterprise, and called for ever earnest and ever heroic endeavor."[29]

Barnum's need for a legitimate gallery to counter his sensational displays of purported freaks of nature on view down the street nicely encapsulates some of what was at stake in the fine line between of the real and the fake that I outlined in the introduction to this project. Spectacular attractions such as Peale's mastodon or Barnum's mermaid, like the moon hoax and the Cardiff Giant affair, gave observers the sense that they were participating in a form of public debate through sensory experience. The conventional reading of Barnum's museum and his many humbugs is that by witnessing the objects—firsthand or through printed accounts—visitors could, in theory, decide for themselves what was real and what was imaginary. This is certainly true. Seeing became both a vernacular as well as a more scientific organizing principle for establishing rules of the universe, from the solar system to the Galapagos Islands. But unlike miraculous vision, which depended on the necessary preexistence of faith and belief on the part of the beholder, those negotiating technological vision needed some sort of discursive, scientific legitimation of the object of vision before they could imbue it with import and meaning. Enthusiasm for, and trust in, encyclopedic knowledge and technological optimism in the seemingly infinitely observable world enabled a lay culture of humbugs and hoaxes in the nineteenth century. For many American spectators at this time, it did not always matter if the things they saw were real. Many came to see the hoax itself. Even if the particular items were proven to be fakes, they wanted to believe that new worlds existed in the firmament, that mythical creatures—mermaids and giants—were present in this world, and that with the right technologies of vision, they might one day be able to see them for themselves.

CHAPTER 3

Camera Vision and the Quest for Indexical Truths

Today the Rochester Historical Society is hard to find. Once located in a nineteenth-century Greek Revival mansion on the city's elegant East Avenue, in late 2018, due to budget cuts, its collections were moved to a rental space in an industrial lot on the outskirts of the city. Included in the crowded warehouse space are objects once owned by Susan B. Anthony, a variety of American Civil War artifacts, and a card table that reportedly was used by the Fox sisters. The pair rose to international fame in the mid-nineteenth century for their seeming ability to communicate with the spirit world. On March 31, 1848, fourteen-year-old Margaretta (Maggie) and eleven-year-old Kate devised a means for translating strange knocking sounds that seemed to emanate from the bowels of their house in Hydesville, New York, a small farming town southeast of Rochester. The sisters deciphered these noises through a method that linked the knocks to letters of the alphabet, thereby revealing what they claimed were messages from a previous visitor to the house, a peddler they called Mr. Splitfoot, who they alleged had been brutally murdered and buried in the basement by an earlier tenant. Soon after these events transpired, the Fox family deserted the ostensibly haunted house and sent Kate and Maggie to nearby Rochester to live with their older sister, Leah. Rochester at this time was part of the area known as the Burned-Over District for the number of new religious movements that had "burned" through it, and news of the Fox sisters' psychic powers spread quickly.[1]

In Rochester the sisters were embraced by many prominent citizens, including the influential Amy and Isaac Post, radical Quakers and local activists for abolition and women's rights. After holding a series of events for the local Rochester community where they communicated with spirits through rapping sounds, the sisters soon went on the road, holding séances and communicating with the dead, often to large, sold-out audiences. Although they later confessed that the whole thing began as an April Fool's Day trick on their mother and admitted to faking the sounds by cracking their knuckles and joints and using a variety of devices that allowed them to knock without being seen, the Spiritualist movement had taken off. By the end of the nineteenth century there were an estimated thirteen million Spiritualists and thirty-five thousand mediums in North America, several million followers in England, and a few hundred thousand in Germany and France. Queen Victoria had her own personal medium who provided regular contact with her deceased husband, Prince Albert; the Princess of Wales and the Empress of Russia also had spiritualist practices; and Abraham Lincoln and his wife, Mary Todd Lincoln, reportedly held séances at the White House.[2]

Historian Ann Braude defines Spiritualism as a "movement aimed at proving the immortality of the soul by establishing communication with the spirits of the dead."[3] But how to substantiate these communications as real? Spiritualists regularly communicated through psychics known as mediums, who helped spirit visitors and their messages take some sort of physical form. The presence of spirits was usually experienced through sensory phenomena: sight, sound, touch. In many ways, the success of the movement was dependent on its associated material culture. The truth claims of mediums depended on the things that augmented or aided their quests for spirit materializations. These included such objects as spirit trumpets, which helped magnify voices from beyond; planchettes such as the Ouija board that spelled out supernatural messages; slate tablets for automatic writing and drawings; precipitated paintings and spirit photographs that claimed to capture likenesses of the departed; and tables such as the one in the Rochester Historical Society.

Whether the Fox sisters actually used the table attributed to them is unclear; its provenance has been traced to the Farley family, who lived around the corner from the oldest sister, Leah Fish, in Rochester, but not directly to the younger Foxes.[4] Regardless, it is interesting for what it reveals. At first glance the table looks like a standard, mahogany-veneered Victorian fold-over card table. A two-piece, matchbook-style top sits on pedestal base that allows it to swivel into place and fold out. Like many card tables from the time, it contains a hollow storage space between the base and the top. What makes this card table different from others of its kind, however, is the small wooden ball on a metal rod attached to a spring inside the storage compartment. The rod sticks out just slightly from one side of the tabletop. When pushed it compresses the spring, which is fastened to a string that runs through the pedestal and can be attached to someone's foot, leg, or shoe. When the rod is released or the string is pulled and then released, the ball hits the bottom of the tabletop and causes a knocking sound (see fig. 25).

While it is unlikely that the Fox sisters used this table with any regularity, if at all (they claimed in their confessions that their earliest knockings in

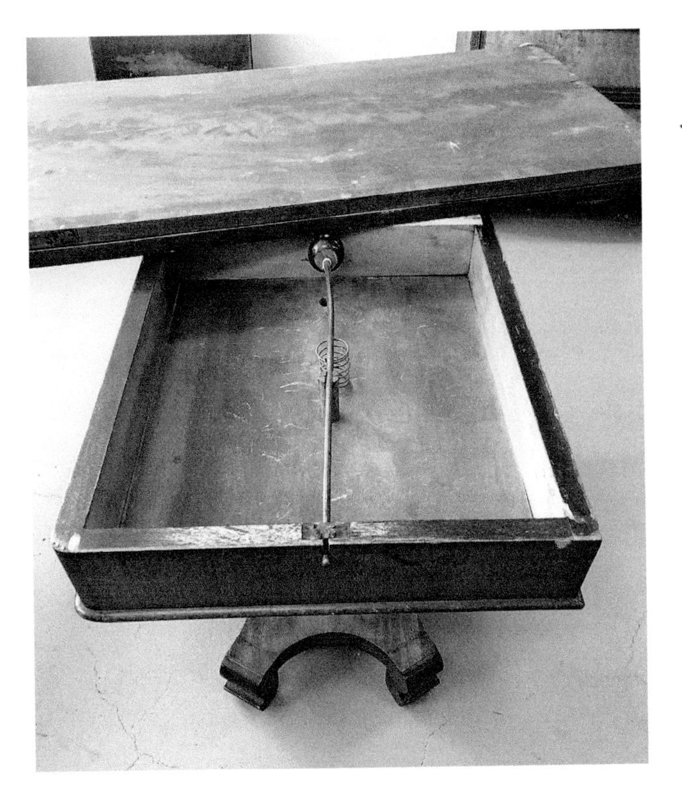

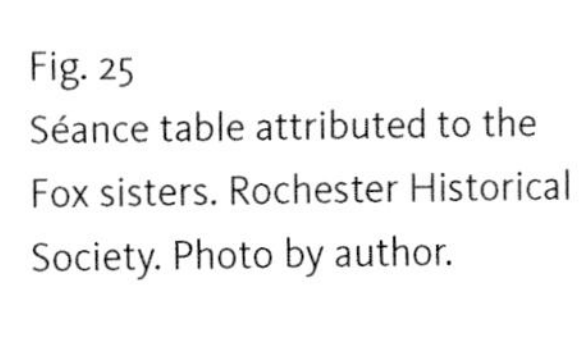
Fig. 25
Séance table attributed to the Fox sisters. Rochester Historical Society. Photo by author.

their Hydesville house came from apples tied to strings and that they later used their joints to make the rapping sounds), similar tables were employed by other mediums. For example, the Reverend H. Mattison in his 1853 book *Spirit Rapping Unveiled* described an account by Hiram Pack, "a respectable manufacturer of cabinet furniture," who testified to him in March 1853 that he made two "medium tables . . . both of which had machinery concealed in them for producing 'raps' at the will of the operator." Like the Rochester table, Pack's contained a pulley system hidden in the table's core to produce loud knocking sounds. Pack explained to Mattison that he "was not sufficiently acquainted with the machine and the matter of working it . . . my business was simply to make the tables for the reception of the 'spirits.'" He concluded, "I have done this in two instances and am ready to do it in twenty more if I can be paid for it. . . . If people will give a dollar a piece to hear a little hammer strike inside a table bed, and run crazy about it, it is not my fault."[5]

The Reverend Mattison's book was one of many texts exposing tricks to unveil duplicitous mediums. Fear of fraud became so prevalent that checking the props, and sometimes the mediums themselves, often became part of the practice of séances. For example, in his 1913 exposé of the Bangs sisters, David Phelps Abbot describes searching their skirts for hidden canvases before sitting for a spirit portrait.[6] Nevertheless, Spiritualists continued to validate and explain their practices to believing audiences. The Spiritualist press was full of accounts

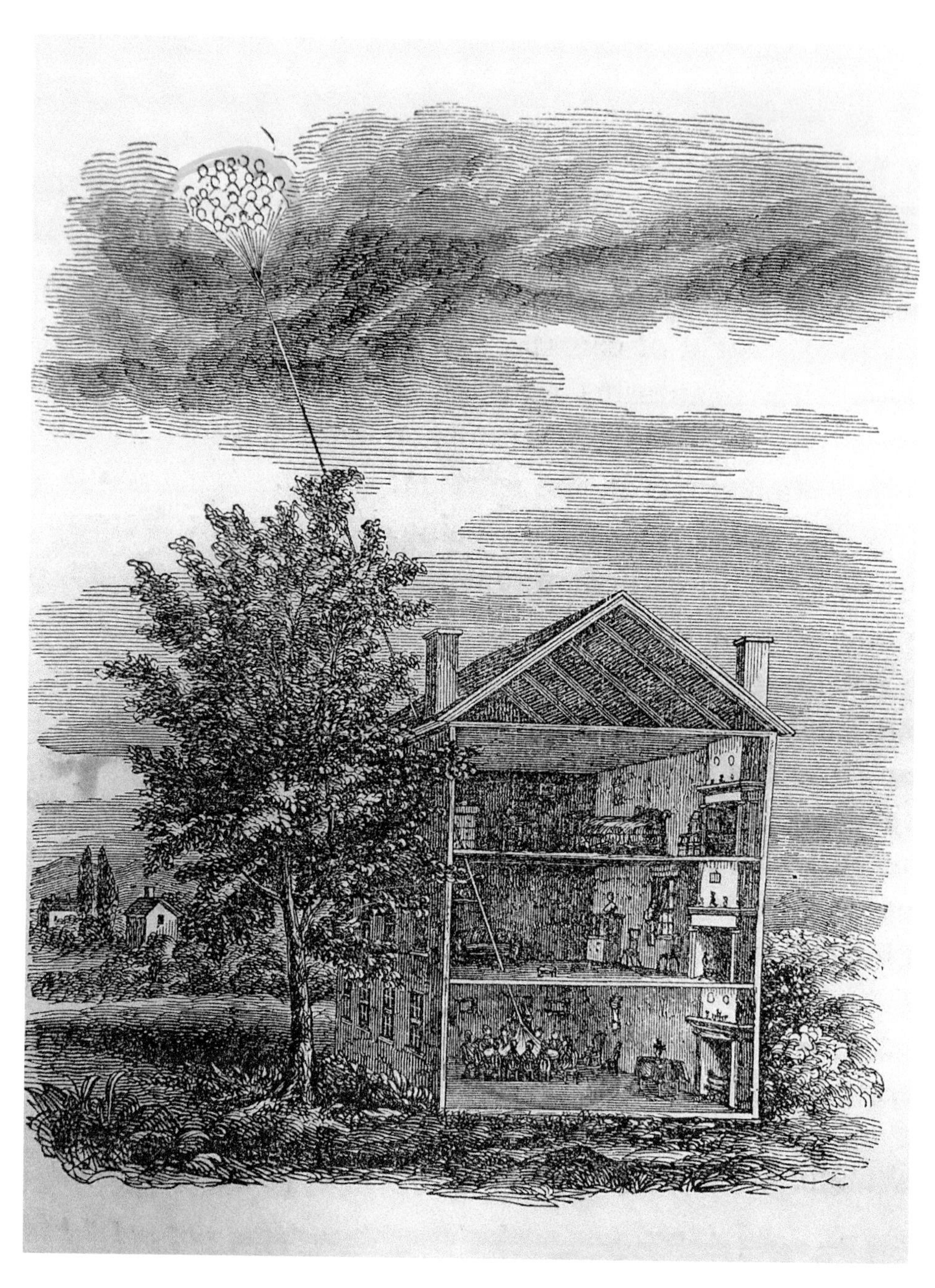

Fig. 26 Illustration of celestial telegraph with note: "The above engraving is designed expressly to illustrate the process of *table-moving.*" From Andrew Jackson Davis, *The Present Age and Inner Life* (New York: Partridge and Brittan, 1853).

of successful encounters, and numerous books and pamphlets elaborated on the best ways to communicate with the departed. For example, a nineteenth-century pamphlet entitled *Table Rapping and Automatic Writing* by Alexr. Verner, F.A.I.P. (the founder and principal of the British Psychological Institute), begins with the assertion that "in nearly every well-regulated family we generally find one or more of the members possessed of psychic power, but they are often at a loss to know how to develop that power." Verner suggests that it "is the best to start with table tilting." Instructions follow:

> Procure a round table and let the members or friends of the family sit around it, with their hands lightly resting on the table, palms downward, and in a short time a particular magnetic vibration will be felt; that, as a rule, gives warning that there is a spirit present. . . . [G]ive the spirit communicating certain rules to work by when answering questions, etc., such as three raps or tilts to mean "yes"; one rap or tilt to mean "no"; two raps to mean "doubtful"; and four raps or tilts to mean "good-night."[7]

Andrew Jackson Davis, often referred to as the "John the Baptist" of the Spiritualist movement, not only provided directions for achieving success with table rapping but tied his explanation for how such communication worked to a form of spiritual telegraphy. In his 1853 book *The Present Age and Inner Life,* he explained:

> We are *negative* to our guardian spirits; they are *positive* to us; and the whole mystery is illustrated by the workings of the common magnetic telegraph. The principals involved are identical. The spirits (improperly so called) sustaining a *positive* relation to us, are enabled through mediums, as electronic conductors, to attract and move articles of furniture vibrate the wires of a musical instrument, and, by discharging through the potencies of their wills, currents of magnetism, they can and do produce rappings, on principles strictly analogous to the magnetic telegraph and may move tables, or tip them, to signify certain letters of the alphabet.[8]

Davis included detailed engravings of the process in the text. One image depicts a three-story house, the back of which is removed like a Victorian dollhouse, to reveal a number of people sitting around a table on the first floor. A corresponding group of figures appears in the clouds above the building. They are connected by a cable of some sort to those assembled below (see fig. 26). Davis described the scene as such:

> Elevated above the cloud-region, is seen the spirit-circle in telegraphic correspondence with the mundane party in the lower story of the dwelling.

> The influence from the upper circle is seen passing down through the roof and floors to the surface of the table, where it imperceptibly radiates and emits invisible rays in every direction, and fills the *substance* of the table as water saturates a sponge. This is a true copy from nature. The descending line, it may be remarked, proceeds in an *oblique* direction, in order to exert a leverage influence on the substance to be moved. But when the "sounds" are desired to be produced, this line descends almost perpendicularly, as will be hereafter shown. The diameter of this magnetic current, which is fine and very strong, as I have frequently seen, varies in size from that of a knitting-needle to a child's little finger.[9]

Jackson was not the only Spiritualist to evoke new technologies such as electromagnetic telegraphy to validate communication between earthly and celestial realms.[10] The theosophist Louis Cahagnet published *The Celestial Telegraph* in 1851, and the *Spiritual Telegraph* was the name of a popular New York City newspaper "devoted to the illustration of Spiritual Intercourse" (according to its masthead), which ran from 1852 to 1860.

Spiritualists often deployed a mix of miraculous and technological legitimation to justify the validity of their objects of vision. Electromagnetic telegraphy and the modern Spiritualist movement arose simultaneously. Just four years before the Fox sisters initiated their communication with Mr. Split-foot, on May 24, 1844, Samuel Morse successfully sent the first electromagnetic telegraph with the message "What hath God wrought?" from Washington, DC, to Baltimore. Morse reportedly had conceived of the idea while traveling back from Europe by ocean steamer a decade before, after discussing Michael Faraday's recent experiments with electromagnetic induction and diamagnetism with his fellow passengers. By 1848, over six thousand miles of telegraph cable had been laid, allowing messages to be transmitted through a series of clicks that corresponded to letters of the alphabet (in a manner not dissimilar to the technique the Fox sisters used). While scholars have explored the links between Spiritualism and the telegraph (and other new forms of technology) to explain communication across celestial realms, the central role played by material objects in substantiating these encounters is often overlooked.

Moreover, Davis's admonition that "we are *negative* to our guardian spirits; they are *positive* to us" also suggests a relationship between spirit communication and newly emerging forms of photographic technology that depended on negatives to produce positive images. Indeed, one of the primary ways that Spiritualists attempted to concretely document the existence of a spirit world was through the use of photography to capture and record paranormal data in a form of what I am calling camera vision. Even though spirit photography, like spirit telegraphy, is well-trod scholarly territory, I include it in this project for a number of reasons. Camera vision provides an ongoing example of the ways in which often well-educated audiences are willing to suspend rational thought in the service of larger desires to believe in ghosts and visions. It also demonstrates the ways in which new forms of technology have been used to buttress and legitimize these desires as real.

From its earliest incarnations, photography has been regarded as somewhat of a conjuring trick and has played with viewers' ideas and expectations about the relationship between representation and reality, fantastic visions and visualizations of everyday life. Writing in March 1839 in response to the first daguerreotypes, for example, the British journal *The Spectator* announced that "an invention has recently been made public in Paris that seems more like some marvel of a fairy tale or delusion of necromancy than a practical reality."[11] "Daguerreotype" is both a noun and a verb; it refers to the early photographic process that used mercury vapor to fix unique positive images on iodine-sensitized silver plates as well as to the plates themselves. Perfected by (and named for) the French diorama maker Louis-Jacques-Mandé Daguerre, in collaboration with the chemist Joseph Nicéphore Niépce, daguerreotypes dominated the photographic market for the first two decades of photographic reproduction. To publicize his invention, Daguerre, the consummate showman, circulated mass-produced broadsides across Paris, explaining:

> The discovery I am announcing to the public . . . consists in the spontaneous reproduction of themes of nature received in the camera obscura—not with their colors but with great delicacy of tonal gradations. With this process, without any notion of drawing, without any knowledge of chemistry or physics, it will be possible to take in a few minutes, the most detailed views of the most picturesque sites. The daguerreotype is not an instrument to be used to draw nature, but a chemical and physical process which *gives her the ability to reproduce herself.*[12]

Daguerre positioned himself as a magician backed by science and technology. From the very beginning, he yoked the rhetoric of photography to a sensory and spectacular conception of visual truth. He also promoted the notion that with the right technology and application of chemicals, nature could spontaneously "reproduce herself," an idea that would resonate with the international Spiritualist community for decades to come.

While the first physical photographic images were not created until the nineteenth century, the desire to capture images directly from nature—both real and imagined—dates back to antiquity. In the fifth century BCE, the Chinese philosopher Mo Ti was the first to use what the German astronomer Johannes Kepler would call the "camera obscura"—or dark room technique—to capture an inverted image by directing light rays through a small hole. Mo Ti called this his "collecting place" or "locked treasure room."[13] Aristotle also experimented with the idea of the camera obscura, using solar eclipses as his light source. In the first century AD, the Islamic scholar and scientist Alhazen used lanterns to achieve a similar effect. Leonardo da Vinci included descriptions of a camera obscura in his notebooks from 1490 as a device to help him achieve linear perspective, and in the early seventeenth century Kepler built the first portable "camera," using a tent that deployed convex lenses and a series of mirrors to capture images. It wasn't until 1816, however, that the first "photograph" was taken by Niépce, who used a camera to project negative images onto paper coated with silver chloride. Niépce continued to experiment with other washes—finding success with a combination of bitumen of Judea fixed with lavender oil—to capture images in a process he called heliography (or sun writing), which he described as "*reproducing spontaneously*, by the action of light, with gradations of tints from black to white, the images received in the *camera obscura*." In a letter to his brother, Niépce described his process as such: "I succeeded in obtaining a *point de vue* . . . using my *Camera Obscura* and my largest stone. The image of the objects is represented with a clarity, an astonishing fidelity, complete with myriad details and with nuances of extreme delicacy. To get the effect, one must look at the stone from an oblique angle . . . and I must say my dear friend, this effect is truly something magical."[14]

By highlighting its "astonishing fidelity" and its "magical" qualities, Niépce simultaneously stressed the natural and supernatural potential of his invention and the experience of both to the physical act of looking at the material object from an "oblique angle." He also set up a duality that would dominate photo discourse for centuries between realness and the construction of realness in photographic reproductions. In this form of camera vision, the device both substantiates and manipulates what is in front of its lens as a form of reality. Daguerre, learning of Niépce's chemical experiments, began corresponding with him, collaborating until his death in 1833 to perfect his daguerreotype process. Among Daguerre's biggest, and most important, supporters was the esteemed astronomer and member of the French legislature Francois Arago, who secured for Daguerre a lifetime pension from the French Académie in exchange for the rights to his process, thereby linking technologies of vision to national identity.

The daguerreotype dominated the photographic imagination in the mid-nineteenth century, in large part, I would argue, because both the object and the process straddled the worlds of art and science; it allowed for projection and interpretation by scientists and artists alike in articulating the possibilities of camera vision and its transformative possibilities in this world and beyond. In an article in the January 12, 1839, edition of the London *Literary Gazette*, for example, the journalist Hippolyte Gaucheraud celebrated the many applications of the daguerreotype, writing, "This discovery seems like a prodigy. It disconcerts all the theories of science in light and optics, and, if borne out, promises to make a revolution in the arts of design."[15] Similarly, after viewing his first daguerreotype, the French painter Paul Delaroche wrote in a letter to Arago that "the drawings obtained by this means are at once remarkable for the perfection of the details and the richness and harmony of the whole. Nature is reproduced in them not only with truth, but with art."[16] The French magazine *L'Artiste* also highlighted the spontaneous and natural properties of the process, announcing to its readers that "all things, big and little, engrave themselves instantly with a kind of camera obscura."[17]

News of Daguerre's invention spread quickly (see fig. 27). Samuel Morse, who was in Paris to promote his telegraph machine, met Daguerre twice in March 1839—once to show him how his telegraphic apparatus worked and then to see Daguerre's pictures. Upon his return to New York, Morse published an account of their encounter in the *New York Observer*, describing the daguerreotype as "one of the most beautiful discoveries of the age" and as "Rembrandt perfected." Morse also lauded the device's potential for both art and scientific transformation:

> One of Mr. D.'s plates is an impression of a spider. The spider was not bigger than the head of a large pin, but the image, magnified by the solar microscope to the size of the palm of the hand, having been impressed on the plate, and examined through a lens, was further magnified, and showed a minuteness of organization hitherto not seen to exist. You perceive how this discovery is, therefore, about to open a new field of research in the depths of microscopic nature. We are soon to see if the minute has discoverable limits. The naturalist is to have a new kingdom to explore, as much beyond the microscope as the microscope is beyond the naked eye.[18]

Morse was among the first to receive the details of the photographic process when Daguerre made it available, and he soon opened the first daguerreotype studio in the United States with his brothers Sidney and Richard. Soon other studios opened across the country. By 1841 New York City had over one hundred daguerreotype studios, and by 1853 there were thirty-seven of them on Broadway alone. "Daguerromania" had taken hold of the United States (see fig. 28).

Edgar Allan Poe, who sat for his portrait, called the daguerreotype "the most important, and perhaps the most extraordinary, triumph of modern science." He further exclaimed, "All language must fall short of conveying any just idea of the truth, and this will not appear so wonderful when we reflect that the source of vision itself has been, in this instance, the designer. Perhaps, if we imagine the distinctness with which an object is reflected in a positively perfect mirror, we come as near the reality as by any other means."[19] Poe's exuberant language captured the feeling of wonder and amazement that surrounded early imaging technologies and the extraordinary sense of possibility afforded by modern

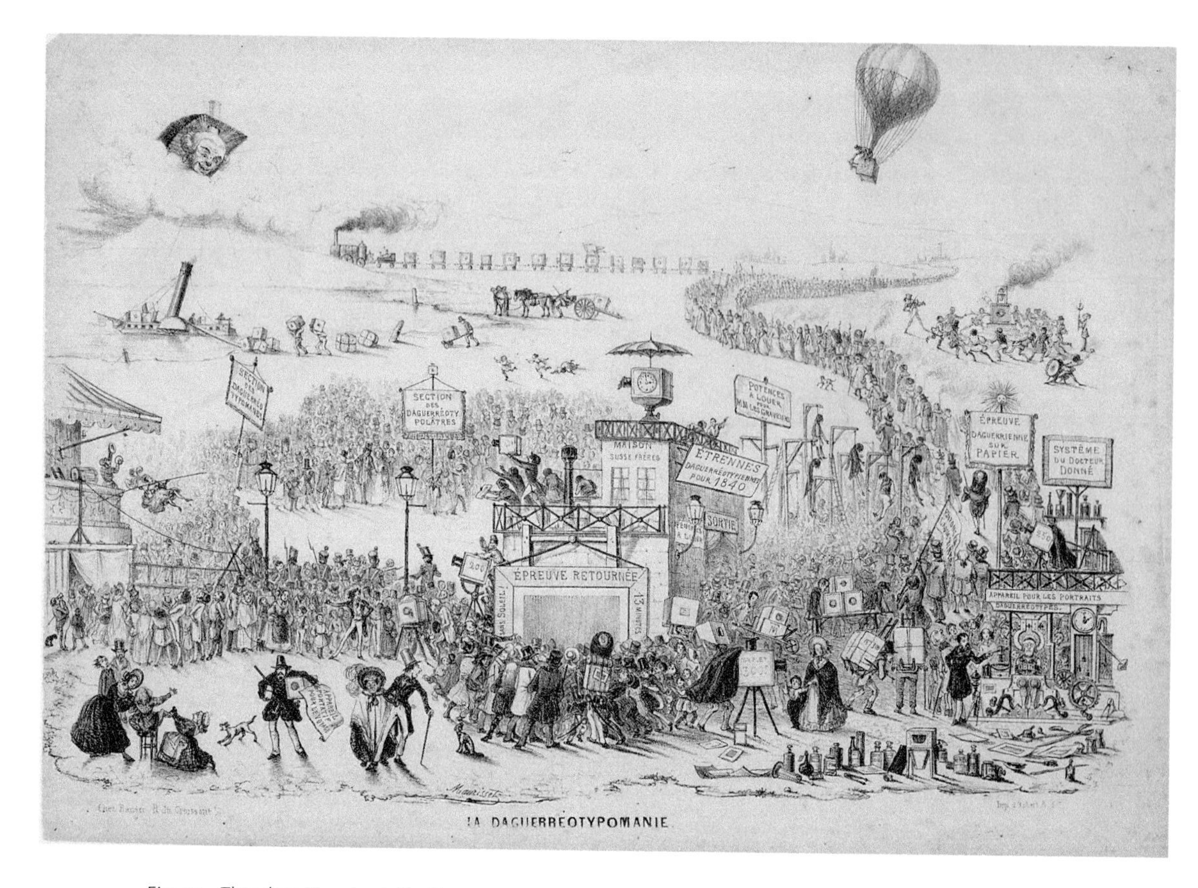

Fig. 27 Theodore Maurisset, "La Daguerreotypomanie," *La Caricature, Revue morale, judiciaire, littéraire, artistique, fashionable et scénique* 58 (December 8, 1839). Lithograph. George Eastman Museum. Gift of Eastman Kodak Company, ex-collection Gabriel Cromer 1980.0461.0002. Courtesy of the George Eastman Museum.

science as a form of truth. Poe's musings were not mere hyperbole. As Alan Trachtenberg has argued:

> From the beginning the daguerreotype excited people into states of awe, wonder, reverence clashing with disbelief, and provided a *frisson* of something preternatural, magical, perhaps demonic. A flickering image on mirrored metal, encased like a jewel in a decorated box, the daguerreotype seemed a simulacrum of the real: too real to be understood as just another kind of copy of the world, too immediately compelling to seem only a likeness. Its effect derived, too, from the image's capacity to negate itself when viewed in another light at another angle, to cancel itself into shadow, and rematerialize, as it were from within itself.[20]

Contemporaneous with Daguerre, the British gentleman scientist William Henry Fox Talbot also had been working on a system for making what he called

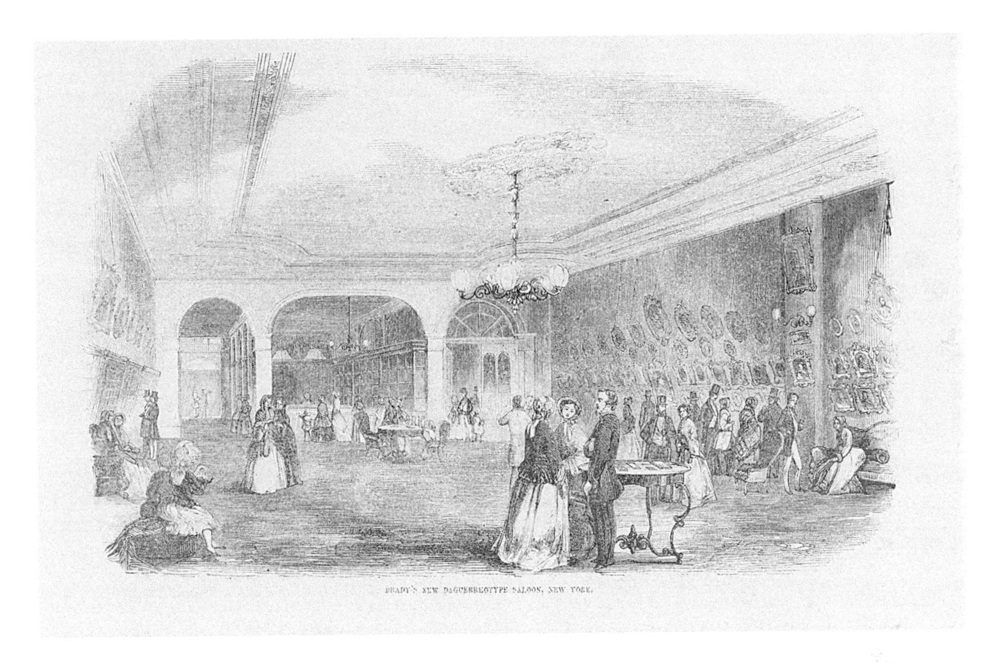

Fig. 28 Unidentified artist, "Brady's New Daguerreotype Saloon, New York," June 11, 1853. Wood engraving on paper. National Portrait Gallery, Smithsonian Institution.

"photographic drawings." Fox Talbot discovered that a sheet of paper coated with salt and a solution of silver nitrate would darken in the sun and that a second coating of silver nitrate would keep it from fading or darkening further. He first used this process to make imprints of botanical specimens by placing leaves and flowers under plates of glass on his treated paper. He further experimented with the chemistry and placed sheets of his sensitized paper into mini camera lucidas that his wife called his "little mouse traps," and placed them around his home. The resulting images, he wrote, "without great stretch of the imagination might be supposed to be the work of some Lilliputian artist. They require indeed examination with a lens to discover all their minutiae," thus capturing more than the naked eye could see. Talbot called the resulting prints, which he fixed with a solution of gallic acid, calotypes, after the Greek word for beauty, *kalos*. Learning of Daguerre's experiments in France, in January 1839 he wrote to the British Royal Society to establish his own timeline. "In the summer of 1835 I made . . . a great number of representations of my house in the country. . . . And this building I believe to be the first that was ever yet known *to have drawn its own picture*."[21]

Talbot's claims that the building drew its own picture established one of the tropes that would come to dominate the discourse around photography: the idea that the photograph is indexical, or that it has a "real relation" to that which it denotes. As I briefly explained in chapter 1, the concept of indexicality was first articulated in the 1860s by Charles Sanders Peirce in his theory of semiosis, or the study of signs. For Peirce signs took one of three forms: icon, index, or symbol. Photographs in theory can fit into all three categories. They have physical properties in common with their objects, thus making them icons; yet they also require cultural interpretation, which render them symbols. Photographs, Peirce argues, belong to the class of index because "they are in certain respects exactly like the objects they represent . . . they were physically forced to correspond point by point to nature."[22]

Much has been written about photography and the concept of indexicality, and whether or not this relationship works. I am not interested in rehashing those arguments here. What is important to note is that from the earliest photo experiments, practitioners and critics alike conceived of camera vision as a form of visual truth rooted in the idea that photographs have a natural relationship with their referents—and that these relationships depend on sensory experiences to validate them as true.[23]

Oliver Wendell Holmes, for example, believed that photography was "a process of visual representation that separated the form of objects from the physical objects themselves." For Holmes, photography was "the mirror with a memory."[24] Nevertheless, despite repeated claims to truth in representation, from the daguerreotype on, every photographic process has been subject to flaws and mistakes—double exposures, blurred images, scratched negatives, chemical spots, the list goes on—and because these errors often were not visible until the plates were developed, an air of mystery surrounded early photographic processes. In *The Interpretation of Dreams,* Sigmund Freud conceived of the psyche as "an instrument that carries out our mental functions as resembling a compound microscope or a photographic apparatus,"[25] or what Walter Benjamin would call "the optical unconscious." This dreamlike sense of mystery surrounding early photographs is in part what made photography so attractive to Spiritualists, from the most earnest to the most duplicitous. As Nancy Martha West has argued, "the paradox of spiritualism was also, in a sense, the paradox of photography" (and I would add of modernity in general), since "each argued for a new way of viewing the world, for a vision in which surface became intelligible and where everything, even the most banal objects, became legible and meaningful texts."[26] Photographs of ghosts and spirits, much like the Cardiff Giant or the Feejee Mermaid, thus became a form of evidence for those who wanted to believe that such things were real. The visions captured on film acted as techno-legitimations of the supernatural world backed up by the indexical nature of camera vision.

The first documented claims of capturing ghostly visions on glass or paper took place in the late 1850s in Europe. In 1858 in Dijon, France, there were reports of the sudden appearance of the image of a recently deceased gentleman on the window of his home. In Paris, stories spread of an incident involving a recently widowed Polish count who wanted to take a photograph of his home before he moved his grieving children elsewhere. According to a contemporary account in the French *Revue Spiritualiste*, the count commissioned a photographer to take an image of the family in front of the building. When he developed the images, a transparent presence appeared to peek out from the shutters of one of the upstairs windows. The family and their associates read the spectral vision as their recently deceased loved one who had come to say goodbye.[27] Writing of both events, Z. J. Pierart, the editor of the *Revue Spiritualiste*, concluded, "If the spirit of Mr. Bader, the former citizen of Dijon, had the ability to make a photographic impression on a pane of glass—which is of course beyond the laws of photography—there is no reason why such a marvel cannot be repeated to obtain similar splendid results as those achieved by the Polish nobleman in his country villa."[28]

Spiritualists regularly used the logic of early photography and camera vision to explain the emergence of mysterious pictures and messages from beyond. While it would be easy to characterize these images—which took various shapes—as forms of miraculous encounter much like those I discussed in the first chapter, many believers went to great lengths to explain their existence as not just as authentic forms of communication with the spirit realm but as proof of the immortality of the soul backed by science and technology. Regarding precipitated paintings, for example, witnesses often deployed rhetoric similar to that used by Niépce, Daguerre, and Talbot to explain how portraits of the deceased seemingly materialized on the canvas out of the air.

According to Ron Nagy, the leading contemporary authority on spirit art, "a precipitated spirit painting is a work of art, usually a portrait, that appears on canvas without the use of human hands during a spiritualist séance."[29] Nagy makes it clear that while precipitated portraits are not photographs, they bear a similar indexical relationship to the spirits they claim to represent. Historically, precipitated spirit painting has been associated with two pairs of mediums: the Campbell brothers, Allan Campbell and Charles Shourds (the two men were not actually brothers but rather a romantic couple who posed as bothers likely to avoid discrimination); and the Bangs sisters, Mary "May" and Elizabeth "Lizzie" Bangs. The Campbell brothers practiced during the summers in the Spiritualist community of Lily Dale, New York, an hour southwest of Buffalo. The spirits that made themselves visible in their portraits included Abraham Lincoln and Napoleon. The Bangs sisters were members of a notorious Chicago-based family of mediums. Despite being arrested on multiple occasions for fraud, they were quite successful. An article in the *Washington Post* from April 17, 1888, notes that "Lizzie and May Bangs, under the firm name of the Bangs Sisters, conduct the leading spiritualistic establishment in Chicago. . . . Their elegant parlors have been crowded by day as well as by night and money flowed into their coffers in large streams."[30] Unlike the Campbell brothers, who tended to call forth portraits

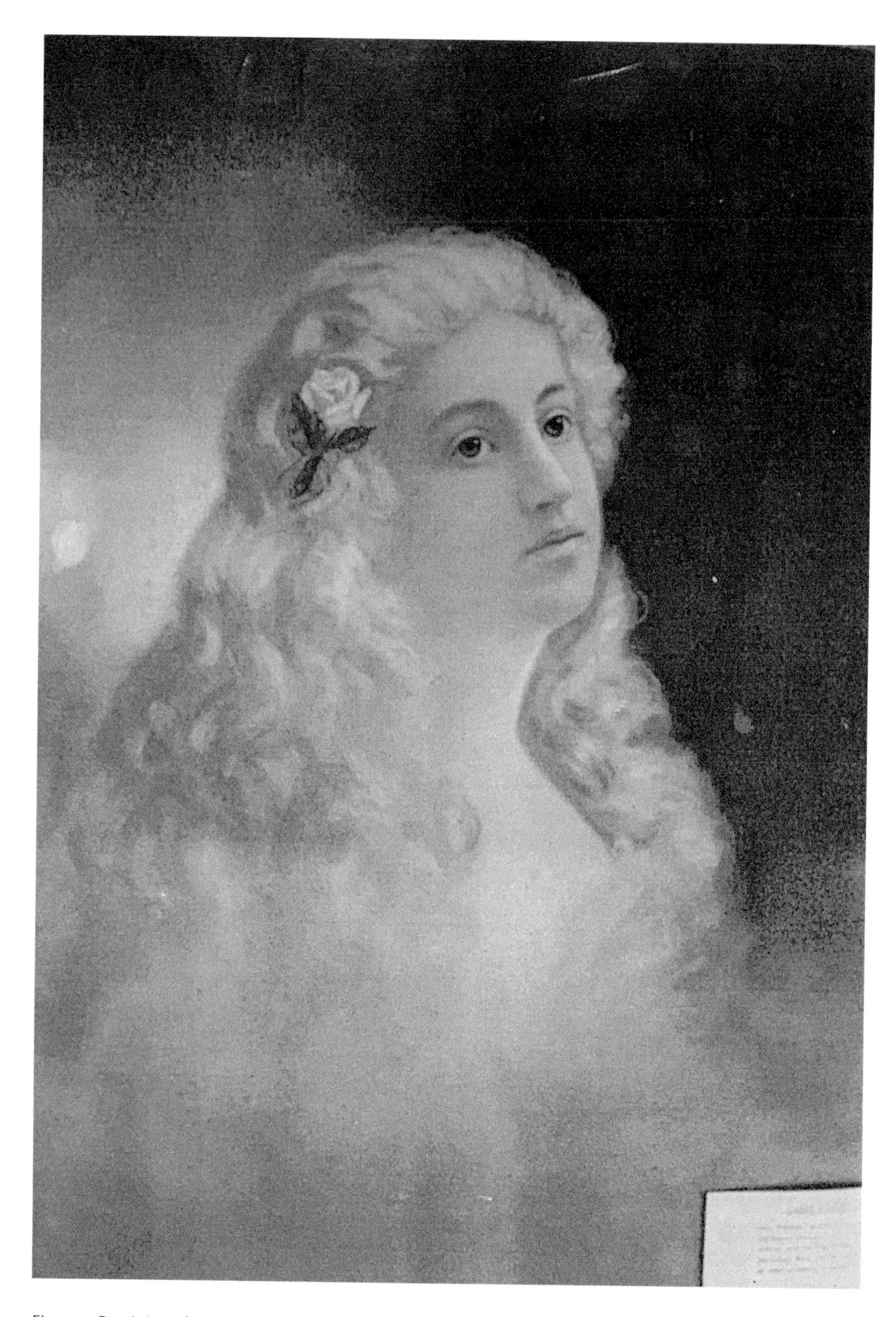

Fig. 29 Precipitated painting from the Maplewood Hotel, Lily Dale, New York. Photo courtesy of Kendall DeBoer, October 2019.

of historical figures, the Bangs sisters worked with clients to contact deceased family members and other lost loved ones, often for very large sums of money (see fig. 29).

Dr. and Mrs. E. H. Thurston of Hagerstown, Indiana, for example, visited the Bangs sisters at their cottage at the Spiritualist camp in Chesterfield, Indiana, in April 1905 with the hopes of procuring a portrait of their deceased daughter. Dr. Thurston described how, along with his wife, he inspected the canvases they were using "under the noonday sun" to "assure myself that they were not chemically prepared, at the same time to secretly mark them for identification." After further inspection of the séance room to ensure that it was free of mechanical manipulation or tricks, Dr. Thurston sat down with the Bangs sisters, who began the process of calling forth a portrait. He and his wife sat directly in front of the sisters, who were "seated on each side of the table," where they each "supported the canvas in an upright position with one hand." After a short period, "a dark shadow passed over the canvas, followed by the outline of the head and body . . . the perfect features of our daughter appeared, with the eyes closed; a few more seconds, and the eyes opened and before us was the beautiful spirit of our deceased daughter, perfectly lifelike in every feature."

Thurston made it clear that the portrait was not a photograph. "Being somewhat familiar with photography and photographic processes, especially solar print work," he explained, "we are fully convinced that the picture is not the product of any photographic process, and we desire to say right here there was positively no evidence whatsoever of any trick, or slight-of-hand performance; everything was perfectly straightforward and honest, as far as the physical eye could discern." For Thurston and his wife, the painting convinced them that they were in the presence of their daughter's spirit. It substantiated their belief in celestial communication. He concluded his account, "We went away from that cottage at beautiful Camp Chesterfield more convinced than ever before of the continuity of life after death and the beautiful philosophy of spiritualism."[31]

Other mediums, however, did use photography to materialize the presence of spirit visitors. The first individual to intentionally practice the craft of spirit photography was a Boston engraver named William H. Mumler, who in October 1861, while experimenting with photographic processes in a friend's studio, "tried to take a picture of myself and found that a second figure had appeared in the picture." Mumler later explained in his autobiography, *The Personal Experiences of William H. Mumler in Spirit Photography*, that he assumed "the picture I had taken was not perfectly clean and that the figure that had formed must have remained on the glass plate." Yet further experiments led him to believe that "the power through which these forms were produced lay far beyond human control." Mumler's wife was a well-known local medium and they socialized with the Spiritualist community. Mumler showed the ghostly image, which he claimed bore a striking resemblance to a deceased cousin of his, to one of their

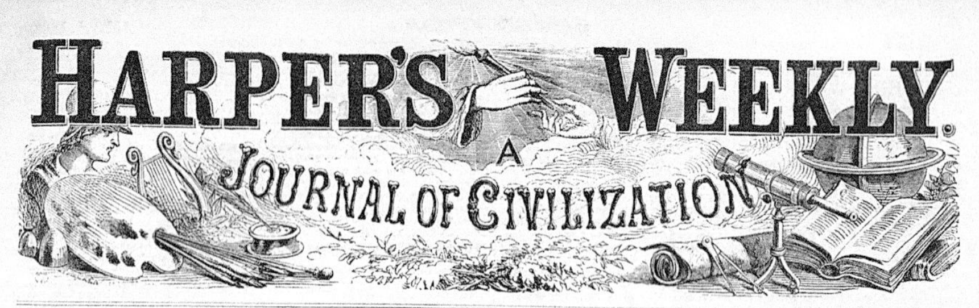

VOL. XIII.—No. 645.] NEW YORK, SATURDAY, MAY 8, 1869. [SINGLE COPIES, TEN CENTS. $4.00 PER YEAR IN ADVANCE.

SPIRITUAL PHOTOGRAPHY.

THE case of the people against WILLIAM H. MUMLER, of 630 Broadway, is one so remarkable and without precedent in the annals of criminal jurisprudence that we devote this page to illustrations bearing upon it. The charge against Mr. MUMLER is that, by means of what he terms spiritual photographs, he has swindled many credulous persons, leading them to believe it possible to photograph the immaterial forms of their departed friends.

The case has excited the profoundest interest, and, strange as it may seem, there are thousands of people who believe that its development will justify the claims made by the spiritual photographer. We shall not attempt to give an expression to our own opinions, but simply to follow the developments of the case through the testimony offered during the first few days of the trial.

It is through the instrumentality of Marshal JOSEPH H. TOOKER that the case has been brought before the courts. He deposes that he was ordered by Mayor HALL to investigate the case, which he did by assuming a false name, and by getting his photograph taken by Mr. MUMLER. After the taking of the picture the negative was shown him, with a dim, indistinct outline of a ghostly face staring out of one corner; and he was told that the picture represented the spirit of his father-in-law. He, however, failed to recognize the worthy old gentleman, and emphatically declared that the picture neither represented his father-in-law, nor any of his relations, nor yet any person whom he had ever seen or known. With this evidence the prosecution rested.

The counsel for the defense have brought forward a number of witnesses who testify to the genuineness of spiritual photographs taken for them by Mr. MUMLER. WILLIAM P. SNEED, a photographer, of Poughkeepsie, testifies that MUMLER succeeded in producing spiritual photographs at his gallery in Poughkeepsie, and he was unable to discover how it was done. Judge EDMONDS, one of the most distinguished advocates of Spiritualism, deposed that he had two photographs taken by MUMLER; the spirit form in one of them he thought he could recognize, but not the one in the other. He said: "I believe that the camera can take a photograph of a spirit, and I believe also that spirits have materiality—not that gross materiality that mortals possess, but still they are material enough to be visible to the human eye, for I have seen them; only a few days since I was in a court in Brooklyn when a suit against a life assurance company for the amount claimed to be due on a certain policy was being heard. Looking toward that part of the court-room occupied by the jury, I saw the spirit of the man whose death was the basis of the suit. The spirit told me the circumstances connected with the death; said that the suit was groundless, that the claimant was not entitled to recover from the company, and said that he (the man whose spirit was speaking) had committed suicide under certain circumstances; I drew a diagram of the place at which his death occurred, and on showing it to the counsel, was told that it was exact in every particular."

A large number of witnesses deposed that they recognized the forms of departed friends (in some cases of those long dead) in the photographs taken for them by MUMLER. The most striking case was that of a gentleman of Wall Street, whose deceased wife's features both he and his friends distinctly recognized in a photograph taken for him in this way.

If there is a trick in Mr. MUMLER's process it has certainly not been detected as yet. To all appearances spiritual photography rests just where the rappings and table-turnings have rested for some years. Those who believe in it at all will respect no opposing arguments, and disbelievers will reject every favorable hypothesis or explanation. Mr. MUMLER has certainly been very fortunate. He has been believed in, in the first place, by a large number of people. He has obtained, again, a good price for his photographs; for who could expect spirits to be called "from the vasty deep" for less than ten dollars per head? And, finally, he has been prosecuted, and thus extensively advertised. Beyond this, the trial, like all legal prosecutions of this nature, will amount to nothing.

In addition to our illustrations of specimens of Mr. MUMLER's spirit photographs, we give also representations of similar photographs taken by Mr. ROCKWOOD of this city. The latter were taken by natural means, but not so as to escape detection as to the trick resorted to to secure the result. Mr. MUMLER has certainly the advantage of a longer experience in the business.

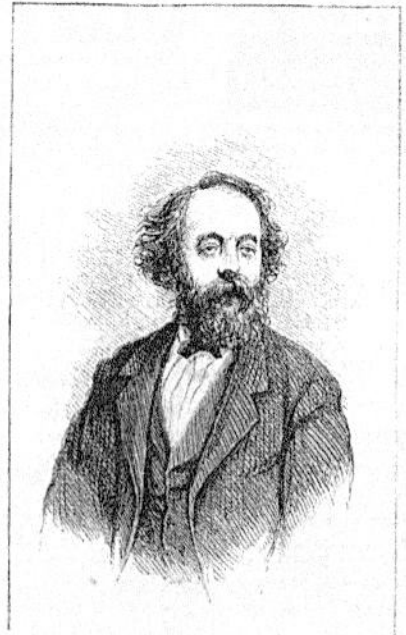
W. H. MUMLER.

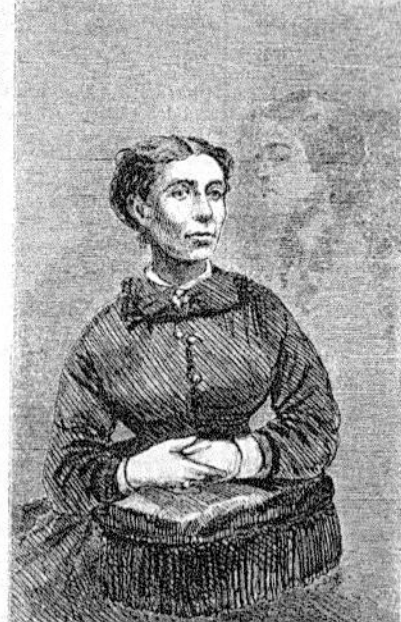
MRS. W. H. MUMLER.—BY MUMLER.

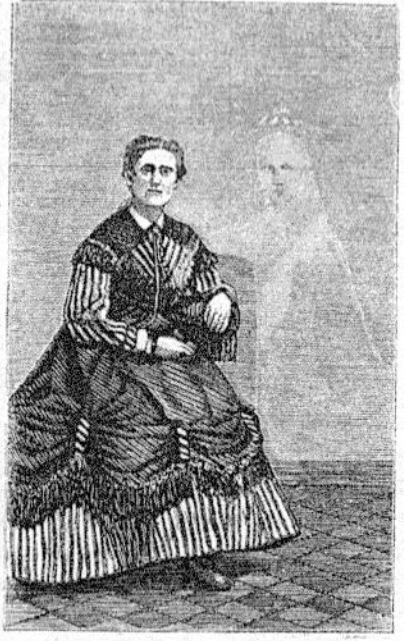
SPIRIT PHOTOGRAPH BY MUMLER.

SPIRIT PHOTOGRAPH BY MUMLER.

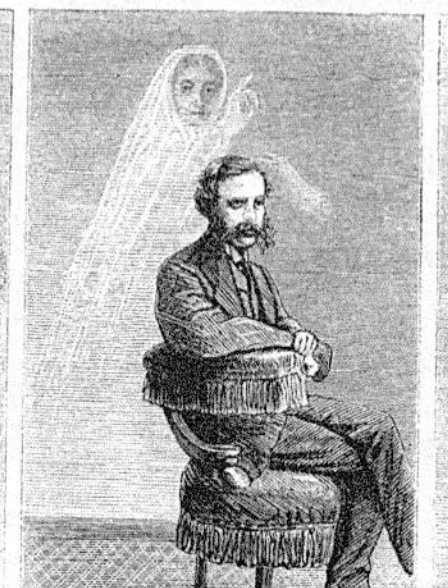
SPIRIT PHOTOGRAPH BY MUMLER.

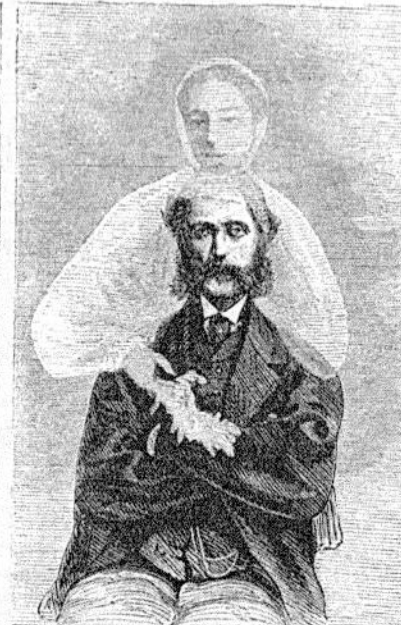
SPIRIT PHOTOGRAPH BY MUMLER.

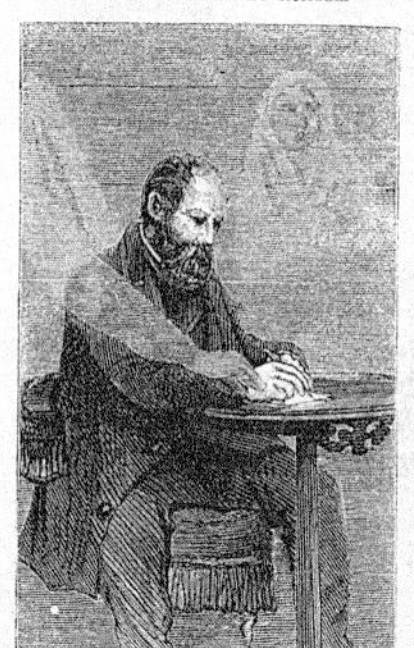
SPIRIT PHOTOGRAPH BY MUMLER.

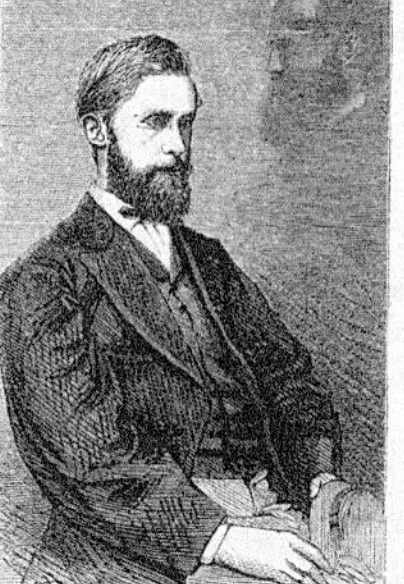
P. V. HICKEY.—BY ROCKWOOD.

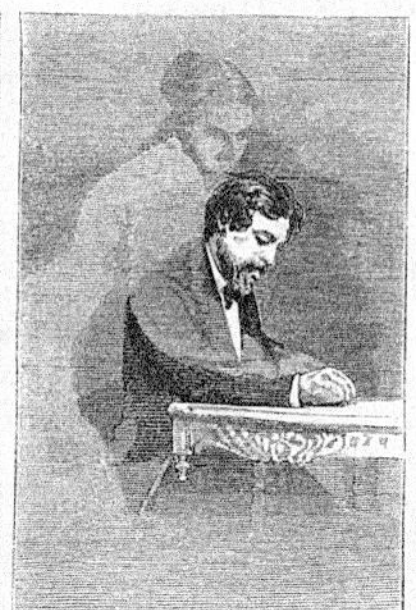
C. B. BOYLE.—BY ROCKWOOD.

SPIRITUAL PHOTOGRAPHY.—[SPECIMENS FURNISHED BY MUMLER AND ROCKWOOD.]

Fig. 30 "Spiritual Photography," *Harper's Weekly*, May 8, 1869. Image from Hathi Trust.

sympathetic friends who brought the story to the Spiritualist press. Soon images of Mumler and his spirit "extra" spread across Boston, drawing to his studio those who wanted their own photographs with ghostly presences (see fig. 30). As demand for his photographs grew, he quit his job as an engraver to devote himself full-time "to the art of photography."[32]

Demand for Mumler's services were high—in large part motivated by the desires of those who had recently lost loved ones during the ongoing American Civil War for some sort of otherworldly contact. In 1869 Mumler opened a studio in New York City, where he charged the exorbitant sum of ten dollars a sitting, over five times the current rate for photographic portraits. Despite his high price, people flocked to his studio to have their picture taken with the likenesses of their deceased loved ones. As Jen Cadwallader has pointed out, with spirit photographs, "the relative positions of mourned and mourner are reversed . . . it is now the mourned who watches the mourner."[33] Among the many famous people who employed Mumler's skills, the most celebrated was Mary Todd Lincoln. Mrs. Lincoln, who had lost three of her four sons as well as her husband, was an ardent Spiritualist. When she visited Mumler's studio in 1871 she entered in full mourning dress, her face covered by a black veil. According to Mumler's own account, "When I came out I found her seated with her veil still over her face. I asked if she intended to have her picture taken with her veil. She replied, 'When you are ready, I will remove it.'"[34] Mumler claimed afterward that he did not know who the grieving widow was when she entered his studio since she registered with a false name and her face was covered until the last moment. It was only upon developing the plates and seeing the image, which seemed to contain the likeness of Abraham Lincoln, did he realize who she was.

From the start, Mumler had his critics. As early as February 1863 one of his portrait sitters claimed to recognize the spirit image in his picture as belonging to someone he knew was still alive. Later that year, Oliver Wendell Holmes took cause with the entire enterprise, writing in the *Atlantic Monthly*, "But is it enough for the poor mother, whose eyes are blinded with tears, that she see a print of drapery like an infant's dress, and a rounded something, like a foggy dumpling, which will stand for a face: she accepts the spirit portrait as a revelation from the world of shadows." Holmes concluded that "the weak people who resort to these places are deluded."[35]

In 1869 the New York City's Mayor's Office launched a sting operation to expose Mumler as a fraud. Using an alias, City Marshal Joseph Tooker visited Mumler's studio to sit for a portrait. According to a contemporary account in the London-based journal *The Illustrated Photographer*, "After the taking of the picture, the negative was shown to [Tooker], with a dim, indistinct outline of a ghostly face starting out of one corner; and he was told that the picture represented the spirit of his father-in-law. He, however, failed to recognize the worthy old gentleman, and emphatically declared that the picture neither represented his father-in-law, nor any of his relations, nor yet any person he had ever seen."[36] The case went to trial in April 1869 in the Tombs Police Court. It was covered widely in the press and drew huge crowds to the courthouse, including many who felt that Mumler's innocence would legitimize not just spirit photography but also Spiritualism itself. In many ways, the Mumler case also put photography on trial. As art historian Michael Leja has pointed out, "Earlier in the decade many Americans had learned to discern truths in the Civil War photographs of Mathew Brady and Alexander Gardner; now photography was being revealed to the same public as yet another field for the practice of humbug."[37] Among those who testified for the prosecution was the father of the "humbug," P. T. Barnum himself. Barnum had long been a critic of Mumler, whom he accused repeatedly of swindling grieving clients, and he volunteered to bear witness against him. To prepare for his testimony, Barnum hired the respected photographer Abraham Bogardus to take his portrait and include a spirit presence in order to demonstrate how easy it would be for any trained photographer to insert "extras" into their images. He later explained that he asked Bogardus "to take my photograph with a spirit on it; I could detect no fraud on his part, although I watched him closely; the spirit on my photograph was that of the departed Abraham Lincoln. I didn't feel any spiritual presence."[38]

During the trial Barnum made a point to differentiate between his own "humbugs" and those of Mumler. When asked by the defense attorney, John D. Townsend, "How long have you been in the humbug business," He replied, "I was never in it. I never took money from a man without giving him the worth of it four times over. These pictures that I exhibited I did so as a humbug, and not as a reality, not like this man who takes $10 from people."[39] When questioned specifically about exhibits such as the Feejee Mermaid, Barnum rejoined to much laughter in the gallery, "The mermaid, at the time it was exhibited, was represented to be as I represented it, and I have not seen anything to the contrary."[40] Leja suggests that we see this extended courtroom exchange as "more than an entertaining game of cat and mouse."[41] Rather, he argues, "the Socratic irony of Barnum's masterly maneuvering suited [a] new culture of deception. Barnum feigned innocence while communicating wit and shrewdness, absurdly persistent as he stonewalled in the face of the evidence." Indeed, the New York *World* reporting on Barnum's testimony at the trial exclaimed, "Who will pretend a trust in the preposterous pretensions of a spiritual photographer when this child-like spirit, this marvel of credulity, this son of Connecticut in whom there is no guile, repudiates and disavows him."[42]

Barnum's testimony highlights the difference between his notion of "humbugs" and outright fraud. There was an ethics to Barnum's humbugs. With a wink and a nod, he included his audience in his deceptions—which he often revealed as fakes from the outset. Mumler and mediums like the Bangs sisters, however, intended to deceive for their own reward. By charging over five times the going rate for portraiture for his enhanced photographs, Mumler made enormous profits with his spirit "extras." Similarly, the Bangs sisters explicitly targeted wealthy patrons for their services. An article in the *Chicago Daily Tribune* answered the question "Who buys them, or rather who pleads for them and, incidentally, pays for these medium's troubles?" with "Well, such as these: doctors, lawyers, and women, of course. What do they pay for these works of art? Anywhere from $15 to $150." The *Tribune* regularly covered the Bangses' exploits, which included "one prominent paying customer . . . the Reverend Dr. Isaac K. Funk of the dictionary publishers Funk and Wagnalls" who "reportedly paid $1500 to the sisters for a number of paintings."[43] Funk was one of many wealthy widowers whom the sisters swindled, often by convincing them that they had received messages from their departed relatives, in some cases to marry them.

May Bangs married four times. She met her first husband, the wealthy chemical manufacturer Henry H. Graham, at an 1887 séance at which, according to the *Tribune*, Bangs told the newly widowed Graham that his dead wife had contacted her and said he should marry the medium, adding that his deceased infant had also sent a message: "Dear papa: I would like this lady for my new mamma."[44] After they divorced, May married Jacob Lesher, a millionaire leather manufacturer. According to the *New York Times*, the medium "proposed to him three times before he was finally won over by the assurance that the spirit of Lesher's mother was urging the match and that he himself would become 25 years younger and would never again be ill."[45]

Unlike the Bangs sisters, who were convicted on multiple occasions for various trespasses, Mumler ultimately was found not guilty of fraud; nevertheless, his reputation and his business suffered as a result of the trial and he stopped taking spirit photographs. The Mumler case was one of the earliest to use photographs as a form of evidence at trial for both sides (prefiguring the Rodney King trial by over a hundred years). The trial and its extended media coverage educated the public not just about the technicalities of photographic processes and printing, but also demonstrated that photographs have "the power to deceive."[46] The tension between the idea that photographs reveal indexical truths but can also act as forms of deception continued to be a source of debate within the Spiritualist community, whose numbers surged again during the First World War. Indeed, fifty years after Mumler stood trial for fraud, Sir Arthur Conan Doyle, the creator of the world-renowned detective Sherlock Holmes, defended camera vision and the idea that one could capture the supernatural in a photographic image. He fully articulated his defense of the practice in two book-length treatises he published in 1922, *The Case for Spirit Photography* and, more famously, *The Coming of the Fairies*.

The Coming of the Fairies describes in detail his experiences with Elsie Wright and Frances Griffiths, two young girls who lived in Cottingley, a small village outside of West Yorkshire, England, who in 1917 claimed to take photographs of fairies and other wood sprites in the fields near their home. Doyle used the images of the two girls frolicking with the fairies in an essay he was writing for the Christmas 1920 edition of *Strand Magazine*, claiming that the images conclusively proved the existence of mystical creatures in the English countryside (see fig. 31).

Doyle's embrace of the supernatural surprised many who equated his views with those of his fictional character, Sherlock Holmes, whose detection method was rooted in the meticulous observation of discernable facts. Yet despite the often-fantastic nature of his subject matter, Doyle's methods were not that different from those of his famous sleuth. He repeatedly justified his defense of Spiritualism in rational terms. In a lecture to the London Spiritualist Alliance on October 25, 1917, for example, he explained that "the subject of psychical research is one upon which I have thought more and have been slower to form my opinion on than any other subject whatsoever. . . . It is only within the last year or so that I have finally announced that I was satisfied with the evidence, that I have not been hasty in forming my opinion."[47] Responding to queries regarding the lack of scientific evidence to support his claims, he countered, "For what is science? Science is the consensus of scientific men, and history has shown that it is slow to accept a truth. Science sneered at Newton for twenty years. Science proved mathematically that an iron ship could not swim and science declared that a steamship could not cross the Atlantic."[48]

Doyle was not alone in his attempts to use science and technological vision to justify his belief in ghostly visions and to legitimize other supernatural phenomena. He was an early member of the Society for Psychical Research, an organization formed in Cambridge, England, in 1892 to investigate paranormal phenomena in a seemingly scientific manner. Other members of the Society included future British prime minister Arthur Balfour, American philosopher William James, the naturalist Alfred Russell Wallace (Charles Darwin's collaborator), and a host of other scientists and philosophers committed to demonstrating that the spiritual world not only existed but—like the natural world—that it was knowable, traceable, and classifiable. Scholars at Harvard and the University of Pennsylvania set up organizations devoted to the investigation and practice of Spiritualism as well. Advances in scientific instruments such as the microscope and the telescope further encouraged Spiritualists: if you could see a world in a drop of water and send messages across long distances through telegraphs, why could you not communicate with the dead?

But, again, how to substantiate these claims? In both his studies of spirit photography Doyle presents his evidence through the proof of camera vision, much like he presented evidence in his Sherlock Holmes stories. He begins his *Case for Spirit Photography*, for example, with the assertion that "one must not limit one's investigation to a single case, where errors of observation and

A. Conan Doyle 465

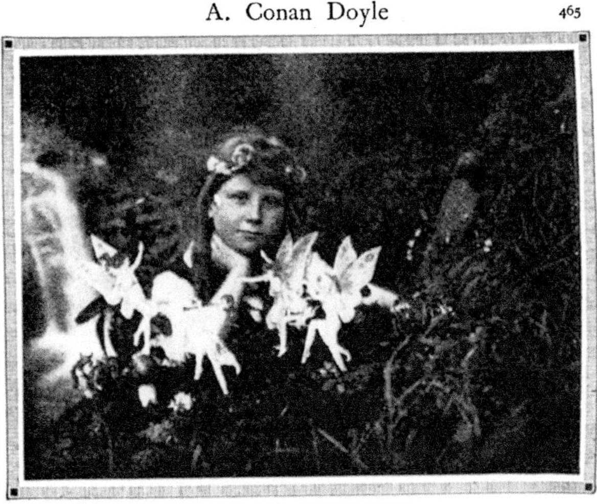

ALICE AND THE FAIRIES.

ALICE STANDING BEHIND THE BANKS OF THE BECK, WITH FAIRIES DANCING BEFORE HER. SHE IS LOOKING ACROSS AT HER PLAYMATE IRIS, TO INTIMATE THAT THE TIME HAD COME TO TAKE THE PHOTOGRAPH.

(An untouched enlargement from the original negative.)

photographer of thirty years' practical experience whom I knew I could trust for a sound opinion. Without any explanation I passed the plates over and asked what he thought of them. After examining the "fairies" negative carefully, exclamations began: "This is the most extraordinary thing I've ever seen"—"Single exposure!"—"Figures have moved!"—"Why, it's a genuine photograph! Where ever did it come from?"

I need hardly add that enlargements were made and subjected to searching examination—without any modification of opinion. The immediate upshot was that a "positive" was taken from each negative, that the originals might be preserved carefully untouched, and then new negatives were prepared and intensified to serve as better printing mediums. The originals are just as received and in my keeping now. Some good prints and lantern slides were soon prepared.

In May I used the slides, with others, to illustrate a lecture given in the Mortimer Hall, London, and this aroused considerable interest, largely because of these pictures and their story. A week or so later I received a letter from Sir A. Conan Doyle asking for information concerning them; some report, I understood, having reached him from a mutual friend. A meeting with Sir Arthur followed, and the outcome was that I agreed to hasten my proposed personal investigation into the origin of the photographs, and carry this through at once instead of waiting till September, when I should be in the North on other matters.

In consequence, to-day, July 29th, I am just back in London from one of the most interesting and surprising excursions that it has ever been my fortune to make!

We had time, before I went, to obtain opinions on the original negatives from other expert photographers, and one or two of these were adverse rather than favourable. Not that any would say positively that the photographs were faked, but two did claim that they *could* produce the same class of negative by studio work involving painted

Fig. 31
"Alice and the Fairies," *Strand Magazine* 60 (July–December 1920). Image from Hathi Trust.

deduction may creep in, but must take a broader view of which will embrace an account of a long series of cases, vouched for by men and women of the highest character and incompatible with any form of fraud." In chapter 4, "Evidential Tests and Their Results," he further explains, "Each of these cases which I have given is impressive, I hope in itself, but the cumulative effect should be overpowering. . . . One or two might conceivably be the result of imperfect observation or incorrect statement, but it is an insult to common sense to say that so long an array of honorable witnesses, with their precise detail, with their actual photographic results, and with the complete exclusion of any possible trickery, should all be explained in any normal fashion."[49]

Similarly he begins *The Coming of the Fairies* with the claim that "this narrative is not a special plea for that authenticity, but is simply a collection of facts the inference from which may be accepted or rejected as the reader may think fit."[50] However, he later acknowledges that "the series of incidents set forth in this little volume represent either the most elaborate and ingenious hoax ever played upon the public, or else they constitute an event in human history which may in the future appear to have been epoch-making in its character."[51] Because he believes in the direct correlation between the photographs and their objects of vision, *The Coming of the Fairies* is a memorandum on the indexical properties of photography. Doyle repeatedly stressed the relationship between the images of the fairies and their existence in the material world. He explains "that all that *can* be photographed must of necessity be physical" but that "just as there are many starts in the heavens recorded by the camera that no human eye has ever seen directly, so there is a vast array of living creatures whose bodies are of that rare tenuity and subtlety that they lie beyond the range of our normal senses."[52]

The book contains painstakingly detailed accounts of the various attempts by Doyle and his collaborator in the endeavor, the theosophist Edward Gardner, to substantiate the images' authenticity. Doyle was about to leave on an extended trip to Australia and New Zealand when he first encountered the images of the Cottingley girls and their fairies. Rather than cancel his trip, he instead dispatched Gardner as his real-life John Watson to investigate the validity of the images. He includes his entire correspondence with Gardner on the matter in his manuscript. Gardner is meticulous in his reporting. In a letter dated July 12, 1920, for example, Gardner explains that he brought the original negatives of the images to a Mr. Snelling, an expert in the manufacturing of photographic devices. Two things stood out to Snelling: that the negatives of the fairy photographs were "one exposure only," and that "all the figures of the fairies moved during exposure, which was 'instantaneous.'"[53] Shortly after this meeting, Gardner brought the negatives to the Kodak Company's offices in Kingsway where he met Mr. West, another photography expert who conducted his own examination of the plates. Neither West nor Gardner "could find any evidence of superposition or other trick."[54]

Throughout the text Doyle uses scientific language to justify his claims, asserting that "fairies are on the same line of evolution as the *winged* insects" and explaining the lack of shadows on the images as "due to the presence of ectoplasm, as the etheric protoplasm has been named, [which] has a faint luminosity of its own, which would largely modify shadows."[55] Midway through the book he provides a detailed taxonomy of the spirits present in the Cottingley woods according to the famous clairvoyant Geoffrey Hodson, whom he and Gardner enlisted to help with their investigation. These include gnomes and fairies, water nymphs, wood elves, water fairies, brownies, golden fairies, and fairy bands.[56] Doyle then provides an encyclopedic description of each, using pseudoscientific categories and language. Gnomes, for example, have coloring of "the palest of green, pink and mauve. Much more in the wings than in the bodies, which are very pale to white. The gnome is described as seeming to be in black tights, reddish brown jersey, and red pointed cap."[57] The excitement Doyle feels upon seeing the images of the young girls with the fairies jumps off the page.

He sees himself as an explorer on the cusp of a new world, exclaiming at one point in the text:

> The recognition of their existence will jolt the material twentieth-century mind out of its heavy ruts in the mud, and will make it admit that there is a glamour and a mystery to life. Having discovered this, the world will not find it so difficult to accept that spiritual message supported by physical facts which has already been so convincingly put before it. All this I see, but there may be much more. When Columbus knelt in prayer upon the edge of America, what prophetic eye saw all that a new continent might do to affect the destinies of the world? We also seem to be on the edge of a new continent, separated not by oceans but by subtle and surmountable psychic conditions. I look at the prospect with awe. May those little creatures suffer from the contact and some Las Casas bewail their ruin! If so, it would be an evil day when the world defined their existence. But there is a guiding hand in the affairs of man, and we can but trust and follow.[58]

The girls took five photographs over four years. Doyle included their first two images, taken in the summer of 1917, in his *Strand* essay. He titled one image "Iris and the Dancing Gnome." The other he called "Alice and the Fairies" and captioned it with the following description: "Alice standing behind the banks of the Beck, with the Fairies dancing before her. She is looking across at her playmate Iris, to intimate that the time had come to take the photograph." A note accompanies the caption that this is "an untouched enlargement from the original negatives."[59] In "Alice and the Fairies," the young girl stares out at the viewer in a form of direct address. With her hand on her chin, flowers in her hair, and seemingly ensconced in nature, she resembles a character from a fairy tale or popular tableau. The images are playful and nostalgic, yet also derivative and knowing. The two photographs fit solidly within the tradition of Victorian portraiture; they evoke the romantic photographs taken by Julia Margaret Cameron and Charles Dodgson (also known as Lewis Carroll), as well as the idealized paintings of the Pre-Raphaelite artists William Holman Hunt, John Everett Millais, and Dante Gabriel Rossetti.

The Pre-Raphaelite Brotherhood, founded in 1848, was a secret society of young artists—painters, writers, and photographers—who were opposed to the British Royal Academy of Art's promotion of the Renaissance ideal as exemplified in the work of Raphael. Inspired by John Ruskin's call for artists to "go to Nature in all singleness of heart, and walk with her laboriously and trustingly," they believed that art should represent serious subjects with maximum realism but also depict symbolic and allegorical subjects.[60] Their principal themes came from the Bible, but they also drew inspiration from other literary texts, in particular from the works of Shakespeare, Spenser, and Tennyson. Doyle was not a member, although he was familiar with the Brotherhood and their philosophies. His Sherlock Holmes story "The Adventures of Charles Augustus Milverton" was inspired by the real-life tale of the art dealer and alleged blackmailer Charles Augustus Howell, who gained notoriety for persuading the Pre-Raphaelite painter Dante Gabriel Rossetti to dig up the poems he buried with his wife, Elizabeth Siddal. He also would have certainly been familiar with Lewis Carroll; thus his choice of pseudonyms for the girls in the images is telling, particularly his substitution of "Alice" for Frances, since Alice immediately connotes Carroll's photographs of Alice Liddle—in many ways the embodiment of Victorian girlhood, simultaneously innocent and knowing—and his whimsical stories of her in Wonderland.

The stylized fairies also seem straight out of the iconography of Victorian fairy lore. Dressed in fashionable attire, they seem to dance in the foreground of the images. As more than one contemporary viewer pointed out, they look like they came out of the pages of a beauty magazine, with one noting in particular "the elaborate Parisian coiffure of the little ladies."[61] Depictions of fairies were popular throughout the nineteenth and twentieth centuries across Europe, but particularly in Britain. *Grimm's Fairy Tales* were translated into English in 1824; Sir Walter Scott published his *Letters on Demonology and Witchcraft,* which contained detailed accounts of fairy evolution, in 1830; and Peter Pan first appeared as a character in J. M. Barrie's 1902 novel *The Little White Bird,* and again two years later in the eponymous play. Artists such as Richard Dadd, John Anster Fitzgerald, Daniel Maclise, and Sir Joseph Noël Paton regularly painted fairy scenes from Shakespeare's *A Midsummer Night's Dream* and *The Tempest,* as well as imagery taken from the poetry of Milton and Spenser. Edwin Landseer, John Everett Millais, and J. M. W. Turner included depictions of fairies in their works as well. Alex Owen, writing in 1994, argues compellingly that "Cottingley was undoubtedly one of the last manifestations of a glorious Victorian and Edwardian fairy tradition." Moreover, he contends that the incident "affords a fleeting glimpse of the interior world of two early-twentieth-century working-class girlhoods, and the way in which the fanciful realizations of childhood were appropriated and recast by a small group of middle-class men."[62] Indeed, much like the Fox sisters before them, who initially were playing an April Fool's Day trick on their mother, these two young girls were just having some fun. Once their cause was taken up by respected members of their communities—even after they confessed that they were fantastic deceptions—their fanciful play became the basis for new ways of seeing, in many ways beyond their control.

The Cottingley fairy photographs encapsulate the ways in which the idea of camera vision, as a marker of indexical truth, allowed true believers such as Doyle to insist that their visions were real and to ground them in a form of pseudoscience, much like Andrew Jackson Davis did with spiritual telegraphy. Doyle was not interested in what the fairies were wearing and doing. Rather, his mission was to verify the integrity of the negatives on which they appeared to substantiate the ecosystem in which they lived—alongside gnomes and brownies and elves and nymphs—as real. If the negatives were undoctored he believed he could conclusively prove the existence of fairies through photographic evidence. He held fast to the idea that photography was indexical and that what the camera saw was a form of truth. If the figures appeared on the negative, he reasoned, they must exist in real life. The idea that the fairies may have been part of the original image but still not real, however, seemed not to occur to him, despite the popularity of composite photographs at the time.

Composite photographs result from the process of combining several distinct negatives into one image. The French photographer Édouard Baldus, one of the founding members of the Société Héliographique—the first photographic organization in the world—regularly retouched his negatives to remove unwanted elements and often pieced together different negatives to create panoramic views of the architectural works he documented as part of his Missions Héliographiques, a project spearheaded by the Historic Monuments Commission of France to photograph historic buildings, bridges, and monuments—many of which were being razed under the direction of Baron Georges-Eugène Haussmann as part of Napoleon III's vast modernization project.[63] Similarly, Gustav Le Gray, whom many historians consider "the most important French photographer of the nineteenth century," often used different negatives in composing his works: one for the body of the image and the other for the sky, since clouds were notoriously hard to capture in early photographs.[64] Both of these photographers used montage and other manipulation techniques to make their images seem more realistic to contemporary viewers; in other words, their photographic works became more accurate through darkroom artifice.

The first to perfect the composite process as a creative form was the Swedish-born artist Oscar Gustave Rejlander, who began his career as a genre painter, specializing in cozy scenes of domestic life. Believing that photography would help make him a more skilled painter and draftsman, he taught himself the basics of photography in one afternoon. Rejlander was committed to the idea that photography required "the same operations of mind, the same artistic treatment and careful manipulation whether it be executed in crayon, grey-in-grey, paint of any description, or by photographic agency," and advocated for the recognition of photographers as legitimate artists.[65] Rejlander's most ambitious work, *Two Ways of Life* (1857), is an allegory depicting the choice between what he presented as a life of virtue and one of vice. Over a six-week period, Rejlander photographed each of his models and background sections separately. He then then combined the more than thirty negatives onto two pieces of paper, which he connected, rephotographed, and reproduced as a single large print.[66] Many contemporary viewers were critical of the blatantly anti-indexical character of

Rejlander's work, which they felt betrayed the true nature of photography as a document of life rather than a work of art.

Henry Peach Robinson perfected his friend and teacher's composite technique in his own work. Like Rejlander, Robinson felt that photography should be respected as an art form in its own right. In his 1869 book *Pictorial Effect in Photography: Being Hints on Composition and Chiaroscuro for Photographers,* Robinson outlined his methods and encouraged aspiring art photographers to consider issues of composition, contrast, and color in creating their images in much the same way that a painter might in producing a work on canvas.[67] To achieve what he called the "pictorial effect," Robinson felt that it was sometimes necessary to stage photographic images. He often shot his work in his studio and used controlled lighting, a variety of props, and costumed models to achieve the mood he wanted. Yet while he embraced artifice, he shied away from outright deception, distinguishing between what he considered artistic truth and actual fact. He explained to his readers:

> It would be possible, by double printing, to make a very passable photograph of a centaur or a mermaid, but the photographer would discredit his art; he would not be believed, and would deserve to be set down amongst charlatans and Barnums. He would be worse than the great showman, who, to his credit, confessed himself a humbug, while the photographer would expect the world to believe his work to be a truth.

A photograph, Robinson asserted, "must represent truth." But Robinson put forward the notion that fact and truth accounted for two separate things. A fact is "a reality" while truth is the "absence of falsehood." Truth, therefore, could exist in photographic art, without an absolute adherence to the reality.[68]

Robinson's concept of truth as "the absence of falsehood" ran counter to notions of indexicality and instead was rooted in more Victorian poetic concepts of the real, or what Tennyson referred to as the "lucid veil."[69] Robinson's most famous work, *Fading Away* (1858), straddles the line between reality and illusion. Using five different negatives to achieve the emotional effect he wanted, Robinson composed the work, which depicts a young girl on her deathbed—either in the late stages of consumption or suffering from a broken heart—surrounded by her mourning family. As with *Two Ways of Life,* many viewers found the work troubling for both its artifice and for its intimate subject matter. In his subsequent works, Robinson often turned directly to literature. In *The Lady of Shalott* (1861), for example, he used two negatives to depict the death scene from Alfred, Lord Tennyson's 1842 poem of the same name. Tennyson's four-part ballad recounts the Arthurian legend of the death of a mysterious and tragic heroine who breaks free from her imprisonment in a tower upstream from Camelot, where she had been cursed to weave scenes she sees only through a mirror that reflected the

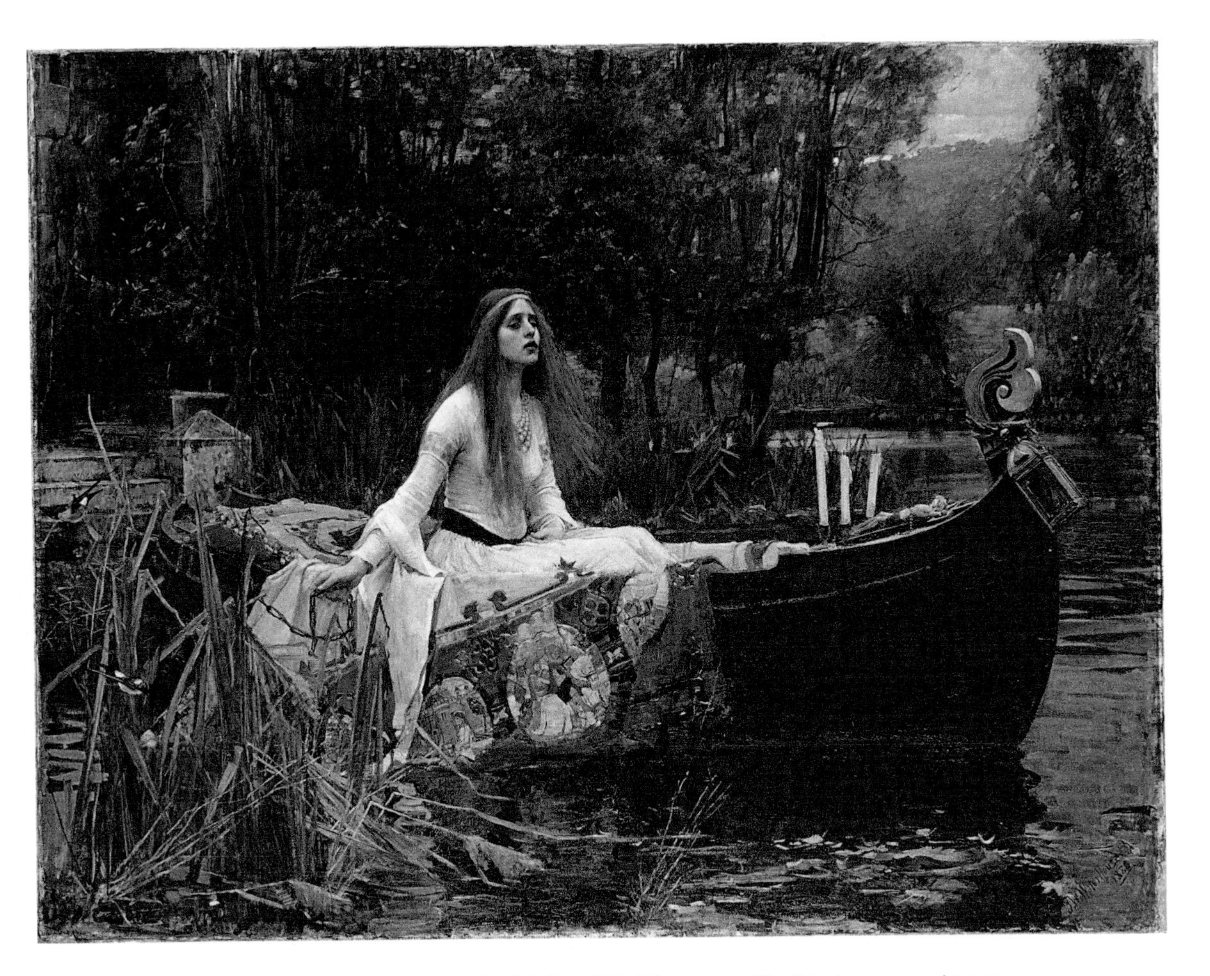

Fig. 32 John William Waterhouse, *The Lady of Shalott*, 1888. Oil on canvas. The Tate Museum, archive no. N01543. Photo © Tate.

world around her. Upon glancing the heroic Lancelot in her mirror, she looks up from her tapestry and, Tennyson writes, "The mirror crack'd from side to side / 'The curse is come upon me,' cried The Lady of Shalott."[70] The lady flees the island in a boat inscribed with her name, only to freeze to death in search of her perceived love. The poem, which many contemporary readers interpreted as an allegory for the tragic artist cursed to observe the world from a distance, was popular among Pre-Raphaelite painters who turned to medieval themes, particularly those that illustrated the tensions between female sexuality and death in Victorian England (see fig. 32).

Robinson's fidelity in this image was to the verse in Tennyson's poem, not to what things looked like in real life (see fig. 33). To create the photograph, he explained, "I made a barge, crimped the model's hair . . . laid her on the boat in the river among the water lilies, and gave her a background of weeping willows, taken in the rain so that they might look dreary."[71] As with *Fading Away*, many

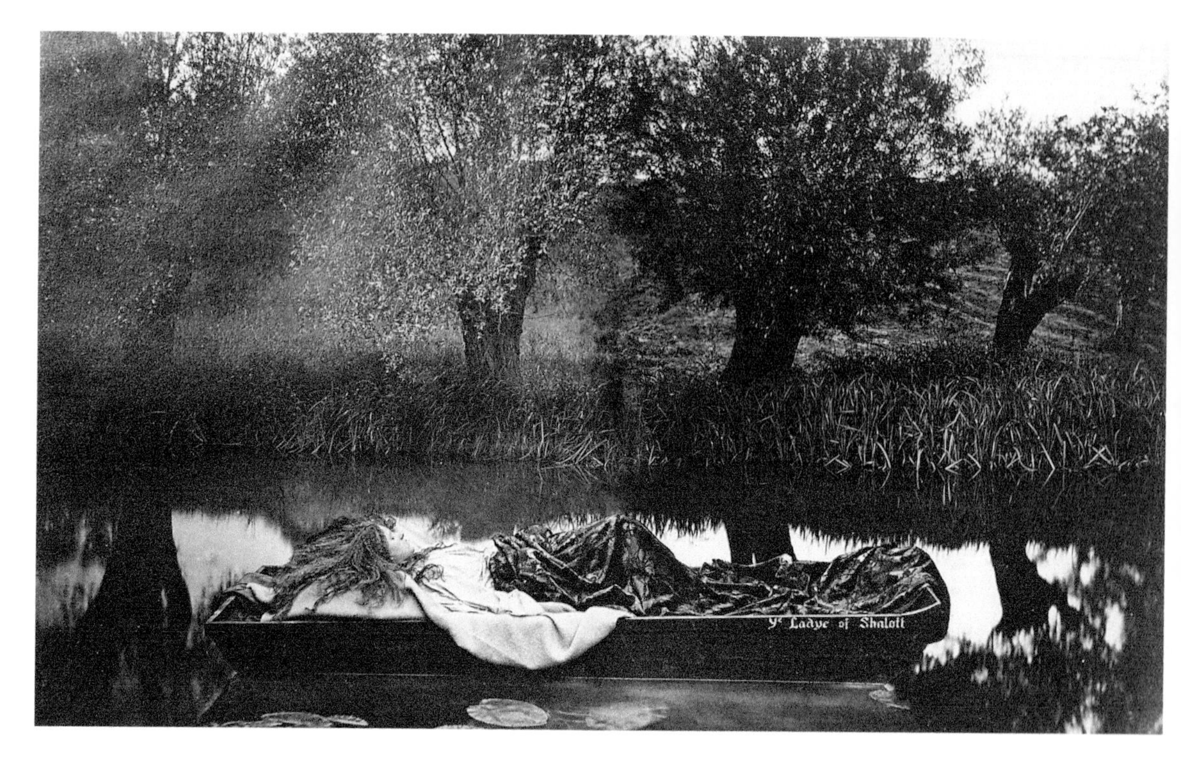

Fig. 33 Henry Peach Robinson, *The Lady of Shalott*, 1860. Albumen print. Image courtesy of The Amelia at the Amelia Scott.

objected to the work for not adhering to reality. One critic complained that he did "not like the boat, which is not a boat but a punt," and could not understand why the "lady lay at the stern of the boat. How could she turn around in it after casting off?"[72] Another was bothered by the lack of movement in the water. Rather than treat the work as an illustration of the poem, they held it to documentary standards and to the idea that the camera should reproduce a version of reality with little to no room for poetic license.

All these debates over the vexed relationships between photographic artifice and notions of reality were covered in the popular press, and Doyle—as well as his Spiritualist contemporaries—certainly would have been familiar with them. Doyle was an avid amateur photographer. He also was a regular contributor to the *British Journal of Photography*. Thus his refusal to consider that the two young girls may have used a form of composite photography or manipulated their scenes to secure their images of the Cottingley fairies suggests that, in this instance, he was willing to suspend what he might have known as rational possibility in order to more readily see what he wanted to believe. His conviction that spirits and fairies existed allowed him to see the visions on the negatives as authentic. He repeatedly deployed the logic of camera vision and the certainty of photographic indexicality and taxonomic reasoning to substantiate his defense of the photographs, and hence the fairies, as real.

For many years after the publication of their images in *Strand Magazine*, Elise and Frances stayed quiet about their source material. Finally, in a 1982 interview with reporter Joe Cooper, Frances acknowledged that the two young girls had constructed the fairy figures themselves and then photographed them as part of a hoax. Using pictures from *Princess Mary's Gift Book* as their source material, they drew their own images on cardboard paper, cut them out using Frances's mother's tailoring shears, and secured them to the landscape using hatpins. Regarding the 1917 photograph of her, Frances lamented to Cooper, "My heart always sinks when I look at it. When I think about how it has gone all around the world—I don't see how people could believe they're real fairies. I could see the backs of them and the hatpins when the photo was being taken."[73] When she was asked in a 1985 interview on British television series *Arthur C. Clarke's World of Strange Powers* why they kept quiet for so long, Elsie answered that she and Frances were too embarrassed to admit the truth after fooling Doyle: "Two village kids and a brilliant man like Conan Doyle—well, we could only keep quiet." In the same interview Frances said, "I never even thought of it as being a fraud—it was just Elsie and I having a bit of fun and I can't understand to this day why they were taken in—they wanted to be taken in."[74]

Like Barnum and the Fox sisters before them, in many ways the young girls were merely playing with their audiences. Yet their photos of the fairies, like celestial telegraphy, theories of precipitation, and new photographic imaging tools and processes, seemed to provide an indexical form of evidence for those who wanted to use new technologies of seeing to produce material objects as the proof that would substantiate the presence of spirits here on earth. What differentiates camera vision from miraculous vision—which relies on similar forms of deep belief—and technological vision—which also depends on a form of discursive-scientific justification—is that the power of camera vision comes from the conviction that there is an intrinsic relationship between the object of vision and its material representation. Popular belief in the veracity of a photographic image as opposed to something "created" enabled viewers to see in the manipulated images of ghosts and fairies evidence of the fantastic and wonderous. It gave them proof of what they were looking for in this world as well as in the next. The following chapter explores what happens when the truth claims of photography are called into question through more postmodern forms of vision.

CHAPTER 4

Untitled

Postmodern Vision and the Triumph of the Pseudo-Event

In December 1896 William Randolph Hearst, in search of stories that would help boost sales for his newly purchased daily paper, the *New York Journal*, offered the well-known reporter Richard Harding Davis $3,000 a month to travel to Havana, Cuba, to cover tensions that had arisen on the island between Spanish authorities and Cuban insurgents.[1] Davis, who had made his name as a heroic, adventure-seeking journalist for *Harper's Weekly*, soon set off for the island along with the popular artist Frederic Remington, who was there to provide the drawings to illustrate Harding's stories. The trip did not get off to an auspicious start. For the voyage Hearst had lent the men his new, steam-driven, 112-foot yacht, the *Vamoose*, but the luxury boat was totally unfit for the trip and after three failed attempts the captain had to turn back and return to Key West. Upon reaching Cuba (via a regularly scheduled passenger steamer), they were then barred from the war zone. According to a now apocryphal story recounted by regular Hearst journalist James Creelman, the bored and discouraged Remington sent Hearst a telegram stating "Everything is quiet. There is no trouble here. There will be no war. Wish to return," to which Hearst supposedly replied, "Please remain. You furnish the pictures and I'll furnish the war."[2]

While many since have disputed the accuracy of this story, the idea that Hearst supplied the war to boost newspaper sales fits well with accounts of both Hearst's temperament and the antics of the nineteenth-century penny press to gain readers. According to Arthur MacEwen, the editor of his first journalistic endeavor, the *San Francisco Examiner*, Hearst subscribed to the idea that

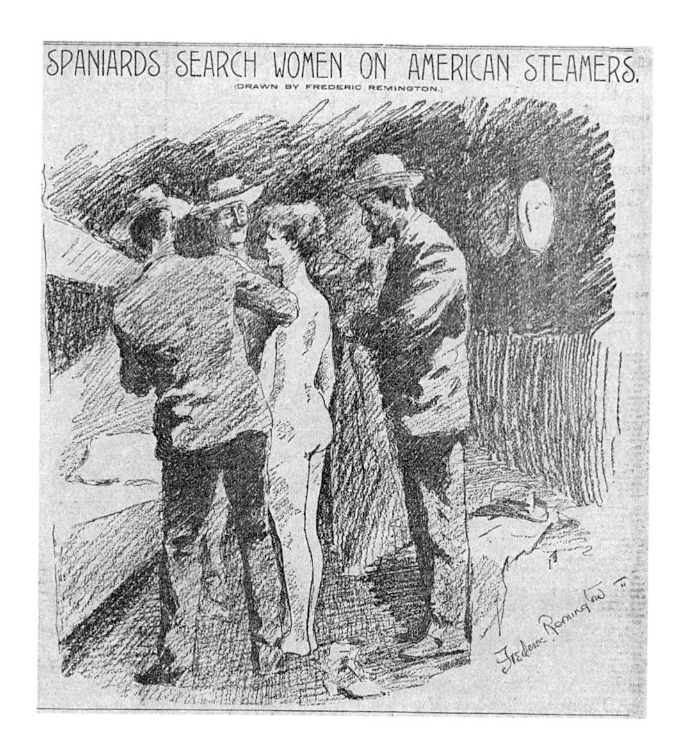

Fig. 34
Frederic Remington, "Spaniards Search Women on American Steamers," 1898. Ink on paper. *New York Journal*, February 12, 1897. Courtesy of the Library of Congress.

"news is anything that makes a reader say, 'Gee Whiz!' Or, put more soberly, 'News is whatever a good editor chooses to print.'"[3] Similarly, David Nassaw in his Hearst biography *The Chief*, writes that the fact that "there are no accounts of Hearst's life nor are there histories of the Spanish American War that do not include some sort of discussion of the role of the Yellow Press in general and Hearst in particular in fomenting war in Cuba . . . is a tribute to his genius as a self-promoter."[4] Nevertheless, after a week of waiting for something worth reporting to actually happen, Remington left Cuba and returned to the United States. Davis, however, stayed and on February 10, 1897, wired the *Journal* a story that recounted how Spanish police had boarded an American ship bound for Key West to strip-search three Cuban women whom they suspected were carrying messages to rebel leaders back in Florida. Focusing on the gendered trespass of the officers, Hearst made the story front-page news on February 12, under an oversized headline that asked, "Does Our Flag Protect Women? Indignities Practiced by Spanish Officials on Board American Vessels."[5]

Remington, who was back in New York City, provided a half-page drawing of one of the women surrounded by Spanish officers going through her things (see fig. 34). The sketch depicts the naked profile of a young woman surrounded by three men who tower over her in an enclosed space. All three men wear suits as well as panama-style hats, and two have visible facial hair (the other we can only see from the back). One man has his arm on her naked shoulder while another leers at her backside. The woman's bare bottom is fully exposed to the reading audience, and her white skin seems to glow on the yellow newsprint. While not exactly tawdry, Remington pushes the boundaries of propriety by displaying the woman's naked body and visible buttocks. He also plays on a number of easily recognized visual stereotypes to signal the various ethnic and gendered missteps at play in his vision of the story: his swarthy Spaniards have beards and mustaches and wear straw hats associated with Latin America as they paw at the seemingly defenseless naked woman. A handwritten headline at the top of the image announces that "Spaniards Search Women on American Steamers." The plural women implies that this is but one in a series of offenses involving lascivious Spanish men and innocent white women. Although a smaller note at the bottom of the page acknowledges that this is "an imaginary incident pictured by Frederic Remington for the *New York Journal*," the image—realistic or not—works to extend perceived social and cultural transgressions by the Spanish in Cuba into the broader imagination of the American public.

The issue sold nearly a million copies. Soon after, however, Joseph Pulitzer's *New York World*, the *Journal*'s main competitor, contested the veracity of Davis's story, citing an interview with Celmencia Arango, one of the women in the encounter, who claimed that she was not actually strip-searched by male officers. Davis, who took the *World*'s challenge as a "reflection of his integrity," responded in a two-page story in the *World*. Under the headline "Mr. Davis Explains," he blamed the absent Remington: "I never said that she was searched by men. . . . Mr. Frederick Remington, who was not present, and who drew an imaginary picture of the scene, is responsible for the idea that the search was conducted by men. Had I seen the picture before it appeared, I should never have allowed it to accompany my article."[6] Davis, who understood that the visual narrative of Remington's image superseded the details of his written report, resigned from the *Journal* as a result and never worked for the Hearst press again. Despite the loss of his star reporter, Hearst did not give up on the Cuba story. While his papers regularly ran explosive and sensational stories such as the one about a child who bit into a stick of dynamite thinking it was a piece of candy, or risqué dispatches by Stephen Crane from the Tenderloin district full of sex and violence, the *Journal* lacked a dedicated daily audience. War in Cuba, Hearst hoped, would provide serial fodder for his readership, thus binding them to his publication on a daily basis.

Hearst's directive to Remington to "furnish the pictures" underscores the importance of images in influencing public opinion, regardless of their veracity. Remington was in New York when the incident he illustrated transpired in Cuba. He made no claims to truth in his visual interpretation (he even included a disclaimer). Nevertheless, although Davis was there to validate the story, Remington's scandalous illustration in effect trumped the actual events as described in Davis's text because of the outrage it inspired. Like the *New York Sun*'s account of life on the moon that I discussed in the second chapter of this book, the underlying goal of Hearst's Cuba stories was to attract readers and sell newspapers. In both situations, readership increased. Unlike the moon hoax, however, which the readers ultimately knew was fabricated, a version of the events in Cuba actually transpired. Readers did not need to suspend their belief systems or question the larger account being reported. There was indeed trouble brewing in Cuba. Many equated the sketch depicting a naked woman surrounded by lecherous men as the truth of the story, even though it was concocted in Remington's studio 1,300 miles from the source. Remington's illustration cemented the belief that things had gone awry in Cuba and that the United States needed to respond on some level. The images worked to frame, and in some cases to create, the news being reported. As I will discuss below, episodes such as this one mark the emergence of what Daniel Boorstin would call the pseudo-event, or highly choreographed media events organized merely for the publicity they generate. They also, I argue, lay the foundation for a form of what I am calling postmodern vision, where images are divorced from—and in some cases lack—historical referents, yet nevertheless make claims to larger truths.

Although Davis resigned from the *New York Journal* in protest to protect his journalistic integrity, Hearst did not stop looking for a narrative hook to help foment upheaval in Cuba and sell more papers. He found his prize narrative in the story of Evangelina Cosio y Cisneros. The fiery daughter of a jailed Cuban insurgent, Cisneros had been arrested for attempted murder and was awaiting trial in a Havana jail when a *Journal* reporter, who was touring the prison in search of stories for the press, first encountered her. The paper published several versions of the reasons for Cisneros's imprisonment before settling on the melodramatic tone that would come to frame the case. In the first version, Cisneros was accidentally arrested in a mass sweep of the area in which she lived; in the next, the paper claimed that she was jailed on account of her "aristocratic blood"; finally, according to the *Journal*, she had been unjustly incarcerated after attempting to defend her chastity against the advances of an unscrupulous Spanish officer who demanded sexual favors in exchange for her father's release. Again, Hearst played on the gendered transgressions of mendacious Spanish men and innocent light-skinned women. According to Creelman, upon hearing of her arrest, Hearst told the newsroom that this story would "do more to open the eyes of the country than a thousand editorials or political speeches" and that they should "telegraph to our correspondent in Havana to wire every detail of this case. Get up a petition to the Queen Regent of Spain for this girl's pardon. Enlist the women of America. Have them sign the petition. . . . Have distinguished women sign first. Cable the petitions and the names to the Queen Regent. Notify our minister in Madrid." Hoping to make a national issue of the case, Creelman asserts that Hearst avowed "that girl must be saved if we have to take her out of prison by force or send a steamer to meet the vessel that carries her away—but that would be piracy, wouldn't it?"[7]

Hearst did not resort to piracy to save his "Cuban Joan of Arc," but, in addition to spearheading a petition—which received hundreds of signatures from prominent American women such as Julia Ward Howe, Clara Barton, Julia Grant, and Varina Davis—and sending it to the Queen Regent of Spain, as well as to the Pope, he dispatched a "brash and fearless young reporter," twenty-nine-year-old Karl Decker, to rescue Evangelina—and wrote about his heroic exploits for the *Journal*. According to Cisneros's autobiography—written later that year in collaboration with Decker, illustrated by Remington, and published by Hearst—Decker enlisted two colleagues to rent a vacant house next to the prison. On October 5, Evangelina received a visit from one of Decker's colleagues who alerted her to their escape plans and gave her a package of candy laced with a strong narcotic. That evening, Evangelina shared the candy with her cell mates, knocking them out. Shortly after midnight, Decker and his partners attempted to break into the prison, but they could not get through the steel bars. The following night they succeeded in breaking through. Once again, Evangelina drugged her cell mates—this time by spiking their coffee with laudanum she had received for a toothache. Decker and his two accomplices then smuggled the young girl out of a window and across the roof boards to their rented house next door. Next, they transferred the young girl to a house on the outskirts of Havana, where, despite regular searches across the city, she remained for two and a half days. On the afternoon of October 9, Evangelina—outfitted as a man wearing trousers, a blue shirt with a butterfly tie, and a large slouch hat; puffing on a cigar; and carrying forged papers identifying her as Juan Sola—boarded a ship bound for Florida.

While later accounts contradicted this narrative—and instead revealed that Decker had merely bribed the guards to let her out—serial accounts of the melodramatic and protracted rescue filled the pages of *the Journal* for days. The paper continued to cover Evangelina's story upon her arrival in New York City, where Hearst installed her in a large suite in the Waldorf Astoria and kept her in virtual seclusion to build up suspense and prepare for her public debut in a parade to Madison Square. The *New York Times* estimated that over seventy-five thousand attended the event to catch a glimpse "of the flower of Cuba." Following a dinner at the glamorous Delmonico's, the *Journal* held a ball in the Waldorf's Red Room. A few days later, Decker accompanied her to Washington, DC, to meet President William McKinley. All of this was, of course, covered—in text and image—on the front pages of the *Journal*.

News outlets have deployed images to influence public opinion since the earliest days of their circulation. Before the advent of photography, papers and magazines employed artists to illustrate articles or depict scenes from current events. With their biting caricatures and satirical sketches, Honoré Daumier and Constantin Guys in France, William Hogarth in England, and Francisco Goya in Spain moved the role of the illustrator from mere description to one of political commentary. In the United States, many large urban papers had artists on their payrolls. Remington joined the ranks of the Ashcan School artists Robert Henri, George Luks, William Glackens, John Sloan, and Everett Shinn, all of whom got their start working as sketch artists for daily newspapers. With advances in photographic technologies and lithographic reproduction, papers began to print photographs—or lithographic reproductions of photographs—to illustrate their text. The explosive market growth of print media in the nineteenth century, as I described in the first chapter, combined with the popular faith in the veracity of photography, which I outlined in the previous chapter, enabled the manufacturing of images to augment—or in the case of the Cuba examples that I just recounted, create—stories that were newsworthy.

Photographic journalists often used their images to sway public opinion. The British photographer Roger Fenton, for example, was hired specifically to document the Crimean War for the British press. The war, which was fought primarily on the coast of the Black Sea, pitted an alliance of British, French, Turkish, and Sardinian armies against Russian forces over territorial disputes in the Holy Land following the decline of the Ottoman Empire. The war was deeply unpopular in much of Europe due to the large number of casualties and the seeming mismanagement of resources. In the winter of 1854–55, a reporter for the *London Times* sent back a series of devastating reports describing the conditions under which British soldiers were living and fighting. Alfred, Lord Tennyson further influenced public opinion with the publication of his poem "The Charge of the Light Brigade," which was written and widely circulated in October 1854 after a particularly brutal battle in which over six hundred soldiers died. Exacerbating public sentiment that the war in the Crimea was a futile endeavor, Tennyson asserted that "Someone had blunder'd: / Their's not to make reply, / Their's not to reason why, / Their's but to do and die: / Into the valley of Death / Rode the six hundred. / Cannon to right of them / , Cannon to left of them / Cannon in front of them / Volley'd and thunder'd; / Storm'd at with shot and shell, / Boldly they rode and well, / Into the jaws of Death, / Into the mouth of Hell."[8]

In May 1855, in an attempt to shore up support in England, the Manchester publisher Thomas Agnew, with backing from the British secretary of state for war, sent Fenton to the Crimea. Fenton arrived in Balaclava with five cameras, all of his darkroom chemicals, seven hundred glass plates, and a photographic van outfitted for sleeping, cooking, and developing his work. He spent nearly four months there in often grueling conditions—at one point he was developing his plates at four in the morning to avoid the high heat of the day. His sponsors back in Britain wanted morally uplifting photos, thus his images included staged portraits of generals in their full military regalia on horseback, nurses attending to soldiers in pristine conditions, and scenes of the harbor at Balaclava filled with ships fully outfitted to do battle. Fenton shot no scenes of dead bodies, maimed soldiers, or unsanitary first aid stations. While not manipulating the images, per se, his sanitized account provided a visual counternarrative to widespread negative reporting. Like Henry Peach Robinson before him, who also evoked Tennyson's verse in his composite photographs, Fenton deployed a type of poetic license to make his work more powerful, though in the name of reportage rather than art. Moreover, as Susan Sontag and Errol Morris have pointed out more recently, Fenton actually did, on occasion, manipulate his scenes (see figs. 35a–b). In her discussion of the role of staging and manipulation in many iconic early war photographs, *Regarding the Pain of Others*, Sontag notes:

> After reaching the much shelled valley approaching Sebastopol in his horse-drawn darkroom, Fenton made two exposures from the same tripod position: in the first version of the celebrated photo he was to call "The Valley of the Shadow of Death" (despite the title, it was not across this landscape that the Light Brigade made its doomed charge), the cannonballs are thick on the ground to the left of the road, but before taking the second picture—the one that is always reproduced—he oversaw the scattering of the cannonballs on the road itself.[9]

Fenton's images, as we now know, were as subjective as Tennyson's verse from which it takes its title. So, it seems, was Sontag's timeline.

The filmmaker Errol Morris, who is also interested in the constructed nature of the two images of the "Shadow of the Valley of Death," challenges the authority with which Sontag constructs a timeline of Fenton's photographic practice. In the introduction to his book *Believing Is Seeing*, Morris asks how Sontag could claim such knowledge without having seen the landscape in which Fenton took his photographs, let alone suggest that Fenton "oversaw the scattering of the cannonballs on the road itself"?

Morris went so far as to travel to the Crimea to chart the trajectory of the sun in Sebastopol to gauge the presence of shadows in the very spot in which Fenton took his photographs in an attempt to conclusively figure out which image came first in the sequence. Yet despite the pseudoscientific veneer to his process, he ultimately concludes, "What we see is not independent of our beliefs. Photos provide evidence, but no shortcut to reality. It is often said that seeing is believing. But we do not form our beliefs on the basis of what we see; rather, what we see is often determined by our beliefs. Believing is seeing, not the other way around."[10] Unlike Doyle and Moctezuma, both of whom I discussed earlier in this project and who I also argue saw what they wanted to believe, Morris's conclusions regarding the links between seeing and believing (and believing and seeing) are more self-reflexive and playful and align with more postmodern notions of fidelity in representation. While still attempting to "prove" a point, he never loses sight of the constructed nature of not just images but also their truths.

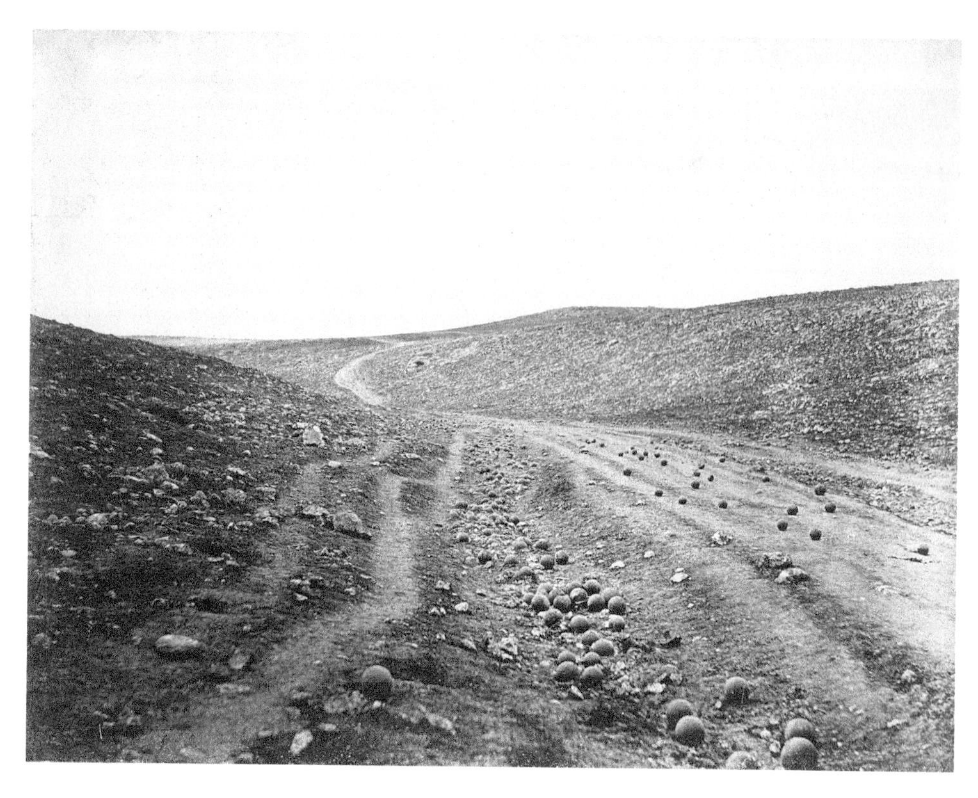

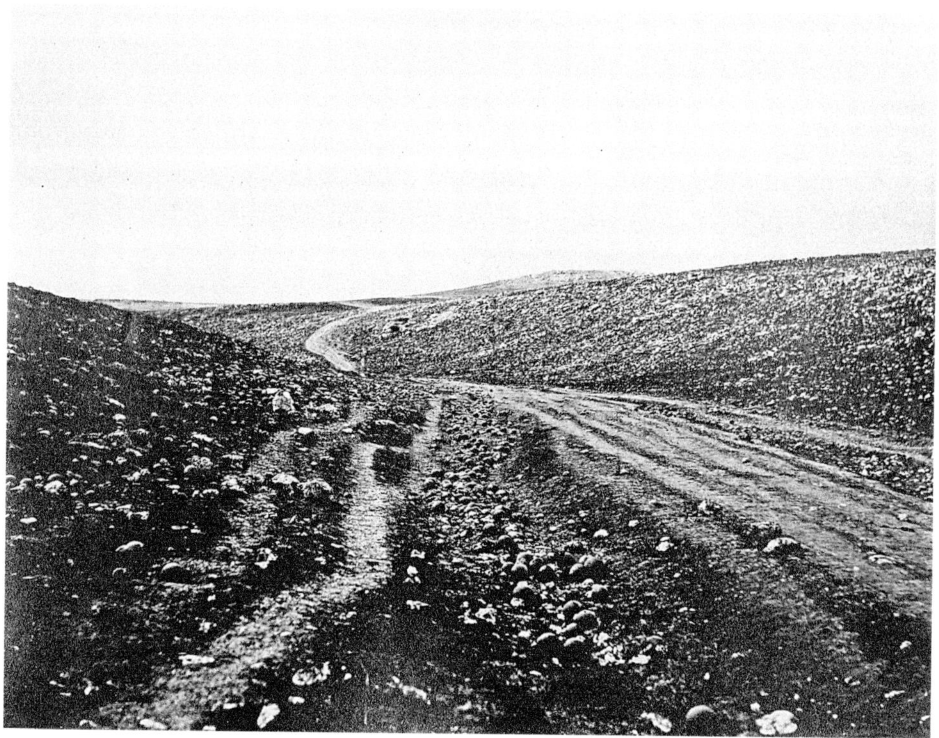

Fig. 35 Roger Fenton, two images for the "Valley of the Shadow of Death," 1855. Courtesy of (a) the Library of Congress and (b) the Mary Evans Picture Library, London.

Photography also played a major role in influencing public opinion in the American Civil War. Initially anticipating that the conflict would be short, many Northern photographers marketed their skills as portraitists to make inexpensive images of soldiers in their uniform on tin (known commonly as tintypes) as keepsakes for their loved ones while they were away. The war, however, lasted much longer than originally anticipated and was much bloodier than anyone could have imagined. Over four years, 2.9 million men served and over a million suffered casualties, including 623,000 deaths. As a result, the role of photography in the conflict changed from providing keepsakes to one of reportage and propaganda.

In July 1861 the well-known photographer Mathew Brady, along with his cameraman Timothy O'Sullivan, journeyed south from his studios in New York City to shoot images of the First Battle of Bull Run in Manassas, Virginia. Less than a month later, on August 17, 1861, the *New York Times* reported, "Mr. Brady, the Photographer, has just returned from Washington with the magnificent series of views of scenes, groups, and incidents of the war which he has been making for the last two months." His photographs, the article continued, "will do more than the most elaborate descriptions to perpetuate the scenes of that brief campaign." Brady and O'Sullivan, along with a group of more than two dozen newspaper correspondents, served at the request of the Union Army Major General Irvin McDowell, who wanted a team of reporters to travel together and "wear a white uniform to indicate the purity of their character."[11] Aside from the battle at Bull Run, which he witnessed from afar, Brady did not spend much time at the front. Instead he oversaw a stable of field photographers from his offices in New York City. Brady regularly showed their work in his New York and Washington, DC, galleries with his own attribution; indeed, most of their images bore the imprint "Photography by Brady." Regarding a show of images from the Battle of Antietam in his New York gallery in 1862, for example, the *New York Times* wrote, "Mr. Brady has done something to bring home to us the terrible reality and earnestness of war. If he has not brought bodies and laid them in our dooryards . . . he has done something very like it."[12]

Much of the Civil War work attributed to Brady was taken either by Alexander Gardner, who ran Brady's studio in Washington, DC, or by Timothy O'Sullivan, who worked first with Brady and then for Gardner when Gardner split from Brady and opened his own studio in Washington, DC. Gardner worked as a civilian member of Union General George McClellan's staff. His images of bloated and ravaged dead and injured bodies from the bloody Battle of Antietam in September 1862 changed the nature of war imagery, which until this point tended to valorize battle. Writing in the *Atlantic Monthly* of these images, Oliver Wendell Holmes proclaimed that, through witnessing the photographs,

> we ourselves were on the field upon the Sunday following the Wednesday when the battle took place. It is not, however, for us to bear witness

> to the fidelity of views which the truthful sunbeam has delineated in all their dread reality. The photographs bear witness to the accuracy of some of our own sketches in a paper published in the December number of this magazine. The "ditch" is figured, still encumbered with the dead, and strewed, as we saw it and the neighboring fields, with fragments and tatters. The "colonel's gray horse" is given in another picture just as we saw him lying.[13]

Holmes indicated that anyone wishing to know war should take in these images: "These wrecks of manhood thrown together in careless heaps or ranged in ghastly rows for burial were alive but yesterday. . . . The end to be attained justifies the means, we are willing to believe; but the sight of these pictures is a commentary on civilization such as a savage might well triumph to show its missionaries."

For Holmes, the "wrecks of manhood" in these troubling images captured the essence of the war through the "fidelity of views" of the "dread reality." Yet according to historian William Frassanito, this "fidelity of views" was often manipulated. On occasion, both Gardner and O'Sullivan staged their images to make them more affecting. For example, in the now canonical image of a young Confederate soldier killed in an area known as "the Devil's Den" on the fields of Gettysburg, Gardner and his assistants O'Sullivan and James Gibson dragged the soldier's dead body on a blanket from where he originally lay to a more dramatic spot against a stone fortification. They also tilted his head toward the camera and leaned a musket (as opposed to the sharpshooter's rifle he would have used) against his body (see fig. 36). Photo historian Robert Hirsch contends, "No one questioned Gardner's right to 'set the scene' for the camera since it was accepted as an accurate overall representation of the situation at hand." Rather, he argues, Civil War photographers "expanded the definition of photographic documentation. . . . Photographic truthfulness was not only a question of picturing what chance placed before the camera, but depicting the experience of war." This, he concludes, "established a silent compact between the viewer and the photographer, giving the photographer license to adjust a situation to deliver a truer, more complete sense of a subject."[14]

While today we might see this manipulation of the scene as undermining the authenticity of the shot, for Civil War–era viewers, particularly in the North, notions of photographic truth was in part indexical, in that the images testified to the horror that took place in real time and in actual places, but also, and perhaps more important, it was bound up with the tone and tenor of the composition itself. For critics such as Oliver Wendell Holmes, as well as for many of the photographers themselves, the photographs performed important moral and ethical work. Their ideas of verisimilitude allowed for the rearrangement of bodies and weapons for broader dramatic, and even honorable, effect. Their creations were intended to capture a greater truth about an event that

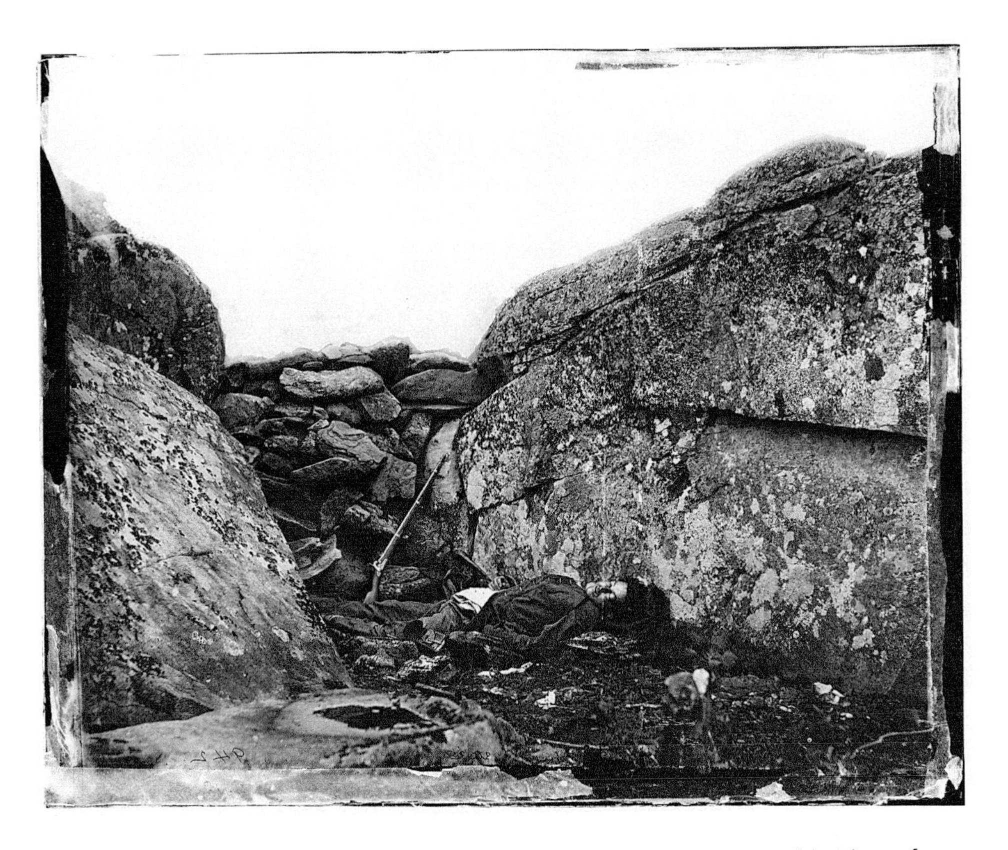

Fig. 36 Timothy O'Sullivan, "Dead Confederate Soldier in Devil's Den," 1863. Courtesy of the Library of Congress.

might not have otherwise lent itself to dramatic imagery. This was not, however, the case for Hearst in his strategic deployment of images later in the century. Hearst's directive to Remington to "furnish the pictures" instead bespeaks a different type of priority, one divorced from an indexical source and focused instead on generating sales and creating what Daniel Boorstin has called the pseudo-event.

Writing in his 1962 polemic *The Image: A Guide to Pseudo-Events in America,* Boorstin tied changing expectations around news and information to the rise of the penny press and what he termed the "Graphic Revolution" that took place during the nineteenth century. He explains, "Man's ability to make, preserve, transmit, and disseminate precise images—images of print, of men and landscapes and events, of the voices of men and mobs—now grew at a fantastic pace [as] . . . by a giant leap Americans crossed the gulf from the daguerreotype to color television in less than a century." He continues, "The competitive daring of giants like James Gordon Bennett, Joseph Pulitzer, and William Randolph Hearst intensified the race for news and widened newspaper circulation" in their competition for readers, and then advertisers, for their daily newspapers. As a result,

Boorstin argues, "verisimilitude took on a new meaning [and] vivid image came to overshadow pale reality."[15]

For Boorstin the pseudo-event is marked by four main criteria. First, planning and staging displaced spontaneity. Second, this planning occurred primarily to be reported and reproduced in media. Questions of veracity are, therefore, replaced by questions of whether the event is newsworthy. Third, its relationship to reality is ambiguous since, he argues, without "ambiguity a pseudo-event cannot be very interesting." And, finally, the pseudo-event usually "is intended to be a self-fulfilling prophecy." The cycle is continuous and produces a seemingly "vicious circle of experience and expectation since 'pseudo-events produce more pseudo-events.'"[16]

In many ways, Boorstin's identification of the pseudo-event and his critique of the rise of the celebrity in postwar American culture is a prescient indicator of what Jean-François Lyotard would identify as "the postmodern condition" seventeen years later. For Lyotard, and many who followed him in theorizing the postmodern, the equation of knowledge with information destabilizes the very possibility of Enlightenment-era grand narratives and comprehensive accounts of historical experience. But rather than decry the loss of totalizing metanarratives, postmodern critics such as Lyotard highlight the possibilities inherent in the performativity of knowledge-producing *petits récits*, or the little narratives that constitute the histories of everyday life. Boorstin's critique of a world "where fantasy is more real than reality" echoes one of the dominant characteristics of postmodern critique—in this case, what French postmodern philosopher Jean Baudrillard termed hyperreality. Like Lyotard, his contemporary, Baudrillard traces the emergence of what he sees as a society of simulation, in which the boundaries between seemingly distinct economic, political, cultural, and social realms break down, subjectivities become fragmented, and the simulacrum—or the copy of something for which there is no original—comes to dominate our expectations of real life. Much like Boorstin's pseudo-event, Baudrillard's travels in hyperreality, or the spaces in which spectators flee what he called the "desert of the real" (amusement parks, shopping malls, and televised sporting events, among other things), often seem more real than life itself.

Unlike Lyotard and Baudrillard, however, Boorstin was still solidly wedded to Enlightenment ideals of truth and complained instead that an American "lives in a world where fantasy is more real than reality, where the image has more dignity than its original. We hardly dare face our bewilderment, because our ambiguous experience is so pleasantly iridescent, and the solace of belief in contrived reality is so thoroughly real. We have become eager accessories to the great hoaxes of the age. These are the hoaxes we play on ourselves."[17] Boorstin uses the concept of the hoax to suggest a delusional state. Yet as I have tried to demonstrate in the previous chapters, hoaxes are often more complicated than they may appear. Stories of biblical giants, spirt extras, frolicking fairies, bat-like moon men, and divine sources of radiant energy have not only persisted for hundreds of years, for many consumers of these stories they have provided a means of making sense of the rapidly changing world around them. Even if we know these stories and visions are not real, these objects of vision give viewers a sense of individual agency to inspect or explore strange new phenomenon and to challenge or confirm their beliefs.

Boorstin was not a postmodernist; on the contrary, his criticism of the conditions that have come to define our notions of postmodernism—a disregard for historical references, a multiplicity of subjectivities, the mutability of materials—are at odds with his allegiance to concepts such as truth and authenticity and his deep distrust of simulated experience and disdain for hoaxes. Missing in his analysis of the pseudo-event is the deep Marxist critique inherent in both Lyotard and Baudrillard's philosophies, or what the Situationist Guy Debord calls "the society of the spectacle." Also missing in all these accounts is an allowance for wonder and enchantment in the face of seemingly spectacular objects of vision.

For Debord the spectacle occurs at the "historical moment at which the commodity completes its colonization of social life." It is marked by "the decline of being into having, and having into merely appearing." Much like for Boorstin, for Debord the "spectacle is not a collection of images, rather, it is a social relationship between people that is mediated by images" and a state in which "all that once was directly lived has become mere representation."[18] Despite their similarities, Debord takes Boorstin to task, criticizing him for describing "the excesses of a world that has become foreign to us as if they were excesses foreign to our world." By locating his reality in a fictional past and denouncing "the superficial reign of images as a product of 'our extravagant expectations,'" Boorstin, he claims, contrasts "these excesses to a 'normal' life" that has no reality in either his book or his era. He alleges that "Boorstin fails to see that the proliferation of the prefabricated 'pseudo-events' he denounces flows from the simple fact that the overwhelming realities of present-day social existence prevent people from actually living events for themselves. Because history itself haunts modern society like a specter, pseudohistories have to be concocted at every level in order to preserve the threatened equilibrium of the present *frozen time*." Debord concludes, "Because the real human life that Boorstin evokes is located for him in the past, including the past that was dominated by religious resignation, he has no way of comprehending the true extent of the present society's domination by images."[19]

For Boorstin, the titular "image" of his book is not only a nostalgic marker for a time and place that never existed, but its predominance in daily life acts as a substitution for what he considers authentic experience. Boorstin's image world is all surface and lacks a depth of experience that he sees present in earlier times. Yet as I mentioned in the introduction to this project, the tension between the visible world and the invisible world, between surface and depth of vision, dates back to antiquity. As Plato argued over two thousand years ago in his parable of the cave, the world we see around us is merely a percept inside our heads, and philosophers and scholars have been grappling with this idea ever since. Nevertheless, Boorstin presents the world of "the image" as a new condition brought on by the proliferation of new media forms in everyday life, the impact of which ranges from politics to the arts. Indeed, in his lament on the effects of the pseudo-event on fine art, Boorstin bemoans the severing of art from notions of the divine. "Like a man," he explains "a work of art has a soul, a life all its own. . . . Every work of art had the fixity, the precise boundaries, which until recently were attributed to God's work in the Creation."[20]

Much like Walter Benjamin before him, Boorstin blames improved technologies, in particular "advances in printing," for altering artistic value. Now, he complains, one can "buy for a few dollars a full-color copy of the 'Mona Lisa' or of Van Gogh's 'Sunflowers' which, properly framed and viewed at a decent distance, was hardly distinguishable from its original." The Graphic Revolution, he continues:

> provides us with mass-produced "originals." Inevitably, then, we come to think that the "original" is to be distinguished from its technically more precise (and often more durable) copy only by its price. Respect for the original comes close to pure snobbery. What is more natural in a democratic age that we should begin to measure the stature of a work of art—especially of a painting—by how widely and how well it is reproduced.[21]

Boorstin's assertion that "the 'original' had a priceless and ineffable uniqueness" certainly evokes Benjamin's account of the loss of the aura in the age of mechanical reproducibility that I discussed in the introduction; however, Boorstin's complaint differs markedly from Benjamin's. His critique is not rooted in immediate concerns about the dangers of an encroaching fascism but rather is focused on his own elitist fears brought on by the blurring boundaries of cultural distinction. Ultimately, for Benjamin, the radical potential of "technological reproducibility emancipates the work of art from its parasitic subservience to ritual." When this happens, "authenticity ceases to be applied to artistic production, [and] the whole total function of art is revolutionized. Instead of being founded on ritual, it is based on a different practice—politics."[22] In the late twentieth century, as many art objects became further liberated not just from ritual but also from notions of authorship and authenticity, the idea of indexical referents was not only called into question; in many cases it was completely disregarded in favor of more postmodern ways of seeing.

While there is no absolute definition of the term postmodern, and there is still much debate over its periodization, I am using the parameters established by art historian Abigail Solomon-Godeau, who defines the postmodern as that identified with the "now fully familiar strategies of appropriation and pastiche; its systematic assault on modernist orthodoxies of immanence, autonomy, presence, originality, and authorship; its engagement with the simulacra; and its interrogation of the problems of photographic mass media representation."[23] For Charles Sanders Peirce and those who followed him, the index is a sign that signifies by means of causality, even if the situation—as in the case of Roger Fenton, Alexander Gardner, and Timothy O'Sullivan—has been manipulated. The postmodern index, however, is more uncanny. With postmodern vision, questions of what is real and what is fake no longer dictate the terms of the viewing experience.[24] As Baudrillard writes, images become "sites of disappearance of meaning and representation, sites in which we are caught quite apart from any judgement of reality."[25] Like Hearst's entreaty to Remington to "furnish the pictures," the postmodern image is often detached from historical causality and even from meaning itself.

As I explained in the previous chapter, the truth claims of photography date back to the earliest days of the practice; but as Lisa Cartwright and Marita Sturken have noted, "The creation of an image through a camera lens always involves some sort of subjective choice." They call this the "myth of photographic truth," following Roland Barthes, for whom the very "principle of myth" is that "it transforms history into nature . . . [and] does not deny things, on the contrary, its function is to talk about them; simply, it purifies them, it makes them innocent, it gives them a natural and eternal justification, it gives them a clarity which is not that of an explanation but that of a statement of fact." Or, as Cartwright and Sturken explain, a mythology "is a hidden set of rules and conventions through which meanings, which in reality are specific to certain groups, are made to seem universal and given for a whole society."[26] Photographic images have played a crucial role in establishing such mythologies. Fenton's images of the Crimea and O'Sullivan and Gardner's photographs from the American Civil War all contributed to the creation and dissemination of mythic national histories and cultural memories; even though many of these images were manipulated in some way, they still had the veneer of having some sort of indexical truth.

Postmodern images make no such claims. On the contrary, contemporary artists such as Sherrie Levine and Cindy Sherman use photography to interrogate modernist attitudes toward reproduction and originality, as well as to call attention to the gendered assumptions inherent in the mythologizing of history and culture through images. Through their work they confront the seriousness of Lyotard and Debord's masculinist critiques and instead make room for a sense of playfulness and artifice in their objects of vision. In her 1981 series of photographs titled *After Walker Evans*, for example, Levine shot photographs of Evans's iconic images of southern sharecroppers from his 1936 collaboration with William Agee for *Fortune* (and later published as their collaborative work

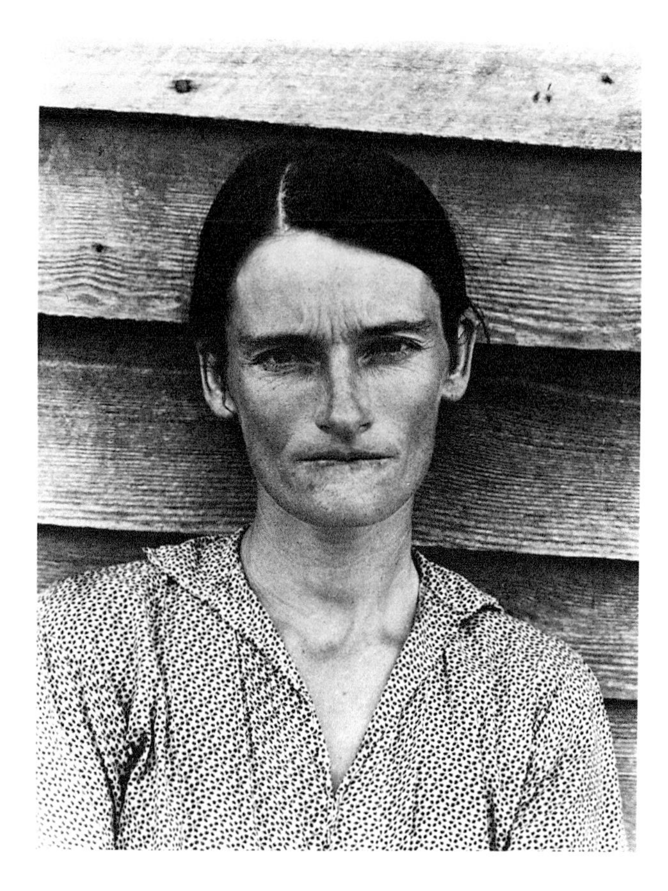

Fig. 37
(a) Walker Evans, Allie Mae Burroughs, Hale County, Alabama, 1936. Film negative, 8 × 10 in. The Metropolitan Museum of Art, Walker Evans Archive, 1994 (1994.258.424). (b) Sherrie Levine (b. 1947), *After Walker Evans 4*, 1981. Gelatin silver print, 12.8 × 9.8 cm (5 1/16 × 3 7/8 in.). The Metropolitan Museum of Art, Gift of the artist, 1995 (1995.266.4). Images copyright © Walker Evans Archive, The Metropolitan Museum of Art. Image source: Art Resource, New York.

Let Us Now Praise Famous Men). Evans's stark black-and-white photographs of the gaunt and economically precarious Burroughs family helped to solidify national narratives of the strength and fortitude of the downtrodden in the Depression-era United States while also stressing the importance of documentary photography to capture (and in some cases to help authenticate) the systemic problems brought on by the financial crisis to buttress the need for social and economic reforms. We now know that Evans and Agee moved the furniture and cropped their images for maximum effect (and had intimate interpersonal relationships with members of the family).[27] Nevertheless, because of their indexical claims—Evans was there, the Burroughs family was real, the conditions were bleak—we continue to see these images as faithfully representing the Dust Bowl during the Great Depression.

Levine's photographs reproduce Evans's prints as seemingly direct copies. In so doing, she calls into question many of the foundational assumptions underlying modernist production, including ideas about the centrality of inspiration, autonomy, and originality in creating autonomous artworks.[28] Who is the author? Who is the subject? Do these questions even matter? For the works in Levine's *After Walker Evans* series, the referents are simultaneously the downtrodden Dust Bowl subjects that Evans captured in his photographs and Evans's

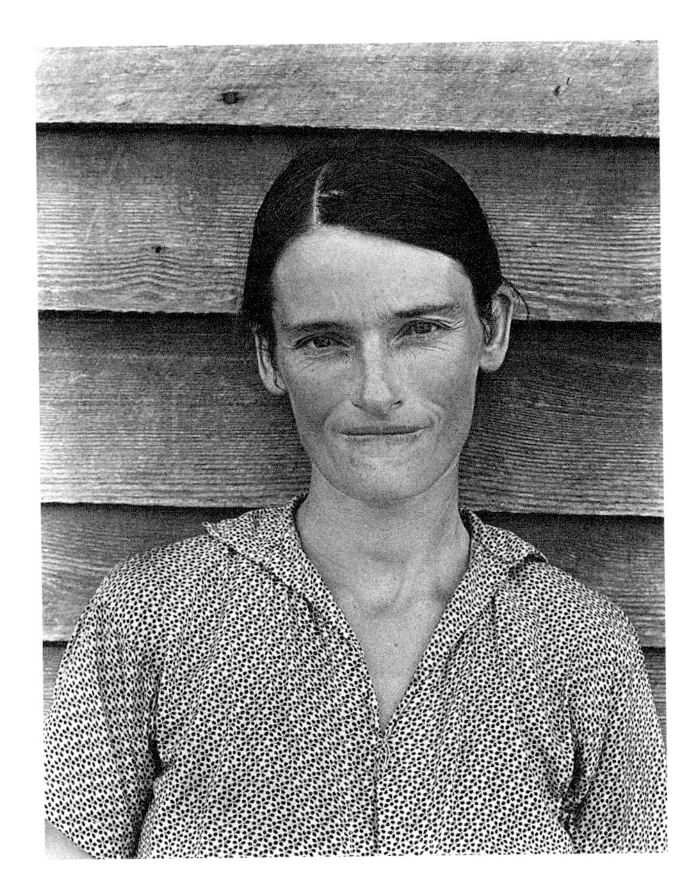

photographs themselves. Evans's prints, which have been reproduced repeatedly, haunt Levine's series. They serve as both indexical and iconic references to the masterwork and in so doing call into question the very practice of documentary photography itself as a form of truth.

Cindy Sherman also plays with our notions of indexicality in her *Untitled Film Still* series. Created between 1977 and 1980, Sherman took portraits of herself in the guise of generic female film characters from earlier in the century. Through her posing, props, and period costumes, she plays with well-known filmic tropes—the vamp, the ingénue, the working girl, the housewife (see fig. 38). Regarding *Untitled Film Still #21*, critic Douglas Crimp wrote in 1979:

> Here is a picture. It shows a young woman with close-cropped hair, wearing a suit and hat whose style is that of the 1950s. She looks the part of what was called, in that decade, a career girl, an impression that is perhaps cued, perhaps merely confirmed by the fact that she is surrounded by the office towers of the big city. But those skyscrapers play another role in this picture. They envelop and isolate the woman, reinforcing with their dark-shadowed, looming facades her obvious anxiety, as her eyes dart over her shoulder . . . at something perhaps lurking outside the frame

> of the picture. Is she, we wonder, being pursued? But what is it, in fact, that makes this a picture of presentiment, of that which is impending? Is it the suspicious glance? Or can we locate the solicitation *to read the picture as if it were fiction* in a certain spatial dislocation—the jarring juxtaposition of close-up face with distant buildings—suggesting the cinematic artifice of rear-screen projection?[29]

Film stills are official studio photographs taken on set during production to be used as promotional material for the film, usually by anonymous photographers employed by the studio. Often included in press kits or sent out with the star's autographs to generate fandom, they are necessary but ultimately throwaway images. Sherman's stills tease the viewer with both their form and their content. They seem familiar but not quite placeable. Is this one from a Hitchcock film? This one from a Sirk? They play with, but ultimately defy, the conventions of the genre and challenge our ideas of authorship and the autonomous work of art because we know that they are actually original (and quite valuable) works of art themselves despite their referents as anonymous and disposable objects. Sherman herself stresses the ambiguity inherent in the works:

> I suppose unconsciously, or semiconsciously at best, I was wrestling with some sort of turmoil of my own about understanding women. The characters weren't dummies; they weren't just airhead actresses. They were women struggling with something but I didn't know what. The clothes make them seem a certain way, but then you look at their expression, however slight it may be, and wonder if maybe "they" are not what the clothes are communicating. I wasn't working with a raised "awareness," but I definitely felt that the characters are questioning something—perhaps being forced into a certain role. At the same time, those roles are in film: the women aren't being lifelike, they're acting. There are so many levels of artifice. I like that whole jumble of ambiguity.[30]

Sherman's pictures recall scenes from movies we may have seen on late-night television (or feel we should have seen but never did). They are simultaneously generic references and stand-alone art works, and Sherman is simultaneously an anonymous female actress performing a part and a well-known artist teasing viewers by playing with the conventions of the form. Her statement that the "women aren't being lifelike; they're acting," speaks not only to the "levels of artifice" and "jumbles of ambiguity" that she evokes; they present another way of seeing that extends beyond her critique of the popular culture she references and the increasingly commodified and academic art world that has embraced her. Like Barnum, she is having fun while also, in a sense, embracing a Cartesian form of wonder as the sudden surprise of the soul.

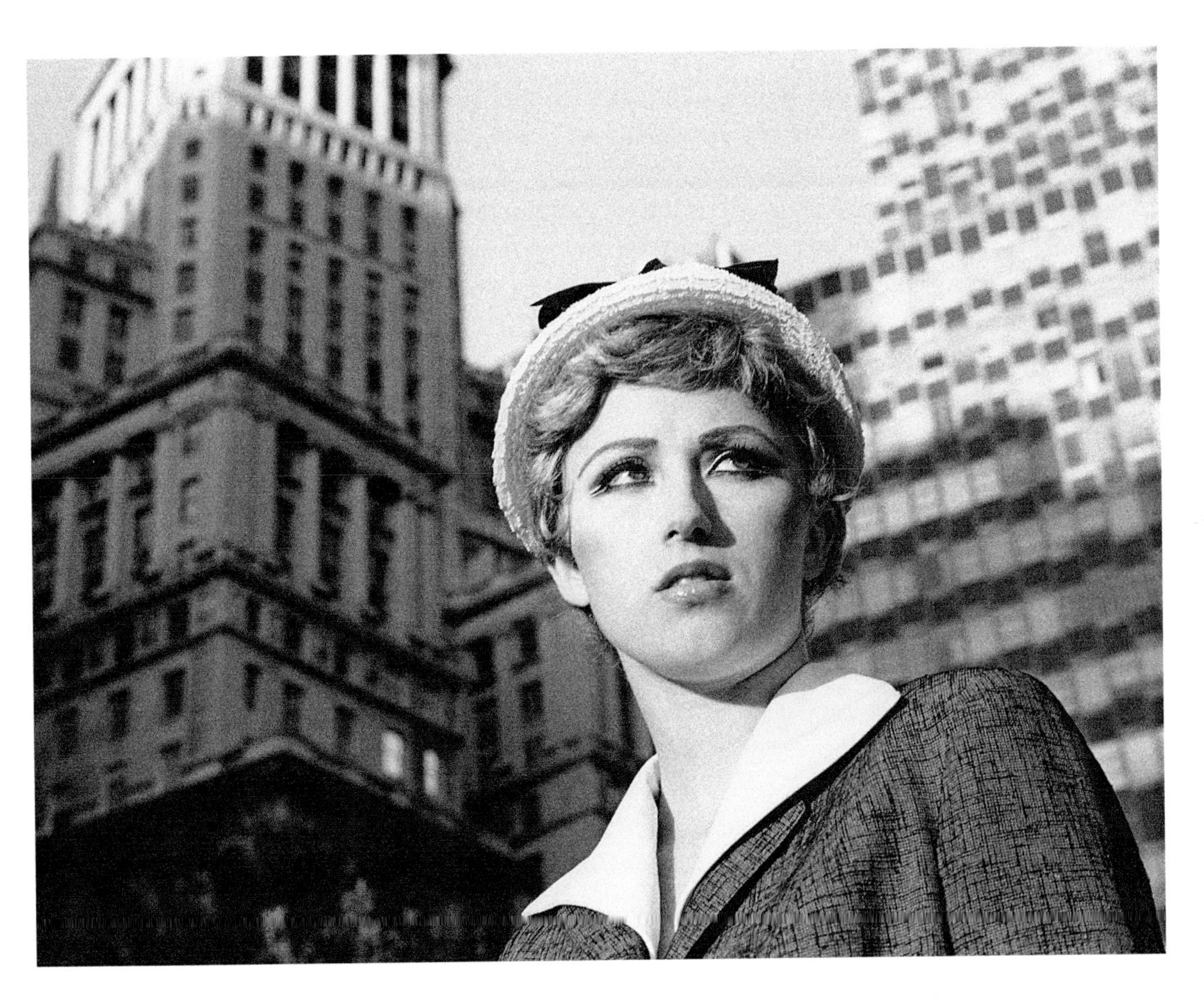

Fig. 38 Cindy Sherman, *Untitled #21*, 1978. Courtesy of the artist and Metro Pictures, New York.

Moreover, despite their titular identification as film stills, the works reference neither a particular film nor its associated production. Rather, they are all highly posed self-portraits, which lends an air of media confusion to them as well. Taken together, or even individually, the works are fun and playful once we know the conceit: They are all staged. They are all Sherman. And, most important, we know that they are all individual works of art each worth millions of dollars, not throwaway promotional film stills. Unlike Brady's photographs or Remington's sketches, they make no claims to represent events in real time, despite their suggestion of a type of indexicality and their broader cultural evocations of what we think we might know.

This type of media confusion, I would argue, today extends beyond the postmodern art world, and, again, the stakes are often high. I began this project by identifying what for me is one of the key moments of disconnect between seeing and believing in the twentieth century: George Holliday's video recording of the 1989 beating of Rodney King and the use of the video in the subsequent trial and not-guilty verdict of the offending officers, despite what seemed to be damning evidence of a brutal assault. By turning eighty-one seconds of pixilated home video into a series of frame-by-frame film stills, the attorneys for Officers Powell, Wind, Briseno, and Koon also fomented a type of media confusion that made it easier for jurors to disregard the visual evidence in front of them as part of a continuing narrative constituting "excessive use of force" and instead to view the images as individual instances that each justified the brutality.

Although the videotape may have ultimately failed to convict the officers (in fact it helped to acquit them), it reentered public discourse almost exactly two years after Holliday shot it, when it ended up in the 1993 Whitney Biennial—one of the most important shows in the contemporary art world.[31] "I knew the videotape was important the first time I saw it," Whitney curator John Hanhardt said of the work. "It represents a new way of seeing the world around us." In an interview with Suzanne Muchnic in the *Los Angeles Times* regarding his choice to include a copy in the exhibition, Hanhardt argued that the Holliday tape "extends the definition of the documentary" and "is paradigmatic of the new relationship media has to its community, and to television itself."[32] The *New York Times* art critic Roberta Smith was less convinced about the work's inclusion in the galleries of the Whitney. "The presence of Mr. Holliday's tape," she wrote in her review, "signals one of the show's basic flaws, which is that it is less about the art of our time than about the times themselves."[33] Similarly, art critic Arthur Danto, writing in *The Nation*, took issue with "the curatoriat of the Whitney Museum of American Art" for including Holliday's videotape in the biennial show: "Now, the King tape certainly demonstrated the power of images and at the same time the limits of art, for no work of art in recent (or perhaps any) time has had a fraction of the effect upon society that the King tape has had upon ours: The broken storefront, the burning city, the many dead—to paraphrase Yeats—all unleashed not so much by an act of police violence as by the fact that it was recorded and shown." But, he continues:

> The images had the effect in part because they were not art, because they were the flat and uninflected effect of reality mechanically registered on videotape: It was the zero degree of visual and moral truth the world beheld; were it to occur to someone that art might have had something to do with it, the effect of the tape would be diminished. I can understand an artist seeking to borrow the power of the King images for, let us suppose, creative purposes of his or her own art . . . without making the tape itself into a work of art; and indeed nothing can or should make a work of art out of that tape. That would put us in just the wrong relationship to it. In fact, any relationship in which we are put to the images other than the relationship in which they put us to the event they transcribe and record is a wrong relationship.[34]

Whether one believes that the video qualified for a spot in the Whitney Biennial, as Hanhardt proclaimed at the time, it certainly "demonstrated the power of images and at the same time the limits of art." Dismissed by the Simi Valley jurors as evidence of a crime, but now framed as "art," it forced Whitney viewers to contemplate what they saw as real versus what they saw as mediated. It may have failed as a certain type of evidence, but it succeeded as another. It transformed a real event into a pseudo-artwork and, as Hanhardt announced, represented a new way of seeing the world around us.

Conclusion

How to Look at a Million Images

Leonardo's *The Last Supper*, Rembrandt's *The Night Watch*, Veronese's *The Wedding at Cana*: these are three of the most canonical paintings in the history of Western art. They are also works that the Welsh filmmaker Peter Greenaway has recently reinterpreted as multisensory experiences in his ongoing *Classic Paintings Revisited* project.

The genesis of Greenaway's work occurred in 2006 when, as part of the celebration surrounding the four hundredth anniversary of Rembrandt's birthday, the Dutch government commissioned him to pay homage to the artist and his masterpiece, *The Night Watch*. Greenaway, building on Rembrandt's use of light as well as his own interest in the adjunct of the cinematic and the theatrical, deployed a series of animated diagrams, digital stills, and a multilayered soundtrack to create a multisensory experience for viewers to the Rijksmuseum. Through overlays of sound and light, Greenaway animated the masterwork. Dogs bark, bells clang, a cannon fires, snippets of conversation float by. The figures in the work appear to move as they gesture to one another across the picture frame. At times the painting looks as if it is deluged by rain, at others engulfed in flames, and in the end, blood seems to drip from its canvas. Through their manipulations, Greenaway and his team transformed the static history painting into a theatrical event transporting viewers back in time to enter the space of the image. Greenaway followed this in situ exhibition with two films about the painting: *Night Watching*, a cinematic *tableau vivant*–like biography of the painting and the artists; and the more documentary thriller *Rembrandt's J'Accuse*, an art historical mystery play that interrogates the murder of one of the central figures in the piece.

The following year, Greenaway took as his subject Leonardo da Vinci's *Last Supper*. In June 2008, he staged a one-night-only event with the original in the refectory of Santa Maria delle Grazie in Milan. Then, using a digital facsimile of the work, he re-created the installation in a variety of locales, including sites in New York and Melbourne. According to the press release from the New York event, "Set within a full-scale replica of the dome of Refectory of Santa Maria delle Grazie in Milan, the home of the original painting, a meticulously detailed facsimile of *The Last Supper* is brought to life through Greenaway's ingenious manipulation of light, sound, and theatrical illusion. Visitors navigate a series of vivid audio-visual environments that provoke new ways of seeing this iconic work."[1] Much like his reinterpretation of Rembrandt's masterpiece, in his reconsideration of *The Last Supper* Greenaway fully animates the mural: the figures seem three-dimensional as they gesture and move, the colors are vivid, and loud religious music fills the air to create a full sensory experience.

Greenaway's digital re-creations challenge our expectations for site-specific works such as *The Last Supper*—where place (the refectory of Santa Maria delle Grazie in Milan) and the original painting are intimately linked. Indeed, Leonardo painted *The Last Supper* in *buon fresco*, mixing his pigment with lime and embedding it into the plaster so that the work is physically part of the wall it adorns. Yet Greenaway's multimedia re-creation allows the painting to leave the wall and travel, thus complicating now-standard Benjaminian notions of the aura, which endows the original artwork with quasi-spiritual properties linked to its presence in place and time. Greenaway's augmentations of masterworks such as *The Night Watch*, *The Last Supper*, and most recently Veronese's *Wedding at Cana* demonstrate how the spaces in which we encounter the works and the technologies we use to experience them continue to influence how and what we see. For example, Leonardo's *Last Supper*, in situ, builds on (and some might say perfects) Leon Battista Alberti's notions of perspective for artistic and architectural representation, as outlined in his 1435 treatise *Della Pittura*, or *On Painting* (see fig. 39). The original work appears as an extension of the dining hall. Leonardo's meticulously precise, grid-like ceiling and his use of a vanishing point in the landscape outside the painted window create the feeling of three-dimensional space. Christ and his disciples seem present in the refectory. Greenaway's manipulations of the work, however, complicate our understandings of perspective further. In his digital resituations, we hear the subjects move and speak; the faded colors of the decaying original are miraculously restored. With Veronese's *Wedding at Cana*, Greenaway reverses his spatial manipulations and digitally returns the painting, which now hangs in the Louvre in Paris, to its original site in the Benedictine refectory on the island of San Giorgio Maggiore outside Venice, exactly where it hung from 1562 (when Veronese

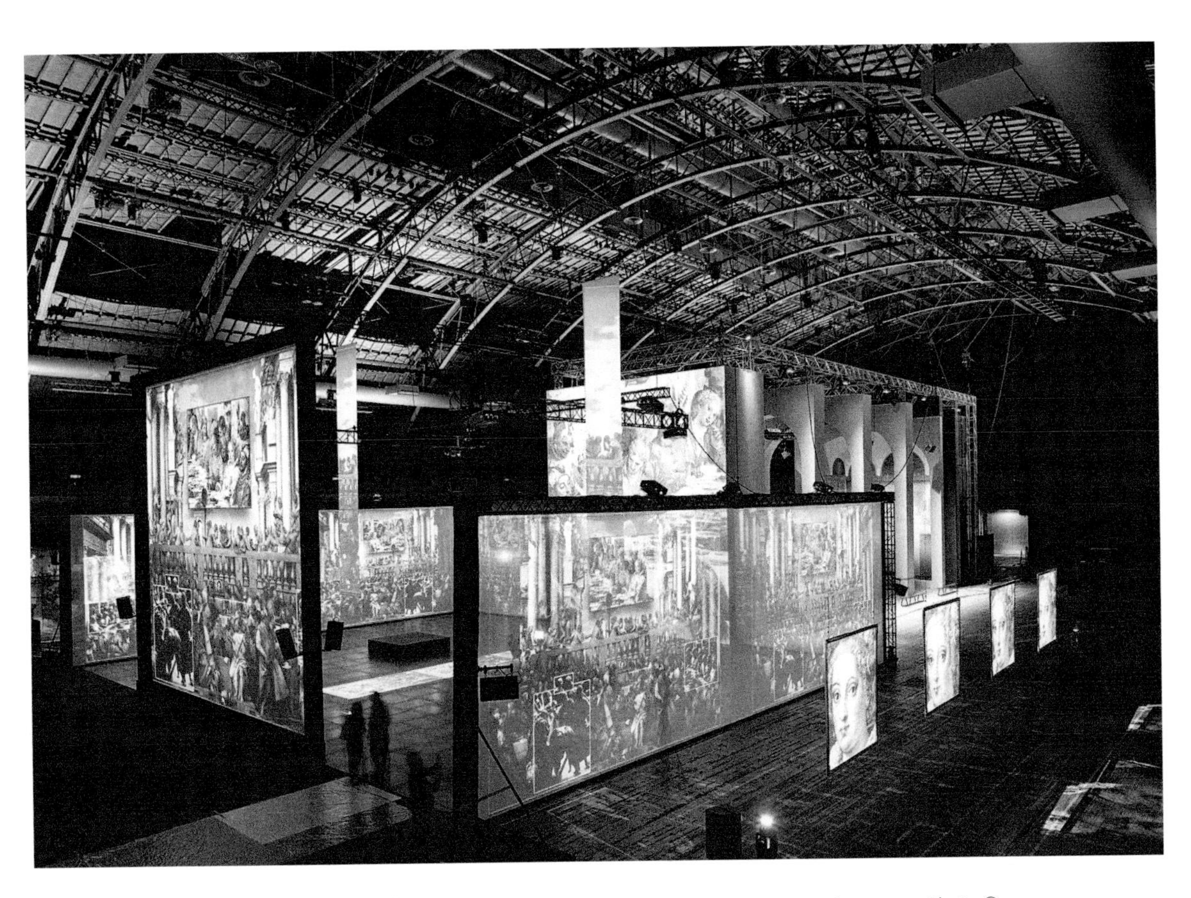

Fig. 39 Peter Greenaway, installation view of *The Last Supper*, Park Avenue Armory, June 2014. Photo © James Ewing / OTTO.

finished it) until 1797, when Napoleon claimed it and took it with him back to France. By resituating the work in its initial location, instead of in the crowded gallery of the Louvre, Greenaway enacts a type of artistic time travel and in so doing attempts to restore the work's original spatial and historical presence.

Regarding the digital projection of works such as Veronese's *Wedding at Cana* back into their original locales, Bruno Latour and Adam Lowe have argued, "Facsimiles, especially those relying on complex (digital) techniques, are the most fruitful way to explore the original and even to help re-define what originality actually is."[2] By placing Veronese's work back in the Benedictine dining room outside of Venice, for example, Greenaway asks viewers to contemplate not just the ways in which vision has been historically constructed and how notions of artistic value and experience have changed over time but also forces us to question the continued utility of the term "aura" in the digital age. Do the crowds of visitors jockeying to see the painting in its current spot in the crowded Italian galleries of the Louvre (where it shares space with the *Mona Lisa*) have a more authentic experience of the painting because it is the original? Can his cinematic projections stimulate something equally as real for visitors to the installation in Venice? Or are we asking the wrong questions by holding on to these criteria for describing what we see and feel when we experience these images as art?

Much like Rembrandt's earlier treatments of light or Leonardo's experimentations with pictorial space, Greenaway's sensory and spatial manipulations have been enabled by new forms of technology. Greenaway conceives of his project as a form of aesthetic liberation. In an interview published in *Digicult*, for example, he explains that he is trying to escape from what he calls the "four bondages" that are keeping the contemporary culture industries hostage. The first he identifies as "that of text." The second is saying "no to the 'framed world' which we must watch from an imposed point of view." Next, he argues, "we should break the chains of slavery put by the categories of entertainment and acting. . . . And finally, we should break the chains of slavery par excellence: the movie camera."[3] Like the great men he references in his *Classic Paintings* canon, he sees himself as a historical actor experimenting with new forms. He explains, "My purpose wasn't to turn classic paintings into movies, or vice versa, but to hybridize these two universes and bridge the gap between them. I wanted to answer two fundamental questions that have been pushing me to undertake this path since the beginning: how would have painting been in presence of electricity? And again: how is it possible to solve the discouraging problem that paintings don't emit sounds and don't move?"[4] By explaining how, in the work of both Caravaggio and Rembrandt, chiaroscuro—or the dramatic use of light and shadow—was brought about by their use of candlelight, Greenaway claims that he, too, is using his available contemporary light sources to reimagine historical works. Moreover, he suggests that his use of digital software turns his projects into "a series of separated and interactive levels. . . . The thin layers of painting, overlapped that represent the criteria of painting in the Renaissance, find a new territory in the layers of video-composition software." In so doing, he likens his artworks to the technological breakthroughs with chiaroscuro, perspective, narrative, and other elements that his canonical forbearers employed. By directly copying and then augmenting the work of venerated masterworks, he sees his projected visions as redefining the work of art in the post-cinematic age and ultimately claims that his "work is [not] doing cinema, but rather it's a creative practice linked to the image supremacy." He concludes with a quote from Derrida: "The image always has the last word."[5]

The idea that images can communicate beyond words is key to the thinking of Lev Manovich as well. For Manovich the "problem with studying visual art, visual culture, and visual media using traditional humanities approaches" is that, "regardless of the methodologies and theories being employed in a given case, all of them use one representational system (natural language) to describe another (images)."[6] Although he never fully defines what he calls "humanities approaches," it is clear that they are all textual- and narrative-based, which for him is inherently limiting and biased. In fact, all forms of visual media share this fundamental thinking. Instead he argues that "if we actually want to start discussing a range of graphical and compositional possibilities . . . we need a new kind of instrument."[7]

Reversing Berger's claim that "seeing comes before words," Manovich, along with his team of scholars in his Software Studies Lab at UC San Diego and now at the City University of New York, has created a sophisticated computer program that uses images to look at millions of images. In our image-saturated culture we make, share, and comment on "billions of new digital artifacts every day." For this, he argues, "we need new methods for seeing culture at its new scale and velocity." Manovich and his collaborators in the lab have been addressing this challenge. Among the questions they ask are:

- "How can we 'observe' giant cultural universes of both user-generated and professional media content created today, without reducing them to averages, outliers, or preexisting categories?"
- "How can work with large cultural data help us question our stereotypes and assumptions about cultures?"
- "What new theoretical cultural concepts and models are required for studying global digital culture with its new mega-scale, speed, and connectivity?"
- "Do we need to develop new theoretical concepts and models to deal with the scale and velocity of user-generated content?"
- "What would 'science of culture' that use computation and big data look like, and what will be its limitations?"[8]

These are big questions. There is something very seductive about Manovich's project and its attempt to flee the bondage of narrative frames and traditional

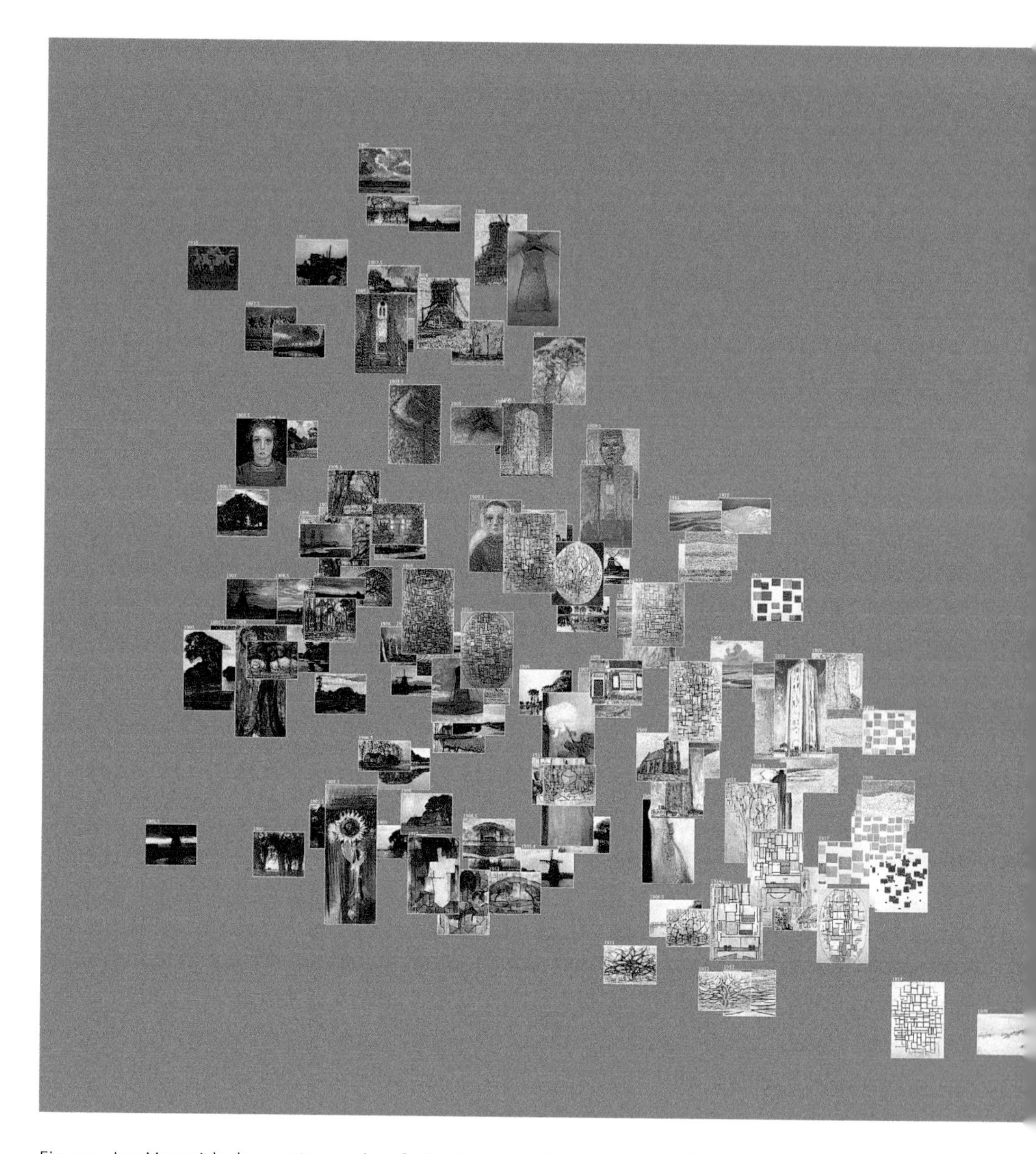

Fig. 40 Lev Manovich, data set image plot of 128 paintings by Piet Mondrian and 123 paintings by Mark Rothko. Cultural Analytics project. Image courtesy of Lev Manovich / Cultural Analytics.

ways of looking and analyzing in search of new methods of seeing and doing. In many ways, his is a utopian project; it is rooted in the deep belief that data reveal larger truths and that we can see them if using the right equipment. In his essay "How to Compare a Million Images," for example, he exclaims that "any reflection on culture begins with an informal comparison between multiple objects in order to understand their similarities and differences." But, he argues, the sample sets for most humanists and social scientists are too small and limited. Regarding a project that looks for trends in Japanese manga, he asserts

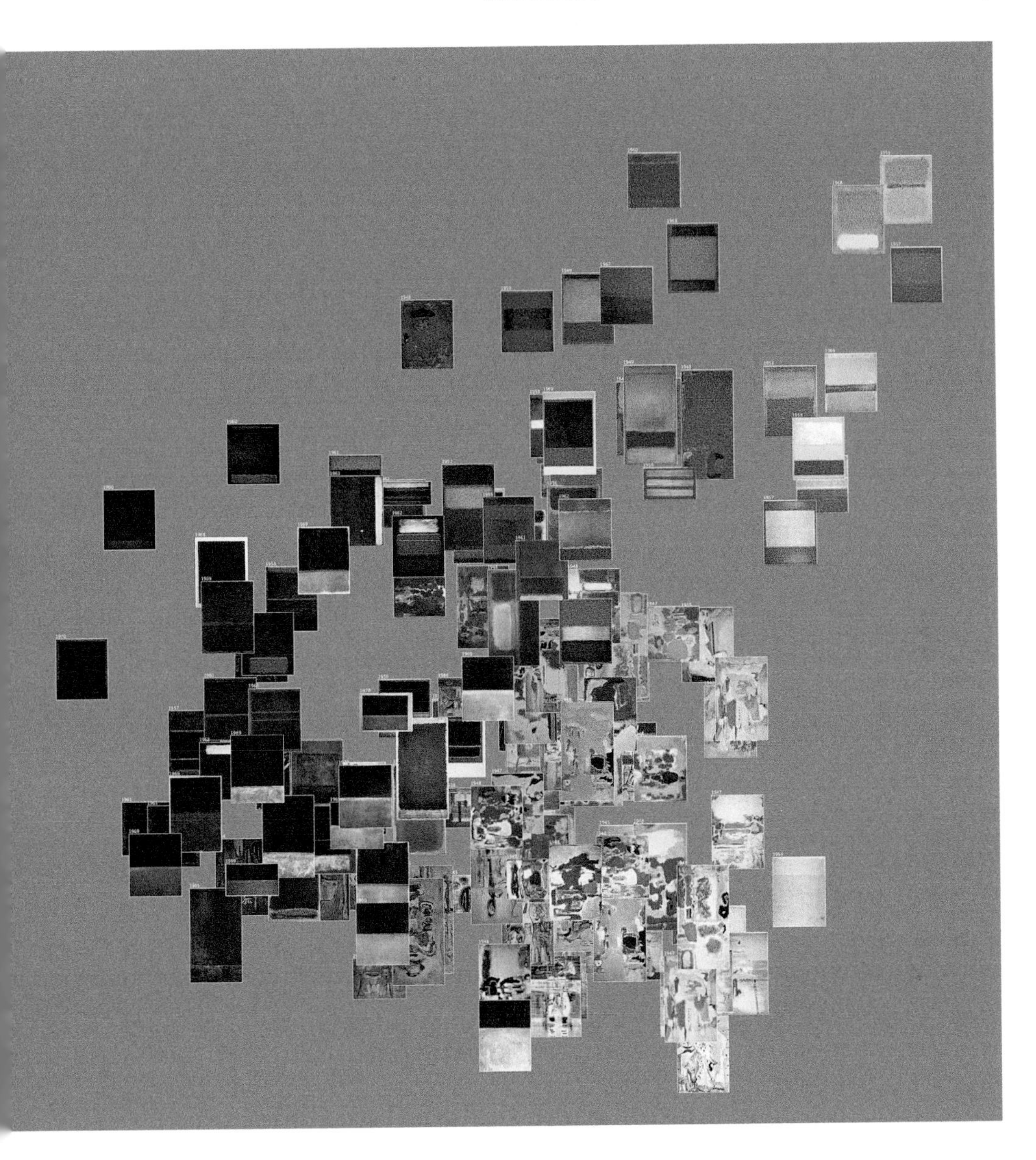

that "if we want our analysis to properly reflect the range of graphical techniques used today by manga artists across thousands of manga books, millions of pages in these books, and tens of millions of individual panels, we need to be able to examine details of individual images and to find patterns of difference and similarity across large numbers of images."[9] Manovich's Cultural Analytics program allows images themselves to determine the search parameters for the larger endeavor, thus expanding the archive beyond the capacity of lone researchers. Another project uses "scatter plots with images superimposed over points . . . to compare a similar number of paintings by Piet Mondrian and Mark Rothko produced over comparable time periods" (see fig. 40). Again, Manovich claims that he is looking at the images through the lens of other images to posit a new way of seeing—a form of image vision, if you will.

One can certainly argue in response to his projects that his data—like all data—are only as good as the codes he and his programmers write to capture and analyze it, and that despite his utopian rhetoric it is still subject to raced and gendered frames. Nevertheless, like the readers of the *New York Sun* almost two hundred years ago who wanted to believe in life on the moon, Manovich's Cultural Analytics promises a new way of understanding the world around us. It allows us to consider new models to make sense of both scientific and artistic practices in the twenty-first century. It forces us to ask, as crazy as it might seem: what happens to our historical understandings of vision and visions when images begin to see for themselves?

Notes

Prologue

1. Lou Cannon, "The King Incident: More Than Meets the Eye on Videotape," *Washington Post*, January 25, 1988, https://www.washingtonpost.com/archive/politics/1998/01/25/the-king-incident-more-than-met-the-eye-on-videotape/2248e35c-178b-47e9-a8db-0734f88b46e0.

2. King juror quoted in Seth Mydans, "The Police Verdict: Los Angeles Policemen Acquitted in Taped Beating," *New York Times*, April 30, 1992, https://www.nytimes.com/1992/04/30/us/the-police-verdict-los-angeles-policemen-acquitted-in-taped-beating.html.

3. Dennis McDougal, "Few L.A. Outlets for Live Coverage of King Trial," *Los Angeles Times*, February 26, 1992, http://articles.latimes.com/1992-02-26/entertainment/ca-2736_1_court-tv-founder.

4. Seth Mydans, "Prosecutor in Beating Case Urges Jury to Rely on Tape," *New York Times*, April 21, 1992, https://www.nytimes.com/1992/04/21/us/prosecutor-in-beating-case-urges-jury-to-rely-on-tape.html.

5. Officer Powell quoted in Goodwin, "Professional Vision," 618.

6. This was actually said by one of the prosecuting attorneys, anticipating this defense. Court TV transcript quoted in ibid., 623.

7. Alexander, "Can You Be BLACK and Look at This?" 80.

8. Sgt. Koons quoted in Seth Mydans, "Their Lives Consumed, Officers Await Second Trial," *New York Times*, February 2, 1993, https://www.nytimes.com/1993/02/02/us/their-lives-consumed-officers-await-2d-trial.html.

9. Meara Sharma, "Claudia Rankine on Blackness as the Second Person," *Guernica*, November 17, 2014, https://www.guernicamag.com/blackness-as-the-second-person.

10. Rankine, *Citizen*. Rankine credits the day the Rodney King verdict was announced with changing her perspective on the American justice system in Sharma, "Claudia Rankine on Blackness as the Second Person."

Introduction

1. Sahagún, *General History*, book 1, p. 47. Montaigne would make a similar point fifty years later in his essay "Of Cannibals," thus establishing one of the dominant tropes of early American conquest and exploration narratives, that the natives were "salvageable" and thus worth saving.

2. Ibid., 49–50.

3. Ibid.

4. The oldest remaining Mayan codex is known as the Dresden Codex. According to the World Digital Library, only four Mayan manuscripts still exist, of which the oldest and best preserved is the Dresden Codex, held in the collections of the Saxon State and University Library. The manuscript was purchased for the Dresden court library in 1739 in Vienna, as a "Mexican book." It consists of thirty-nine leaves, inscribed on both sides, and was originally folded in an accordion-like manner. See https://www.wdl.org/en/item/11621.

5. "Codex" is a term used by scholars in medieval studies to describe illustrated Christian books made of papyrus, parchment, or vellum. See Roberts, "The Codex." It also refers to the screen-fold manuscripts of ancient Mesoamerica. See Boone, *Stories in Red and Black*. Thanks to Janet Berlo for helping me with the historiography of the term and for pointing me toward these texts.

6. Anderson and Dibble, *Florentine Codex*, book 12, p. 44.

7. There is an increasing literature on Malinche that complicates the narrative that she was Cortés's willing collaborator and places her within more complicated feminist, queer, and indigenous readings regarding her assimilation and survival. See for example the essays in Harris and Romero, *Feminism, Nation and Myth*.

8. Thank you again to Janet Berlo for helping me unpack this excerpt from the text.

9. Gillespie, "Blaming Moctezuma," 42.

10. Clendinnen, "Fierce and Unnatural Cruelty," 69.

11. Gillespie, "Blaming Moctezuma."

12. Although the numbers vary by account, between one-third and one-half of the population of Tenochtitlan died of smallpox within two years of the conquest. Also key to the conquest was the exploitation of women as intermediaries between the Spanish and indigenous peoples. See Barr, *Peace Came in the Form of a Woman.*

13. Excerpt from letter published in Markey, "Istoria della terra chiamata la nuova spagna," 202.

14. For the history of the codex's journey from Mexico to Florence, see ibid., 199–221.

15. The notion of the image for Aristotle, and Plato as well, was not necessarily visual in the way we conceive of the term today. Rather it evokes an "inner vision" that transcends bodily sense.

16. Aristotle, *De anima*, 3.7–8, http://psychclassics.yorku.ca/Aristotle/De-anima/de-anima3.htm. Emphasis mine.

17. Plato, *Republic*, 173.

18. Berger, *Ways of Seeing*, 1.

19. For more on the privileging of sight over the other senses—as well as recent challenges to this paradigm—see Smith, *Making Sense of the Past.*

20. Foster, *Vision and Visuality*, ix.

21. Mirzoeff, *Right to Look*, 2, 25.

22. Gordon, *Ghostly Matters*, 7. Regarding power, Gordon writes, "Power can be invisible, it can be fantastic, it can be dull and routine. It can be obvious, it can reach you by the baton of the police, it can speak the language of your thoughts and desires. It can feel like remote control, it can exhilarate like liberation, it can travel through time, and it can drown you in the present. It is dense and superficial, it can cause bodily injury, and it can harm you without seeming ever to touch you. It is systematic and it is particularistic and it is often both at the same time. It causes dreams to live and dreams to die" (3).

23. Dalton, "From Eyesight to Insight," 635.

24. Quoted in ibid., 634.

25. Max Weber articulates this as "disenchantment," or *Entzauberung*, which actually translates to "de-magic-ation." For more on this in Western philosophical thought, see Josephson-Storm, *Myth of Disenchantment.*

26. For Jane Bennett, there is an ethical component to this project. She writes, "Enchantment is something we encounter . . . but . . . is also a comportment that can be fostered through deliberate strategies." These include giving "greater expression to the sense of play" as well as "to hone sensory receptivity to the marvelous specificity of things" and "to resist the story of the disenchantment of modernity." Enchantment, she writes, "provokes moments of joy, and that joy can propel ethics." Bennett, *Enchantment of Modern Life*, 2–3.

27. Thompson famously writes in the prologue to his book, "The working class did not rise like the sun at an appointed time. It was present at its own making." Thompson, *Making of the English Working Class*, 8.

28. Ibid.

29. As Michael Leja compellingly argues in "Scenes from a History of the Image," such a comprehensive history must "venture into many of the disciplines that bear on these activities—optics, theories of vision, history of art, philosophy, psychology, biology, cognitive science, religion. . . . Not much would be excluded" (999).

30. Bloch, *Historian's Craft*, 50.

31. Bynum, "Wonder," 25.

32. Descartes, *Passions of the Soul*, 56.

33. Bynum, "Wonder," 25.

34. Ibid., 23.

35. Descartes, *Passions of the Soul*, 56.

36. Art historian Hans Belting, in his important study *Likeness and Presence*, for example, provides what he calls "a history of the image before the era of art," which for him begins during the Renaissance. Belting acknowledges that "art, as it is studied by the discipline of Art History today," certainly existed in the Middle Ages. But, he argues, after the Middle Ages, "art took on a different meaning and became acknowledged for its own sake—art as invented by a famous artist and defined by a proper theory" (xxi). See also Holmes, *Miraculous Image in Renaissance Florence*. Holmes argues that it was at this same moment that venerated and miracle-working images such as those of the Virgin and Saint Anne began "their extraordinary efficacy as sites of votive petition, sacred intercession, and miraculous manifestations[and] . . . their visual imagery seemed to enact the active agency of the sacred beings represented" (3).

37. Sahagún, *General History*, book 1, p. 53.

38. Art historian Ellen T. Baird, though, holds that the images in the work are "highly Europeanized," in particular the treatment of Moctezuma's death, which she reads through

the visual filter of depictions of Jesus's crucifixion. See Baird, "Sahagún and the Representation of History."

39. Quoted in Kemp, *Leonardo on Painting*, 117–36.

40. Locke, *Essay Concerning Human Understanding*, chap. 1.

41. Ibid., chap. 11. Bishop Berkeley challenged Locke's doctrine though his theory of immaterialism's delineation of what he called "sensible objects" in the fourth of his *Principles of Human Knowledge*:

> It is indeed an opinion strangely prevailing amongst men, that houses, mountains, rivers, and in a word all sensible objects have an existence natural or real, distinct from their being perceived by the understanding. But with how great an assurance and acquiescence soever this principle may be entertained in the world; yet whoever shall find in his heart to call it in question, may, if I mistake not, perceive it to involve a manifest contradiction. For what are the forementioned objects but the things we perceive by sense, and what do we perceive besides our own ideas or sensations; and is it not plainly repugnant that any one of these or any combination of them should exist unperceived?

42. Crary, "Modernizing Vision," 31. Crary elaborates on this in his landmark text *Techniques of the Observer*.

43. Crary further elaborates on the centrality of the concept of the camera obscura to changing notions of perception. For Crary, the "reorganization of knowledge and social practices" from the Renaissance on led to changing notions of the observer, which arose in large part from what he sees as a shift from the seventeenth- and eighteenth-century metaphor of the camera obscura to that of the stereoscope and stereoscopic vision in the nineteenth and twentieth centuries. He writes, "The problem of the observer is the field on which vision in history can be said to materialize to become itself visible. Vision and its effects are always inseparable from the possibilities of an observing subject who is both the historical product *and* the site of certain practices, techniques institutions, and procedures of subjectification." Crary, *Techniques of the Observer*, 5.

44. Unless otherwise noted, English translations are drawn from the Encyclopedia of Diderot & d'Alembert: Collaborative Translation Project, https://quod.lib.umich.edu/d/did.

45. Quoted in Hunt, *Making of the West*, 611.

46. This image was not included in the original volume. It was later mailed out to subscribers and then included in subsequent editions.

47. For a full description identifying these figures, see the information online at the MIT Libraries, https://libraries.mit.edu/exhibits/diderots-encyclopedia-exhibit-preview/introduction.

48. For a facsimile of the *Encyclopédie*, with links to a translation, see http://encyclopedie.uchicago.edu/content/système-figuré-des-connaissances-humaines-0.

49. Quoted in Foucault, *Order of Things*, xv.

50. Ibid., xx. Following Foucault, cultural critic Tony Bennett argues that the impulse toward visualizing power structures was behind the birth of the modern museum as well: "The emergence of the art museum was closely related to that of a wider range of institutions—history and natural science museums, dioramas and panoramas, national and, later, international exhibitions, arcades and department stores—which served as linked sites for the development and circulation of new disciplines (history, biology, art history, anthropology) and their discursive formations (the past, evolution, aesthetics, man) as well as for the development of new technologies of vision." Bennett, *Birth of the Museum*, 59.

51. McGregor, *Sir Hans Sloane*, 31–34. Quoted in Cuno, *Museums Matter*, 12.

52. Caygill, "Sloan's Will." Quoted in Cuno, *Museums Matter*, 13.

53. Trachtenberg, *Reading American Photographs*, 8.

54. Quoted in Gunning, "World as Object Lesson," 125. For more on Goode's collecting strategies, see Hughes, "People's Museum."

55. Pierre Bourdieu calls this "cultural capital." For Bourdieu, taste, an amorphous category based on the aesthetic preferences of social elites, acts as a means of creating symbolic boundaries based on social distinctions. See Bourdieu, *Distinction*. For more on this, see Saab, *For the Millions*, 187–88n18.

56. Written while he was living in Paris (exiled from Nazi Germany), Benjamin produced three versions of the essay between 1935 and 1939. The first, written in French in 1936, was intended for a small group of fellow Marxist academics living in Paris at the time.

The essay was translated into German in1955 and into English in 1968. For more on the history of the text, see the essays in Jennings, *Work of Art*.

57. Benjamin notes in the essay's opening sentence that in theory art has always been reproducible. "Around 1900," however, "technological reproduction not only had reached a standard that permitted it to reproduce all known works of art, profoundly modifying their effect, but it also had captured a place of its own amongst the artistic processes." Yet, he argues, "in even the most perfect reproduction, *one* thing is lacking: the here and now of the work of art—its unique existence in a particular place. It is this unique experience—and nothing else—that bears the mark of the history to which the work has been subject. This history includes changes to the physical structure of the work over time, together with any changes in ownership." Benjamin, "Work of Art," 21.

58. Hansen laments the ways in which "the common understanding of the aura as a primarily aesthetic category" has become "a shorthand for the particular qualities of traditional art that he observed waning in modernity, associated with the singular status of the artwork, its authority, authenticity, and unattainability." Hansen, "Benjamin's Aura," 336. See also Levin, "Walter Benjamin and the Theory of Art History."

59. Benjamin, "Work of Art," 23.

60. Ibid., 24. Moreover, as Shawn Smith and Sharon Sliwinski have argued, "although he rarely acknowledged it directly, Benjamin took many of his cues from Sigmund Freud who repeatedly relied on the metaphor of photography in his own work." Freud credited "the image-making medium within us" as foundational to becoming conscious and the importance of "photographic apparatus"—to figure out the workings of the mind." See *Photography and the Optical Unconscious*, 1–32.

Chapter 1

1. Obstat, *Good Saint Anne*, 14–15.

2. Quoted in "Our Lady in the Old World and New," Texas Tech University, Southwest Collection / Special Collections Library, http://swco.ttu.edu/medieval/OurLadyofGuadalupe.html.

3. According to Gianni Pizzigoni, "the premise of the Catholic *ex voto* is the vow," the solemn promise supplicants make, in a moment of great hardship, to give public thanks to a particular saint if he or she intervenes to avert disaster; the ex-voto, in turn, is "the concrete testimonial of that vow's fulfillment," an object that stands as the material representation of the miracle itself Although painted ex-votos hang on the walls of churches and shrines, they are not ecclesiastically sanctioned professions of faith. The relationship to God and His saints they enact—direct, personal, even a bit irreverent—bypasses pastoral mediation and ecclesiastical rituals of address, which might account for the church's historical ambivalence toward them. See Pizzigoni, *Commentary*, 4–5.

4. Auerbach, *Mimesis*, 6.

5. Plato, *Republic*, 509d4–8, in Taylor, *Plato*, 391.

6. Jay, *Downcast Eyes*, 29.

7. Aristotle, *De anima* 3.3, 428a1–2, http://psychclassics.yorku.ca/Aristotle/De-anima/de-anima3.htm.

8. Jay, *Downcast Eyes*, 37.

9. Quoted in ibid.

10. Ibid., 126n4.

11. John of Damascus, *On Holy Images*, 98.

12. "Medieval Sourcebook: Iconoclastic Council, 754," https://sourcebooks.fordham.edu/source/icono-cncl754.asp.

13. John of Damascus, *Oratio I*, PG 94, cols. 1248c–d. Quoted in Freedberg, *Power of Images*, 401.

14. Augustine, *Summa Theologica*, 1.520.

15. Ibid., 1.405.

16. Daston, "Marvelous Facts and Miraculous," 97.

17. Trexler, *Public Life in Renaissance Florence*, 6–7.

18. Alberti, Vasari, and Leonardo all quoted in ibid., 61–63.

19. Ibid., 62–63.

20. "A practical identity," Trexler writes, "existed between Mary and the image. . . . It is in the nature of a sufficient power—either corpse or image—to embody itself perfectly and integrally in whatever form it happens to take." Ibid., 67.

21. In their 1978 study *Image and Pilgrimage in Christian Culture*, Edith and Victor Turner demonstrate how pilgrimages provide escape from mundane and everyday experience and cut "across the boundaries of provinces, realms, and even empires" (6).

22. A pilgrimage center, from the standpoint of the believing actor, also represents a threshold, a place and moment "in and out of time," and such an actor—as evidence of many pilgrims of many religions attests—hopes to have their direct experience of the sacred, invisible, or supernatural order, either in the material aspect of miraculous healing or in the immaterial aspect of inward transformation of spirt or personality. Ibid., 197.

23. For Orsi a "lived religion approach is to balance carefully and self-reflectively border between familiarity and difference, strangeness and recognizability, whether in relation to people in the past or in another cultural world." Orsi, "Is the Study of Lived Religion Irrelevant?" See also Orsi's introduction as well as the other essays in Hall, *Lived Religion in America.*

24. Thwaites, *Jesuit Relations and Allied Documents*, 51:87–90.

25. Dunn, *Ritual Theory, Ritual Practice*, 130.

26. Ibid., 167.

27. The Basilica of Sainte-Anne-de-Beaupré hosts a website that lists all of the miracles purported to have taken place there. See http://www.sanctuairesainteanne.org.

28. Thoreau, *Yankee in Canada*, 45.

29. Quoted in Steckley, *Beyond Their Years*, 34.

30. Koppedrayer, "Making of the First Iroquois Virgin," 288.

31. See https://www.tekconf.org/st-kateri.

32. Holmes, "Narrative Repatriation of Blessed Kateri Tekakwitha," 87.

33. Berlo and Phillips, *Native North American Art.* The fifth episode of *TimeTraveller* can be viewed at https://vimeo.com/52633125.

34. Castillo, *Memoirs of the Conquistador*, 61.

35. See https://www.catholic.org/about/guadalupe.php

36. Wolf, "Virgin of Guadalupe," 34, 38.

37. Peterson, *Visualizing Guadalupe*, x.

38. Andzaldua, *Borderlands / La Frontera*, 27.

39. Sandstrom, "Tonantsi Cult of the Eastern Nahua."

40. Peterson, *Visualizing Guadalupe*, x.

41. Crary, *Techniques of the Observer*, 5.

42. Ibid., 24.

43. Nicolotti, *From the Mandylion of Edessa.*

44. Geimer, "Self-Portrait of Christ." Quote from Gail, *Visage de Jésus-Christ*, 292–93.

45. Pia quoted in Geimer, *Inadvertent Images*, 102. According to Geimer, these two photographs mark the beginning of the debate over the veracity of the shroud. See also Zaccone, "Fotografia della sindone del 1898." On the history of the reception of Pia's photographs, see Didi-Huberman, "Indice de la plaie absente"; Geimer, "Autorité de la photographie," translated by Thomas Repensek as "Index of an Absent Wound."

46. Pia, "Mémoire," in Loth, *La photographie du Saint Suaire de Turin*, 19. The text of the Italian manuscript is published in Pia, "Prima fotografia della SS. Sindone."

47. Gunning, "What's the Point of an Index?" 39.

48. See https://plato.stanford.edu/entries/peirce.

49. Hartshorne and Weiss, *Collected Papers of Charles Sanders Peirce*, 2:299.

50. For a good overview, see http://csmt.uchicago.edu/glossary2004/symbolindexicon.htm.

51. Doane, "Indexical," 128–29.

52. Barcaccia et al., "Uncovering the Sources of DNA."

53. See https://www.shroud.com/nature.htm.

54. See https://www.csicop.org/specialarticles/show/claims_of_invalid_ldquoshroudrdquo_radiocarbon_date_cut_from_whole_cloth.

Chapter 2

1. Unless otherwise indicated, all quotations in this chapter are drawn from the six-day *New York Sun* serialized moon hoax, beginning on August 25, 1835, reproduced online at http://hoaxes.org/text/display/the_great_moon_hoax_of_1835_text.

2. Grimsted, "Rioting in Its Jacksonian Setting," 364."

3. Quoted in O'Brien, *Story of "The Sun,"* 119

4. Reiss, *Discourse of Modernism*, 140.

5. Quoted in Walsh, *Sins Against Science*, 249.

6. Castagnaro, "Lunar Fancies and Earthly Truths," 265.

7. Crary, *Techniques of the Observer*, 3.

8. Poe, *Works of Edgar Allan Poe*, 198.

9. Rebekah Higgitt, "The Great Moon Hoax and the Christian Philosopher," *Guardian*, February 5, 2015, http://www.theguardian.com/science/the-h-word/2015/feb/05/great-moon-hoax-christian-philosopher-history-science.

10. Dick, "Illustrations of the Omnipotence of the Deity," 37–38.

11. For more on the Burned-Over District, see Cross, *Burned-Over District*.
12. See http://history1800s.about.com/od/popularentertainment/fl/Cardiff-Giant-Hoax.htm.
13. *Syracuse Daily Standard*, October 19, 1869, 1.
14. See https://lockhaven.edu/~dsimanek/cardiff.htm. Emphasis mine.
15. Ibid.
16. Petit, "Joy in Believing," 660.
17. Young, *Bunk*.
18. Canada, *Literature and Journalism*, 9.
19. "Barnum's Speech on Humbugs," *Grand River Times*, November 15, 1854.
20. Harris, *Humbug*, 57.
21. Barnum, *Struggles and Triumphs*, 76.
22. Outwater 86. For more on Barnum and Heth see Eric Lott. *Love and Theft*, 75-81.
23. Harris, *Humbug*, 68.
24. Quoted in ibid., 74.
25. Ibid., 79.
26. Schofield, "Science Education."
27. Trachtenberg, *Reading American Photographs*, 8.
28. Ibid., 12.
29. Barnum, *Struggles and Triumphs*, 118.

Chapter 3

1. Cross, *Burned-Over District*.
2. Krauss, *Beyond Light and Shadow*, 104–5.
3. Braude, *Radical Spirits*, 2.
4. The Rochester Historical Society continues to call the table the "Fox Sisters' Table" despite the lack of evidence directly linking them to it. Brandon Hodge, the curator of the Mysterious Planchette site, has done substantial research on the table and thinks the connection is dubious. I would like to thank Hodge for sharing his work with me. For more on Hodge, see http://www.mysteriousplanchette.com/Curator/curator.html.
5. Quoted in Mattison, *Spirit Rapping Unveiled*, 174.
6. Abbot, *Spirit Portrait Mystery*, 28.
7. Verner, *Table Rapping and Automatic Writing*, 9–10. On the topic of "materialization," Verner further explained that "it is always best to speak to the spirit or vision and question it, then you will be able to see if you know it, and you may ask the apparition if it has any message for you. If it warns you of any important event or accident, or loss of money, or any calamity, it will be best for you to act on that advice; if you do not, it may turn out very serious."
8. Davis, *Present Age and Inner Life*, 66–68. Davis continued, "There is always a super-mundane circle *corresponding* to the structure and conditions of the circle on earth. And each guardian mind in the *spiritual group* contributes its proportion of magnetic emanation, to form a line of communication, just as each person in a *terrestrial group* lends his or her mental and physical influence to mediumize the table. Thus there is an earthly terminus and there is a spiritual terminus to the *fine thread of magnetism*, which perforating and passing through all intervening substances, accomplishes the wonders herein described" (68). For more on the idea of a spiritual telegraph, see Sconce, "Media and Mediums."
9. Davis, *Present Age and Inner Life*, 68.
10. For an outstanding discussion of this, see, in particular, Sconce, "Media and Mediums."
11. *The Spectator*, March 1839. Reprinted in *Museum of Foreign Literature, Science and Art*, n.s., vol. 7 (March 1839): 341–43. Text quotation on 343.
12. Quoted in Newhall, *History of Photography*, 19. Emphasis mine.
13. Quoted in Modrak and Anthes, *Reframing Photography*, 28.
14. Quoted in Hirsch, *Seizing the Light*, 9. Emphasis mine.
15. *Literary Gazette; and Journal of the Belles Lettres, Arts, Sciences, &c.*, January 12, 1839, 28.
16. Quoted in Newhall, *History of Photography*, 11n5.
17. Quoted in ibid., 11n6.
18. Samuel Morse, "The Daguerreotipe" [*sic*], *New York Observer*, April 20, 1839, 62.
19. Edgar Allan Poe, *Alexander's Weekly Messenger* (Philadelphia), January 15, 1840, 2. Reprinted in Brigham, *Edgar Allan Poe's Contributions*, 20–22.
20. Trachtenberg, "Likeness as Identity," 175–76.
21. Hirsch, *Seizing the Light*, 12. Emphasis mine.
22. Hartshorne and Weiss, *Collected Papers of Charles Sanders Peirce*, 2:281.
23. Indexes depend on sensory legitimation. They must be visible, audible, et cetera. For example, the presence of smoke (in one's eyes, or its smell) suggests the presence of fire.
24. Sentilles, "Misreading Feuerbach," 39.
25. Freud, *Interpretation of Dreams*.

26. West, "Camera Fiends," 174–75.
27. Krauss, *Beyond Light and Shadow*, 99.
28. Quoted in ibid., 100.
29. Nagy, *Precipitated Spirit Painting*, 1.
30. *Washington Post*, April 17, 1888.
31. Dr. Thurston's account is printed in full in Coates, *Photographing the Invisible*, 354–57.
32. Mumler quoted in Krauss, *Beyond Light and Shadow*, 102–3.
33. Cadwallader, "Spirit Photography," 15.
34. Quoted in Kaplan, *Strange Case of William Mumler*, 92.
35. Oliver Wendell Holmes, "Doings of the Sunbeam," *Atlantic Monthly*, July 1863, 14.
36. *Illustrated Photographer* (London: Gilbert and Rivington), May 28, 1869, 254.
37. Leja, *Looking Askance*, 27.
38. Quoted in Selzer, *Ghosts of Lincoln*.
39. Quoted in Leja, *Looking Askance*, 48.
40. Quoted in ibid., 50.
41. Ibid., 53.
42. Ibid., 55.
43. *Chicago Daily Tribune*, February 25, 1905.
44. *Chicago Daily Tribune*, April 17, 1890.
45. *New York Times*, July 1, 1915.
46. Leja, *Looking Askance*, 55, 58.
47. Quoted in Stashower, *Teller of Tales*, 333–34.
48. Doyle, *Mystery of Cloomber*, chap. 16.
49. Doyle, *Case for Spirit Photography*, 12, 37.
50. Doyle, *Coming of the Fairies*, n.p.
51. Ibid., 9.
52. Ibid., 122.
53. Edward Gardner, letter to Arthur Conan Doyle, July 12, 1920, reprinted in ibid., 21.
54. Doyle, *Coming of the Fairies*, 23. Gardner published his own account of the matter years later. See Gardner, *Fairies*.
55. Doyle, *Coming of the Fairies*, 37–38.
56. Ibid., 76–80.
57. Ibid., 36.
58. Ibid., 58.
59. Arthur Conan Doyle, "Faeries Photographed: An Epoch-Making Event," *Strand Magazine*, December 1920, 462, 465.
60. Quoted in Wilcox and Newall, *Victorian Landscape Watercolors*, 32.
61. Quoted in Doyle, "Faeries Photographed," 464.
62. Owen, "Borderland Forms," 50.
63. Barry Bergdoll has pointed out that Baldus often painted out the sky in his images to make the architectural forms he was capturing look more monumental while also underscoring the changing urban conditions of Paris at this time. See Bergdoll, "Matter of Time."
64. See http://www.getty.edu/art/collection/artists/1877/gustave-le-gray-french-1820-1884.
65. Rejlander believed that "the same way a painter goes if he wishes to paint, a photographer must go if he wishes to make a composition photograph. The two go together; part here to meet again. Fine art consists of many parts, and a photographic composition commenced in this manner must contain many parts in common with art." Rejlander, "On Photographic Composition," 191.
66. The website for the Metropolitan Museum of Art in New York calls *The Two Ways of Life* "one of the most ambitious and controversial photographs of the nineteenth century." See https://www.metmuseum.org/art/collection/search/294822. Rejlander described the print as portraying "the venerable sage introducing two men into life—the one, calm and placid, turns towards Religion, Charity, and Industry, and the other virtues, while the other rushes madly from his guide into the pleasures of the world, typified by various figures, representing Gambling, Wine, Licentiousness, and other vices; ending in Suicide, Insanity, and Death. The center of the picture, in front, between the two parties, is a splendid figure symbolizing Repentance, with the emblem of Hope." Quoted in Hirsch, *Seizing the Light*, 124.
67. Robinson, *Pictorial Effect in Photography*, n.p.
68. Ibid., 78.
69. For more on notions of Victorian poetic truth, see Shaw, *Lucid Veil*. For more on composite photographs, see Fineman, *Faking It*.
70. Tennyson, "The Lady of Shalott," in *Poems*, lines 115–17.
71. Quoted in "Photographic Contributions to Art: 'The Lady of Shalott,'" *British Journal of Photography* 8 (October 15, 1861): 356.
72. Ibid.
73. Frances Griffiths, interview with Joe Cooper, in Cooper, "Cottingley," 2338–40.
74. Arthur C. Clarke (presenter) and Anna Ford (narrator), "Fairies, Phantoms, and Fantastic Photographs," season 1, episode 6, *Arthur C. Clarke's World of Strange Powers*, ITV, May 22, 1985.

Chapter 4

1. In 1895, a new U.S. tariff on Cuban export led to massive unemployment in Cuba. In

response, Cubans tried to gain independence from Spain. The San Francisco *Examiner*, a Hearst paper, compared Cuba to Armenia and called on the U.S. to intervene in their defense.

2. Schudson, *Discovering the News*, 62.
3. Boorstin, *Image*, 8.
4. Nassaw, *Chief*, 125.
5. Schudson, *Discovering the News*, 62.
6. Richard Harding Davis, "Mr. Davis Explains," *New York World*, February 17, 1897, 2.
7. Creelman quoted in Nassaw, *Chief*, 128.
8. Alfred, Lord Tennyson, "The Charge of the Light Brigade," *Examiner* (London), December 9, 1854, lines 12–25.
9. Sontag, *Regarding the Pain of Others*, 54.
10. Morris, *Believing Is Seeing*, 93.
11. Quoted in Trachtenberg, *Reading American Photographs*, 71. See also Robert Wilson, "The False Heroism of a Civil War Photographer," *Atlantic*, July–August 2011, https://www.theatlantic.com/magazine/archive/2011/07/the-false-heroism-of-a-civil-war-photographer/308543.
12. "Brady's Photographs: Pictures of the Dead at Antietam," *New York Times*, October 20, 1862, 5.
13. Oliver Wendell Holmes, "Doings of the Sunbeam," *Atlantic Monthly*, July 1863, 11.
14. Hirsch, *Seizing the Light*, 83.
15. Boorstin, *Image*, 13.
16. Ibid., 31.
17. Ibid., 37.
18. Debord, *Society of the Spectacle*, 2–5.
19. Ibid.
20. Boorstin, *Image*, 119.
21. Ibid., 125–26.
22. Benjamin, "Work of Art," 25–25.
23. Solomon-Godeau, "Living with Contradictions," 225.
24. For an excellent overview of postmodernism (as well as of modernism and modernity), see Cartwright and Sturken, *Practices of Looking*, 237–77.
25. Quoted in ibid., 237.
26. Ibid., 19.
27. Erroll Morris, "The Case of the Inappropriate Alarm Clock (Part 3)," *New York Times*, October 20, 2009, https://opinionator.blogs.nytimes.com//2009/10/20/the-case-of-the-inappropriate-alarm-clock-part-3.
28. Writing of Levine's work in 1982, Craig Owens declared that she "assumed the functions of the dealer, the curator, the critic—everything but the creative artist." Owens, "Sherrie Levine at A&M Artworks," 148. Similarly, Howard Singerman argues that the images "criticality stemmed from their challenge to authorship, and to the idea of a unique and original work of art . . . as well as from their challenge to what could be seen, to the visual as the final meaning of the work of art and the final arbiter of its quality." Singerman, "Seeing Sherrie Levine," 78.
29. Douglas Crimp, "Pictures," *October* 8 (Spring 1979): 80. Emphasis mine.
30. Sherman, *Complete Untitled Film Stills*, 8.
31. According to Suzanne Muchnic, "Holliday had never heard of the Whitney Biennial until [curator John] Hanhardt contacted Grigg [his attorney] and requested the tape for the exhibition. . . . Grigg met with Hanhardt and museum director David Ross in New York before releasing the tape to the exhibition. Holliday may have been surprised by the museum's request, but 'I wasn't,' Grigg said. 'In spite of the fact that he wasn't consciously making art at the moment of creation, what he did is something very significant.'" Suzanne Muchnic, "Rodney King Beating Footage Comes to the Art World," *Los Angeles Times*, March 10, 1993, http://articles.latimes.com/1993-03-10/entertainment/ca-1355_1_art-world.
32. Ibid.
33. Roberta Smith, "At the Whitney, a Biennial with a Social Conscience," *New York Times*, March 5, 1993, C1.
34. Arthur Danto, "The 1993 Whitney Biennial," *Nation*, April 19, 1993, 533.

Conclusion

1. See http://www.armoryonpark.org/mobile/event_detail/last_supper_peter_greenaway.
2. Latour and Lowe, "Migration of the Aura," 279–80.
3. See https://digicult.it/news/the-image-always-has-the-last-word-cinema-according-to-peter-greenaway.
4. Quoted in ibid.
5. Ibid.
6. Manovich, "How to Compare One Million Images," 261.
7. Ibid., 261–62.
8. See http://lab.culturalanalytics.info/p/about.html.
9. Manovich, "How to Compare One Million Images," 251.

Bibliography

Abbot, David Phelps. *The Spirit Portrait Mystery, Its Final Solution*. Chicago: Open Court, 1913.

Alexander, Elizabeth. "'Can You Be BLACK and Look at This?': Reading the Rodney King Video(s)." *Public Culture* 7, no. 1 (1994): 77–94.

Anderson, Arthur J. O., and Charles E. Dibble, eds. *Florentine Codex*. Santa Fe: School of American Research and University of Utah, 1975.

Andzaldua, Gloria. *Borderlands / La Frontera*. San Francisco: Aunt Lute Books, 1999.

Auerbach, Erich. *Mimesis: The Representation of Reality in Western Literature*. Translated by Willard R. Trask. Princeton: Princeton University Press, 1953.

Baird, Ellen T. "Sahagún and the Representation of History." In *Sahagún at 500: Essays on the Quincentenary of the Birth of Fr. Bernardino De Sahagún*, edited by John Frederick Schwaller, 117–36. Berkeley, CA: Academy of American Franciscan History, 2003.

Barcaccia, Gianni, Giulio Galla, Alessandro Achilli, Anna Olivieri, and Antonio Torroni. "Uncovering the Sources of DNA Found on the Turin Shroud." *Scientific Reports* 5, no. 14484 (2015). https://doi.org/10.1038/srep14484.

Barnum, Phineas T. *Struggles and Triumphs*. 1927. Repr., New York: Arno, 1970.

Barr, Juliana. *Peace Came in the Form of a Woman: Indians and Spaniards in the Texas Borderlands*. Chapel Hill: University of North Carolina Press, 2007.

Baudrillard, Jean. *Simulacra and Simulation*. Translated by Sheila Glaser. Ann Arbor: University of Michigan Press, 1981.

Belting, Hans. *Likeness and Presence: A History of the Image Before the Era of Art*. Chicago: University of Chicago Press, 1997.

Benjamin, Walter. "The Work of Art in the Age of Its Technical Reproducibility." In *The Work of Art in the Age of Its Technical Reproducibility and Other Writings on Media*, edited by Michael Jennings, 19–55. Cambridge, MA: Belknap Press of Harvard University Press, 2008

Bennett, Jane. *The Enchantment of Modern Life: Attachments, Crossings, Ethics*. Princeton: Princeton University Press, 2001.

Bennett, Tony. *Birth of the Museum*. New York: Routledge, 1995.

Bergdoll, Barry. "A Matter of Time: Architects and Photographers in Second Empire France." In *Photographs of Édouard Baldus*, edited by Malcom Daniel, 99–119. New York: Harry N. Abrams, 1994.

Berger, John. *Ways of Seeing*. London: BBC Enterprises, 1972.

Berkeley, George. *The Principles of Human Knowledge*. Dublin, 1710.

Berlo, Janet Catherine, and Ruth Phillips. *Native North American Art*. New York: Oxford, 2016.

Bloch, Marc. *The Historian's Craft*. Translated by Peter Putnam. New York: Alfred K. Knopf, 1954.

Boone, Elizabeth Hill. *Stories in Red and Black: Pictorial Histories of the Aztecs and Mixtecs*. Austin: University of Texas Press, 2000.

Boorstin, Daniel. *The Image: A Guide to Pseudo-Events in America*. New York: Vintage Books, 1962.

Bourdieu, Pierre. *Distinction*. Translated by Richard Nice. Cambridge, MA: Harvard University Press, 1984.

Braude, Ann. *Radical Spirits: Spiritualism and Women's Rights in Nineteenth Century America*. 2nd ed. Bloomington: Indiana University Press, 1989.

Brigham, Clarence S. *Edgar Allan Poe's Contributions to "Alexander's Weekly Messenger."* Worcester, MA: American Antiquarian Society, 1943.

Bynum, Caroline Walker. "Wonder." *American Historical Review* 102, no. 1 (February 1997): 1–26.

Cadwallader, Jen. "Spirit Photography and the Victorian Culture of Mourning."

Modern Language Studies 37, no. 2 (Winter 2008): 8–31.

Canada, Mark. *Literature and Journalism*. New York: Palgrave Macmillan, 2013.

Cartwright, Lisa, and Marita Sturken. *Practices of Looking: An Introduction to Visual Culture*. New York: Oxford University Press, 2003.

Castagnaro, Mario. "Lunar Fancies and Earthly Truths: The Moon Hoax of 1835 and the Penny Press." *Nineteenth-Century Contexts* 34, no. 3 (2012): 253–68.

Castillo, Bernal Díaz del. *The Memoirs of the Conquistador Bernal Díaz Del Castillo, Written by Himself: Containing a True and Full Account of the Discovery and Conquest of Mexico and New Spain*. Vol. 1. Translated by John Ingram Lockhart. 1844. Repr., London: Penguin, 1963.

Caygill, Marjorie. "Sloan's Will and the Establishment of the British Museum." In *Sir Hans Sloane, Collector, Scientist, Antiquary, Founding Father of the British Museum*, edited by Arthur McGregor, 45–68. London: British Museum Press, 1994.

Clendinnen, Inga. "'Fierce and Unnatural Cruelty': Cortes and the Conquest of Mexico." *Representations* 33 (Winter 1991): 65–100.

Coates, James. *Photographing the Invisible: Practical Studies in Spirit Photography, Spirit Portraiture, and Other Rare but Allied Phenomenon*. Chicago: Advanced Thought, 1911.

Connors, Joseph, and Gerhard Wood, eds. *Colors Between Two Worlds: The Florentine Codex of Bernadino de Sahagún*. Cambridge, MA: Harvard University Press, 2011.

Cooper, Joe. "Cottingley: At Last the Truth." *Unexplained* 117 (1982): 2338–40.

Crary, Jonathan. "Modernizing Vision." In *Vision and Visuality*, edited by Hal Foster, 29–49. Discussions in Contemporary Culture 2. Seattle: Bay Press, 1988.

———. *Techniques of the Observer: On Vision and Modernity in the Nineteenth Century*. Cambridge, MA: MIT Press, 1990.

Cross, Whitney. *The Burned-Over District: The Social and Intellectual History of Enthusiastic Religion in Western New York, 1800–1850*. Ithaca: Cornell University Press, 1981.

Cuno, James. *Museums Matter: In Praise of the Encyclopedic Museum*. Chicago: University of Chicago Press, 2011.

Dalton, Stuart. "From Eyesight to Insight: Descartes's Dream of a World Without Images." *Philosophy Today* 61, no. 39 (Summer 2017): 5–39.

Daniel, Malcolm. *Photographs of Édouard Baldus*. New York: Harry N. Abrams, 1994.

Daston, Lorraine. "Marvelous Facts and Miraculous Evidence." In *Wonders, Marvels, and Monsters in Early Modern Culture*, edited by Peter Platt, 76–104. Newark: University of Delaware Press, 1999.

Davis, Andrew Jackson. *The Present Age and Inner Life*. New York: Partridge and Brittan, 1853.

Debord, Guy. *The Society of the Spectacle*. Translated by Ken Knabb. Berkeley, CA: Bureau of Public Secrets, 2014.

Descartes, René. *The Passions of the Soul*. Translated by Stephen H. Voss. Indianapolis: Hackett Publishing, 1989.

Dick, Thomas. "Illustrations of the Omnipotence of the Deity." In *The Christian Philosopher; or, The Connection of Science and Philosophy with Religion*, 32–60. Philadelphia: Key and Biddle, 1836.

Didi-Huberman, Georges. "L'indice de la plaie absente: Monographie d'une tache." *Traverses* 30–31 (March 1984): 151–63.

Doane, Mary Ann. "The Indexical and the Concept of Medium Specificity." *differences: A Journal of Feminist Cultural Studies* 18 (Winter 2007): 128–52.

Doyle, Arthur Conan. *The Case for Sprit Photography*. New York: George H. Doran, 1923.

———. *The Coming of the Fairies*. New York: Hodder and Stoughton, 1922.

———. *The Mystery of Cloomber*. London: Ward & Downey, 1889. http://www.gutenberg.org/ebooks/7964.

Dunn, Catherine. *Ritual Theory, Ritual Practice*. New York: Oxford University Press, 1992.

Fineman, Mia. *Faking It: Manipulated Photography Before Photoshop*. New York: Metropolitan Museum of Art; New Haven: Yale University Press, 2012.

Foster, Hal, ed. *Vision and Visuality*. New York: DIA Foundation, 1988.

Foucault, Michel. *The Order of Things: An Archeology of Human Sciences*. New York: Vintage Books, 1994.

Freedberg, David. *The Power of Images: Studies in the History and Theory of Response*. Chicago: University of Chicago Press, 1989.

Freud, Sigmund. *The Interpretation of Dreams*. 3rd ed. Translated by A. A. Brill. New York: Macmillan, 1913. http://psychclassics.yorku.ca/Freud/Dreams/dreams.pdf.

Gail, Paul de. *Le visage de Jésus-Christ et son linceul*. 2nd ed. Paris: Éditions France-Empire, 1977.

Gardner, Edward. *Fairies: The Cottingley Photographs and Their Sequel*. London: Theosophical Publishing House, 1945.

Geimer, Peter. "L'autorité de la photographie: Révélations d'un suaire." *Études photographiques* 6 (May 1999): 67–99.

———. *Inadvertent Images: A History of Photographic Apparitions*. Chicago: University of Chicago Press, 2018.

———. "The Index of an Absent Wound (Monograph on a Stain)." Translated by Thomas Repensek. *October* 29 (Summer 1984): 63–81.

———. "A Self-Portrait of Christ or the White Noise of Photography? Paul Vignon and the Earliest Photograph of the Shroud of Turin." Translated by Gerrit Jackson. *Grey Room* 59 (Spring 2015): 6–43.

Gillespie, Susan D. "Blaming Moctezuma: Anthropomorphizing the Aztec Conquest." In *Invasion and Transformation: Interdisciplinary Perspectives on the Conquest of Mexico*, edited by Rebecca P. Brienen and Margaret A. Jackson, 25–55. Boulder: University of Colorado Press, 2007.

Goodwin, Charles. "Professional Vision." *American Anthropologist* 96, no. 3 (September 1994): 606–33.

Gordon, Avery. *Ghostly Matters: Haunting and the Sociological Imagination*. Minneapolis: University of Minnesota Press, 2004.

Grimsted, David. "Rioting in Its Jacksonian Setting." *American Historical Review* 77 (April 1972): 361–97.

Gunning, Tom. "What's the Point of an Index? or, Faking Photographs." *Nordicom Review* 1–2 (2004): 39–49.

———. "The World as Object Lesson: Cinema Audiences, Visual Culture and the St. Louis World's Fair, 1904." *Film History: An International Journal* 6, no. 4 (1994): 422–44.

Hall, David, ed. *Lived Religion in America*. Princeton: Princeton University Press, 1997.

Hansen, Miriam. "Benjamin's Aura." *Critical Inquiry* 34 (Winter 2008): 336–75.

Harris, Amanda Nolacea, and Rolando Romero, eds. *Feminism, Nation and Myth: La Malinche*. Houston: Arte Público Press, 2005.

Harris, Neil. *Humbug: The Art of P. T. Barnum*. Chicago: University of Chicago Press, 1973.

Hartshorne, Charles, and Paul Weiss, eds. *The Collected Papers of Charles Sanders Peirce*. Cambridge, MA: Belknap Press of Harvard University Press, 1931.

Hirsch, Robert. *Seizing the Light: A Social History of Photography*. Columbus, OH: McGraw-Hill, 1999.

Holmes, Megan. *The Miraculous Image in Renaissance Florence*. New Haven: Yale University Press, 2013.

Holmes, Paula Elizabeth. "The Narrative Repatriation of Blessed Kateri Tekakwitha." *Anthropologica* 43 (2001): 87–103.

Hughes, Ellen Roney. "The People's Museum: George Brown Goode's Collection of Sporting Goods for the Smithsonian Institution in Victorian America." *Historian* 64, no. 2 (Winter 2002): 295–315.

Hunt, Lynn. *The Making of the West: Peoples and Cultures; A Concise History*. Vol. 2, *Since 1340*. Boston: Bedford / St. Martin's, 2007.

Jay, Martin. *Downcast Eyes: The Denigration of Vision in Twentieth-Century French Thought*. Berkeley: University of California Press, 1993.

Jennings, Michael, ed. *The Work of Art in the Age of Its Technical Reproducibility and Other Writings on Media*. Cambridge, MA: Belknap Press of Harvard University Press, 2008.

John of Damascus. *On Holy Images*. London: T. Baker, 1898.

Josephson-Storm, Jason. *The Myth of Disenchantment: Magic, Modernity, and the Birth of the Human Sciences*. Chicago: University of Chicago Press, 2017.

Kaplan, Louis. *The Strange Case of Louis Mumler, Spirit Photographer*. Minneapolis: University of Minnesota Press, 2008.

Kemp, Martin. *Leonardo on Painting: An Anthology of Writings by Leonardo da Vinci*. New Haven: Yale University Press, 1989.

Koppedrayer, K. I. "The Making of the First Iroquois Virgin: Early Jesuit Biographies of the Blessed Kateri Tekawitha." *Ethnohistory* 40, no. 2 (Spring 1993): 277–306.

Krauss, Rolf. *Beyond Light and Shadow: The Role of Photography in Certain Paranormal Phenomena; A Historical Survey*. Munich: Nazraeli Press, 1995.

Latour, Bruno, and Adam Lowe. "The Migration of the Aura; or, How to Explore the Original Through Its Facsimiles." In *Switching Codes: Thinking Through Digital Technology in the Humanities and the Arts*, edited by Thomas Bartscherer and Roderick Coover, 275–98. Chicago: University of Chicago Press, 2011.

Leja, Michael. *Looking Askance: Skepticism and American Art*. Berkeley: University of California Press, 2007.

———. "Scenes from a History of the Image." *Social Research: An International Quarterly* 78, no. 4 (Winter 2011): 999–1028.

Levin, Thomas Y. "Walter Benjamin and the Theory of Art History." *October* 47 (Winter 1988): 84–90.

Locke, John. *An Essay Concerning Human Understanding*. London, 1689. http://www.gutenberg.org/ebooks/10615.

Loth, Arthur. *La photographie du Saint Suaire de Turin: Authenticité du Suaire, documents nouveaux et concluants, avec reproductions photographiques*. Paris: Oudin, 1910.

Lott. Eric. *Love and Theft: Blackface Minstrelsy and the American Working Class*. New York: Oxford University Press, 1993.

Lyotard, Jean-François. *The Postmodern Condition: A Report on Knowledge*. Translated by Geoffrey Bennington and Brian Massumi. Minneapolis: University of Minnesota Press, 1984.

Manovich, Lev. "How to Compare One Million Images." In *Understanding Digital Humanities*, edited by David Berry, 249–78. New York: Palgrave Macmillan, 2012.

Markey, Lia. "'Istoria della terra chiamata la nuova spagna': The History and Reception of Sahagún's Codex at the Medici Court." In *Colors Between Two Worlds: The Florentine Codex of Bernadino de Sahagún*, edited by Gerhard Wood and Joseph Connors, 199–220. Cambridge, MA: Harvard University Press, 2011.

Mattison, H. *Spirit Rapping Unveiled*. New York: J. C. Derby, 1855.

McGarry, Molly. *Ghosts of Futures Past: Spiritualism and the Cultural Politics of Nineteenth-Century America*. Berkeley: University of California Press, 2008.

McGregor, Arthur, ed. *Sir Hans Sloane, Collector, Scientist, Antiquary, Founding Father of the British Museum*. London: British Museum Press, 1994.

Mirzoeff, Nicholas. *The Right to Look: A Counterhistory of Visuality*. Durham: Duke University Press, 2011.

Modrak, Rebecca, and Bill Anthes. *Reframing Photography: Theory and Practice*. New York: Routledge, 2011.

Morris, Errol. *Believing Is Seeing: Observations on the Mysteries of Photography*. New York: Penguin Books, 2014.

Nagy, Ron. *Precipitated Spirit Painting*. Lakewood, MN: Glade Press, 2012.

Nassaw, David. *The Chief: The Life of William Randolph Hearst*. New York: Mariner Books, 2001.

Newhall, Beaumont. *The History of Photography from 1839 to the Present*. New York: Museum of Modern Art, 1982.

Nicolotti, Andrea. *From the Mandylion of Edessa to the Shroud of Turin: The Metamorphosis and Manipulation of a Legend*. Leiden: Brill, 2014.

O'Brien, Frank M. *The Story of "The Sun."* New York: George Doran, 1918.

Obstat, Nihil. *Good Saint Anne: Her Power and Dignity*. Clyde, MO: Benedictine Books, 1964.

Orsi, Robert A. "Is the Study of Lived Religion Irrelevant to the World We Live In? Special Presidential Plenary Address, Society for the Scientific Study of Religion, Salt Lake City, November 2, 2002." *Journal for the Scientific Study of Religion* 42, no. 2 (June 2003): 169–74.

Outwater, Alice. *Wild at Heart: America's Turbulent Relationship with Nature.* New York: St. Martin's, 2019.

Owen, Alex. "'Borderland Forms': Arthur Conan Doyle, Albion's Daughters, and the Politics of the Cottingley Fairies." *History Workshop,* no. 38 (1994): 48–85.

Owens, Craig. "Sherrie Levine at A&M Artworks." *Art in America* 70, no. 6 (June 1982): 148.

Peterson, Jeannette Favrot. *Visualizing Guadalupe.* Austin: University of Texas Press, 2014.

Pettit, Michael. "'The Joy in Believing': The Cardiff Giant, Commercial Deceptions, and Styles of Observation in Gilded Age America." *Isis* 97, no. 4 (December 2006): 659–77.

Pia, Giuseppe. "La prima fotografia della SS. Sindone." *Sindon* 3, no. 5 (April 1961): 33–50.

Pizzigoni, Gianni. *Commentary: Ex voto votive dal XV al XIX secolo.* Milano: Tipographia Davide Mazza, 2001.

Plato. *Republic.* Translated by Benjamin Jowett. New York: Cosimo, 2008.

Poe, Edgar Allan. *The Works of Edgar Allan Poe.* Edited by Chester Noyes Greenough. New York: Hearst International Library, 1914.

Prince, Carl. "'The Great Riot Year': Jacksonian Democracy and Patterns of Violence in 1834." *Journal of the Early Republic* 5, no. 1 (Spring 1985): 1–19.

Rankine, Claudia. *Citizen: An American Lyric.* Minneapolis: Graywolf Press, 2014.

Reiss, Timothy. *The Discourse of Modernism.* Ithaca: Cornell University Press, 1982.

Rejlander, Oscar Gustav. "On Photographic Composition: With a Description of Two Ways of Life." *Journal of the Photographic Society of London* 65 (April 21, 1858): 191–97.

Roberts, Colin. "The Codex." *Proceedings of the British Academy* 40 (1954): 169–204.

Robinson, Henry Peach. *Pictorial Effect in Photography: Being Hints on Composition and Chiaroscuro for Photographers.* London: Piper & Carter, 1869.

Saab, A. Joan. *For the Millions: American Art and Culture Between the Wars.* Philadelphia: University of Pennsylvania Press, 2004.

Sahagún, Fray Bernardino de. *General History of the Things of New Spain.* Translated by Arthur O. Anderson and Charles E. Dribble. Salt Lake City: University of Utah Press, 1982.

Sandstrom, Alan R. "The Tonantsi Cult of the Eastern Nahua." In *Mother Worship: Theme and Variations,* edited by James J. Preston, 25–50. Chapel Hill: University of North Carolina Press, 1982.

Schofield, Robert E. "The Science Education of an Enlightened Engineer: Charles Willson Peale and His Philadelphia Museum, 1784–1827." *American Studies* 30, no. 2 (1989). https://journals.ku.edu/amsj/article/view/2470/.

Schudson, Michael. *Discovering the News: A Social History of American Newspapers.* New York: Basic Books, 1981.

Sconce, Jeffery. "Media and Mediums." In *Technological Visions: The Hopes and Fears That Shape New Technologies,* edited by Marita Sturken, Douglas Thomas, and Sandra J. Ball-Rokeach, 48–70. Philadelphia: Temple University Press, 2004.

Selzer, Adam. *Ghosts of Lincoln: Discovering His Paranormal Legacy.* Woodbury, MN: Llewellyn, 2015.

Sentilles, Sarah. "Misreading Feuerbach: Susan Sontag, Photography and the Image World." *Literature and Theology* 24, no. 1 (March 2010): 38–55.

Shaw, W. David. *The Lucid Veil: Poetic Truth in the Victorian Age.* London: Athlone Press, 1987.

Sherman, Cindy. *The Complete Untitled Film Stills.* New York: Museum of Modern Art, 2003.

Singerman, Howard. "Seeing Sherrie Levine." *October* 67 (Winter 1994): 78–107.

Smith, Mark M. *Making Sense of the Past.* Berkeley: University of California Press, 2007.

Smith, Shawn, and Sharon Sliwinski, *Photography and the Optical Unconscious.* Durham: Duke University Press, 2017.

Solomon-Godeau, Abigail. "Living with Contradictions: Critical Practices in the Age of Supply-Side Aesthetics." In *Visual Culture: The Reader,* edited by Jessica Evans and Stuart Hall, 224–43. London: Routledge, 1999.

Sontag, Susan. *Regarding the Pain of Others.* New York: Farrar, Straus and Giroux. 2003.

Stashower, Daniel. *Teller of Tales: The Life of Arthur Conan Doyle*. New York: Henry Holt, 1999.

Steckley, John. *Beyond Their Years: Five Native Women's Stories*. Toronto: Canadian Scholars' Press, 1999.

Taylor, A. E. *Plato, the Man and His Work*. 1826. Repr., London: Methuen, 1952.

Tennyson, Alfred. *Poems*. 2 vols. London: Edward Moxon, 1842.

Thompson, E. P. *The Making of the English Working Class*. New York: Vintage Books, 1980.

Thoreau, Henry David. *A Yankee in Canada: With Anti-slavery and Reform Papers*. Boston: Ticknor and Fields, 1866.

Thwaites, Reuben Gold, ed. *The Jesuit Relations and Allied Documents*. Cleveland: Burrows Bros., 1896–1901.

Trachtenberg, Alan. "Likeness as Identity: Reflections on the Daguerrean Mystique." In *The Portrait in Photography*, edited by Graham Clarke, 173–92. London: Reaktion Books, 1992.

———. *Reading American Photographs: Images as History—Mathew Brady to Walker Evans*. New York: Hill and Wang, 1989.

Trexler, Richard. *Public Life in Renaissance Florence*. Ithaca: Cornell University Press, 1980.

Tuner, Victor, and Edith Turner. *Image and Pilgrimage in Christian Culture*. 1978. Repr., New York; Columbia University Press, 2011.

Verner, Alexander. *Table Rapping and Automatic Writing*. Chicago: Advanced Thought, [between 1910 and 1920?]. Undated pamphlet in the Rare Books Collection, University of Rochester Library.

Walsh, Lynda. *Sins Against Science: The Scientific Media Hoaxes of Poe, Twain, and Others*. Albany: State University of New York Press, 2007.

West, Nancy Martha. "Camera Fiends: Early Photography, Death, and the Supernatural." *Centennial Review* 40, no 1 (Winter 1996): 171–206.

Wilcox, Scott, and Christopher Newall. *Victorian Landscape Watercolors*. New Haven: Yale Center for British Art, 1992.

Wolf, Eric R. "The Virgin of Guadalupe: A Mexican National Symbol." *Journal of American Folklore* 71, no. 279 (January–March 1958): 34–39.

Young, Kevin. *Bunk: The Rise of Hoaxes, Humbug, Plagiarists, Phonies, Post-Facts, and Fake News*. Minneapolis: Graywolf Press, 2017.

Zaccone, Gian Maria. "La fotografia della sindone del 1898: Recenti scoperte e conferme nell'archivio Pia." *Sindon*, new ser., vol. 3 (December 1991): 69–94.

Index

Pages in *italics* refer to illustrations.